Chris Webb

The Belzec Death Camp

History, Biographies, Remembrance

Chris Webb

THE BELZEC DEATH CAMP

History, Biographies, Remembrance

ibidem-Verlag
Stuttgart

Bibliographic information published by the Deutsche Nationalbibliothek
Die Deutsche Nationalbibliothek lists this publication in the Deutsche Nationalbibliografie; detailed bibliographic data are available in the Internet at http://dnb.d-nb.de.

Bibliografische Information der Deutschen Nationalbibliothek
Die Deutsche Nationalbibliothek verzeichnet diese Publikation in der Deutschen Nationalbibliografie; detaillierte bibliografische Daten sind im Internet über http://dnb.d-nb.de abrufbar.

ISBN-13: 978-3-8382-0866-4

Printed in the United States of America

FOR

ROBERT KUWALEK & SIR MARTIN GILBERT

Dedicated to the memory of

Billy Rutherford, & Harry Stadler

Foreword

Professor Matthew Feldman
University of Teesside, UK

The death camp at Belzec was the first site in history designed to kill human beings in an industrial manner in static gas chambers on an unparalleled scale. During the Second World War, the Third Reich deployed gassing and mass-cremation technologies in order to literally turn millions of victims into ash. In this sense, the Third Reich's earliest extermination camp at Belzec remains a low-water mark in human relations with one another. Internecine wars and savagery have always pocked human history. But never before had mass murder and modern technology come together to provide a purpose-built, self-contained, assembly-line operation for the destruction of an entire people.

The death camps collectively known as *Operation Reinhard(t)*[1], of which Belzec was the earliest constructed in 1941—it was joined by Sobibor and Treblinka later in 1942—managed this genocidal process brutally, yet bureaucratically. In the months following Nazi Germany's invasion of the Soviet Union on June 22, 1941, mass shootings in the east had proven unsatisfactory and difficult to conceal. Expertise and personnel were then engaged from an earlier gassing program, also using carbon monoxide gas, which had murdered more than 72,000 patients in converted asylum facilities over the preceding two years.[2]

---

1 The spelling of *Aktion Reinhardt* is fraught—the Germans involved in the mass murder programme spelt it with a "t" and without a "t". In this book *Reinhardt* is favored, as the recruitment pledge is spelt that way.

2 For details on the T-4 Operation and its relevance to the development of the Holocaust, see Friedlander, Henry, *The Origins of Nazi Genocide: From Euthanasia to the Final Solution*. University of North Carolina Press, Chapel Hill, 1995.

In a grisly process of trial and error, technicians from the euphemistically-entitled "Euthanasia Program" helped to develop mobile gas-vans, to murder Jews from the Warthegau region, they were murdered in the converted "palace" at Chelmno. By the end of 1941, with the construction of Belzec about halfway completed, the Nazi leadership had decided upon a process of total destruction—one whereby European Jews would be gassed, pillaged, and disposed of, preferably in a secluded place next to a main railway line in Nazi-occupied territory.[3]

It was this method, built from scratch and refined over the coming months, which was to be first perfected at Belzec in June 1942. Victims were sometimes murdered at a rate of 10,000 persons a day—in hermetically sealed chambers, people piled into overcrowded trains before reaching their final destination, corpses pillaged for valuables after being gassed. Later the bodies were burned—these had been buried in mass graves at first, before trial and error made this, too, more efficient—over an enormous human grill, also designed by the overseers of the "Final Solution to the Jewish Question," Heinrich Himmler's *Schutzstaffel*—or SS.[4]

This uniquely insidious project was directed at the Jews of Europe. One of the very few survivors from Belzec, an enslaved worker named Rudolf Reder—kept barely alive as a camp handyman prior to escaping—established as early as 1946 that "Belzec served no other purpose than that of murdering Jews." After witnessing uncountable thousands of his fellow Jews from Poland sent to their deaths, some he knew well, Reder recalled:

> Words are inadequate to describe our state of mind and what we felt when we heard the terrible moans of those people and the cries of the children being murdered. Three times a day we saw people

---

3 For more on Reich Security Main Office role in the Holocaust see Wildt, Michael, *An Uncompromising Generation: The Nazi Leadership of the Reich Security Main Office*, University of Wisconsin Press, London, 2009.

4 R. Breitman, *The Architect of Genocide: Himmler and the Final Solution*, Pimlico, London, 2004; David Cesarani, *Eichmann: His Life and Crimes*, Vintage, London, 2005; Berndt Rieger, *Creator of Nazi Death Camps: The Life of Odilo Globocnik*, Vallentine Mitchell, London, 2007.

> going nearly mad. Nor were we far from madness either. How we survived from one day to the next I cannot say, for we had no illusions. Little by little we too were dying, together with those thousands of people who, for a short while, went through an agony of hope. Apathetic and resigned to our fate, we felt neither hunger nor cold. We all waited our turn to die an inhuman death. Only when we heard the heart-rending cries of small children—"Mummy, mummy, but I have been a good boy" and "Dark. dark"—did we feel something.[5]

This inhumanity was meted out to a minimum of 434,508 people at Belzec, nearly all of them Polish Jews.[6] According to a recent debate in the pages of *East European Jewish Affairs*, the number is likely still higher: perhaps 600,000 Jews were murdered there, or even 800,000.[7] Who knows, for instance, how many unregistered trains, containing some 50 boxcars filled with thousands of terrified Jews, were diverted to Belzec during the height of its activity in Summer-Autumn 1942? Affixing a precise number of victims is as impossible as imagining the individual fate of Jews suffocated at one of the principal charnel houses of the Holocaust—and indeed in human history—Belzec.

Notwithstanding this staggering reality, relatively little has been written to date on Belzec by scholars in English. This is borne out by the scattered references to Belzec in excellent studies on the Holocaust that have been recently published by Christopher Browning, Saul Friedlander, and Peter Longerich.[8] One reason for

---

5 R. Reder, *Belzec*, translated by M. M. Rubel, in Polin, *Studies in Polish Jewry*, vol. 13, 2000, pp. 276, 287.

6 Höfle Telegram, National Archives Kew, HW 16/32.

7 Three articles debating these figures have been published by the academic journal *East European Jewish Affairs:* Robin O'Neil's *Belzec: A Reassessment of the Number of Victims*, 29/1 1999, pp. 85–118; a response by Dieter Pohl and Peter Witte entitled *The Number of Victims of Belzec Extermination Camp: A Faulty Reassessment*; and O'Neil rejoinder *Belzec: Toward a Constructive Debate* 31/1 2001, pp. 15–25.

8 C. Browning, *The Origins of the Final Solution: The Evolution of Nazi Jewish Policy 1939–1942*, Arrow Books, London, 2005; Friedlander, Saul, *The Years of Extermination: Nazi Germany and the Jews 1939–1945*, Weidenfeld and Nicolson London, 2007; Longerich, Peter, *Holocaust: The Nazi Persecution and Murder of the Jews*, Oxford University Press, Oxford, 2010.

this is the relatively stronger documentation left behind at other extermination camps such as Auschwitz-Birkenau, where more than a million Jews were killed, before the SS beat a hasty retreat from the advancing Soviet forces. Another factor is clarified by the extremely small number of survivors from Belzec. And still another reason is the sheer scale of the Final Solution, involving not only the gassing of Jews in their millions, but extended to millions more deaths through shooting, starvation and overwork. That is to say, even the most detailed and comprehensive accounts of the Holocaust of late have but scratched at the surface of Belzec's horrors.

An important exception to the limited Anglophone scholarship on Belzec is provided by Yitzak Arad's groundbreaking work on the *Operation Reinhard(t)* camps. Published in 1987, his scholarly *Belzec, Sobibor, Treblinka* added new insight into the day-to-day running of the camps. Like the other two main *Reinhard (t)* death camps at Sobibor and Treblinka, Belzec comprised four groups of people: Jewish victims; a contingent of around 120 mass murderers (SS and police guards, Ukrainian auxiliaries and auxiliary administrative staff on site); Jews taken from transports to help with the extermination process, who only lived a day or two; and so-called *Hofjuden* (court Jews), who were tailors, carpenters and other skilled workers serving the camp personnel for a period of months before being murdered. Rudolf Reder was only able to escape because he was in the latter category. For the murderers, in turn, deceit and speed were central to the process, in order to blunt resistance and the chances of escape; this also "increased the killing capacity of the camp."

Finally, one particularly chilling feature shared by all three death camps Belzec, Sobibor, and Treblinka: songs by orchestral musicians, often playing to drown out the screams of those murdered by gas or shooting. In Belzec there was a small orchestra, Arad writes, which was used primarily during the transports and to entertain the SS men during their nights of drunkenness and debauchery. The orchestra was made up of six musicians who usually played in the area between the gas chamber and the burial pits.

The transfer of corpses from the gas chambers to the graves was done to the accompaniment of the orchestra.[9]

The Holocaust in the Soviet Union is Arad's most recent and ambitious account, which also sheds new light on the *Operation Reinhard(t)* camps. He devotes a chapter to Belzec here, emphasizing that deportations took place largely from the Polish region of Galicia in the *Generalgouvernement*—an area first occupied by the USSR between September 1939 and June 1941—lasting over a period of seven months. Although the Belzec death camp existed between mid-March and mid-December 1942, a six-week pause was undertaken to expand the killing facilities: Six concrete gassing chambers were installed to murder as many as 2,000 Jews at a time. Thereafter, in the six months comprising the "big deportations" to Belzec, more than 100,000 transported Jews could be murdered in the course of a single month.[10]

Yet in spite of Arad's exceptional contribution to understanding Belzec and the history of *Operation Reinhard(t)* more generally, Dieter Pohl rightly maintained in a pivotal 2004 collection on historical interpretations of the Holocaust that the "three camps of the Aktion Reinhardt, Belzec, Sobibor and Treblinka, became from the spring of 1942, the murder sites of almost half of Polish Jewry, but no scholarly camp monograph has yet been published."[11]

This has been recently remedied with English-language studies in the cases of Sobibor and Treblinka,[12] but not for the earliest of the *Aktion Reinhardt* camps, Belzec.

In this sense alone, the following contribution to Holocaust Studies is worthy of recognition. Over his years of independent research, moreover, Chris Webb has also collected a number of

---

9 Y. Arad, *Belzec, Sobibor, Treblinka: The Operation Reinhard Death Camps*, Indiana University Press, Bloomington, 1987, pp. 27, 227.

10 Y. Arad, *The Holocaust in the Soviet Union*, Yad Vashem, Jerusalem, 2009, ch. 20.

11 D. Pohl, *War, Occupation and the Holocaust in Poland* in Dan Stone, *The Historiography of the Holocaust*, Palgrave, Basingstoke, 2004, p. 99.

12 J. Schelvis, *Sobibor: A History of a Nazi Death Camp*, Berg, Oxford 2007; Chrostowski, Withold, *The Extermination Camp Treblinka*, Vallentine Mitchell, London, 2004.

contemporaneous photographs from Belzec, some of which are included in this edition. Relevant transcriptions from a wartime publication called the *Polish Fortnightly Review*; wartime diaries and subsequent memoirs, excerpts from postwar testimony and trials; as well as sketches and reproductions of Belzec are also included in this book. Intended for a general audience, both the selection and narrative here are intended to give an overview, an impression of Belzec's development and function. Images of the perpetrators are given prominent place: these few orchestrated the murder of hundreds of thousands of men, women, and children. While these previously-unseen images are helpfully included in the pages to follow, several unexpected details are also provided: a brief history of the area; information on the small "Gypsy Camp" at Belzec; and insight into the exhumation and incineration of thousands of corpses after the camp ceased to be operational.

Drawing upon his personal archive and his work on a number of Holocaust educational websites, Webb's book provides details of Austro-German SS and police personnel at Belzec, in addition to many of the Ukrainians and so-called *Volksdeutsche* auxiliaries also serving in the extermination center. These and other findings are part of a lifetime's dedication to making the Holocaust—and specifically the part played by the death camp at Belzec in this process of genocide—better known to a wider audience.

Chris Webb's private undertakings therefore have a very publicly-spirited effect; reminding his readers that, at Belzec, the worst was perpetrated against defenseless Jewish victims, again and again. Taken together, the patchwork of quotations, pictures and testimony comprising this book serves to reinforce the impression that human depravity passed a certain threshold there. The Belzec death camp offers a glimpse of this abyss, when genocide was streamlined—administered and employed against enemies of the Third Reich for no other reason than that they were Jewish.

York, England
November 2014

Author's Introduction

Belzec Death Camp—History, Biographies, Remembrance is an updated and revised edition of my book *Belzec—The Death Camp Laboratory*, which was first published in 2012. This new version has provided a more comprehensive coverage of both the Jewish victims as part of the Roll of Remembrance and the perpetrators. Extensive use has been made of the Bundesarchiv Memorial database to include those German Jews who were deported to Belzec from the Reich, not included in the earlier version.

This work should be viewed as a companion edition to my book on the Treblinka death camp, published in 2014 by *ibidem*-Verlag Stuttgart. This book has been re-written to match the style of the book on Treblinka and to include new information on the victims and the perpetrators and to further increase our understanding of the role that Belzec played in the destruction of Polish and European Jewry. Firstly, I must thank Professor Matthew Feldman from

Teesside University for not only writing the foreword to this book, but also for his long-standing friendship and support. It is thanks to Matthew that I was introduced to Anna Pivovarchuk, who has diligently and skillfully proof-read the manuscript in such a professional manner, for which I must thank her profusely. I must thank Clare Spyrakis, for her work on the cover design.

I must thank both Dr. Robin O'Neil and Michael Tregenza for their groundbreaking research into the grisly world that was Belzec death camp. I am grateful to the current Belzec museum director, Tomasz Hanejko, for all his help and support. I must also mention Tomasz's father Eugeniusz Hanejko,at the Regional Museum Tomaszow Lubelski for allowing the use of a number of photographs from their archives in this book. Also I am indebted to Shaul Ferrero from Yad Vashem and Zvi Oren from the Ghetto Fighters House. I must pay special tribute to Robert Kuwalek who sadly passed away in June 2014, in Lvov. I met him in 2000, when I first went to Lublin. His knowledge on Belzec in particular and the Holocaust in general was second to none, and his tragic early death, has robbed the world of a great talent. Sadly continuing this theme, I must also record my thanks to another Polish researcher, the late Artur Hojan, from the Tiergartenstrasse-4 Association, who helped me with this project, along with co-founder Cameron Munro, who shared some of his research material.

Finally, I must also express my gratitude to the late Sir Martin Gilbert, the well-respected British historian who has allowed me to show his brilliant map of Belzec, and has allowed me to use some of his other maps in my wider research.

Belzec is often referred to as the "Forgotten Camp of the Holocaust"—this book attempts to ensure that the victims of this charnel house are not forgotten.

Chris Webb
February 2015

Abbrevations used in the Footnotes

BA	Bundesarchiv (Federal Archive), Germany
GFH	Ghetto Fighters House, Israel
HHS	Holocaust Historical Society UK
NA	National Archives Kew, UK
NARA	National Archives Washington DC, United States of America
USHMM	United States Holocaust Memorial Museum, USA
YVA	Yad Vashem Archives, Israel

Contents

Part I
The Hell Called Belzec

Chapter I
Aktion Reinhardt: An Overview

Aktion Reinhardt—also known as *Einsatz Reinhardt*—was the code name for the extermination of primarily Polish Jewry from the former *Generalgouvernement* and the Białystok area. The term was used in remembrance of *SS-Obergruppenführer* Reinhard Heydrich, the co-ordinator of the "Final Solution to the Jewish Question" (*Endlösung der Judenfrage*)—the extermination of the Jews living in the European countries occupied by German troops during the Second World War.

On May 27, 1942, in a suburb of Prague, Jozef Gabčík and Jan Kubiš, members of the Czech resistance, ambushed Heydrich in his car while he was en route to his office in Prague, from his home at Panenské Březany. Heydrich died from his wounds at Bulovka Hospital on June 4, 1942.[13]

Four days after his death, approximately 1,000 Jews left Prague in a single train which was designated "AaH" (*Attentat auf Heydrich*). This transport was officially destined for Ujazdów, in the Lublin district, Poland, but the deportees were gassed at the Bełżec death camp in the far southeastern corner of the Lublin district. The members of Odilo Globocnik's resettlement staff henceforward dedicated the murder program to Heydrich's memory, under the code name *Einsatz Reinhardt*.[14]

The head of *Aktion Reinhardt* was *SS-Brigadeführer* Odilo Globocnik, the SS and Police Chief of the Lublin district, appointed to this task by *Reichsführer-SS* Heinrich Himmler. At the Führer's Head Quarters in Rastenburg (a town in present Poland known as

---

13 R. Cowdery, & P. Vodenka, *Reinhard Heydrich Assassination*, USM, Inc., Lakeville, 1994, pp. 49, 63.

14 G. Reitlinger, *The Final Solution*. Vallentine, Mitchell, London, 1953, pp. 105–106.

Kętrzyn), Heinrich Himmler, Friedrich-Wilhelm Krüger, and Odilo Globocnik met at a conference on October 13, 1941, during which Globocnik was authorized to build a death camp at Bełżec. Belzec was the first death camp built using static gas chambers, the first mass extermination camp in the east, was Kulmhof (a town in present day Poland known as Chełmno) and they used gas vans here from early December 1941.[15]

On January 20, 1942, at a villa in Wannsee, a suburb of Berlin, Heydrich organized a conference on the "Final Solution to the Jewish Question in Europe." The conference had been postponed from December 8, 1941, as Heydrich wrote to one of the participants Otto Hoffmann, that it had been necessary to postpone the conference "on account of events in which some of the invited gentlemen were concerned."[16] This referred to the Japanese attack on Pearl Harbor the previous day and the entry of the United States of America into the war. Those who attended the Wannsee Conference included the leading officials of the relevant ministries, senior representatives of the German authorities in the occupied countries, and senior members of the SS, including Heinrich Müller, head of the Gestapo, and Adolf Eichmann, head of Department IV B4, the sub-section of the Gestapo dealing with Jewish affairs.

*

Odilo Lothario Globocnik was born on April 21, 1904, in Trieste, the son of an Austro-Slovene family, and a construction enginner by trade. In 1930 he joined the Nazi party in Carinthia, Austria and after the banning of the Nazi Party in Austria in 1934, earned a reputation as one of the most radical leaders of its underground cells. In 1933 Globocnik joined the SS, which also became a prohibited organization in Austria in 1934, and was appointed *Stellvertretender Gauleiter* (Deputy Party District Leader).[17]

---

15 P. Longerich, *The Unwritten Order—Hiter's Role in the Final Solution*. Tempus, Stroud, 2001, p. 85.

16 Reitlinger, *The Final Solution*, op. cit., p. 101.

17 J. Poprzeczny, *Hitler's Man in the East—Odilo Globocnik*. McFarland, Jefferson, 2004, p. 10.

After serving several short terms of imprisonment, for illegal activities on behalf of the Nazis, he emerged as a key figure in the pre-Anschluß plans for Austria, serving as a key liaison figure between Adolf Hitler and the leading pro-Nazi Austrians.[18]

After the Anschluß of March 1938 Globocnik's star continued to rise, and on May 24 he was appointed to the coveted key position of Party District Leader (*Gauleiter*) of Vienna.

His tenure was short-lived, however, and on January 30, 1939, he was dismissed from this lofty position for corruption, illegal speculation in foreign exchange and tax evasion—all on a grand scale.[19]

After demotion to a lowly SS rank and undergoing basic military training with an *SS-Standarte*, he took part with his unit in the invasion of Poland. Eventually pardoned by Himmler, who needed such unscrupulous characters for future "unsavoury plans," Globocnik was appointed to the post of *SS- und Polizeiführer* (SS and Police Leader) of Lublin on November 9, 1939. Globocnik had been chosen by the *Reichsführer-SS* as the central figure in *Aktion Reinhardt*, not only because of his ruthlessness, but also because of his virulent anti-Semitism.

In Lublin, Globocnik surrounded himself with a number of his fellow Austrians, SS officers like Herman Julius Höfle, born in Salzburg on June 19, 1911. Höfle became Gobocnik's deputy in *Aktion Reinhardt*, responsible for personnel and the organization of Jewish deportations, the extermination camps and the re-utilisation of the victim's possessions and valuables. Höfle was later to play a significant role in mass deportation *Aktionen* in Warsaw and Białystok. Ernst Lerch, from Klagenfurt, became Globocnik's closest confidante and adjutant. Georg Michalsen, a Silesian from Oppeln, was another adjutant, and he, too, participated with Höfle in the deportation of Jews from the ghettos in Warsaw and Białystok. Another, early member of this group was Amon Göth, who cleared the Tarnów, Krakow, and Zamosc

---

18 Reitlinger, *The Final Solution*, op. cit., p. 262.
19 Poprzeczny, *Hitler's Man*, op. cit., p. 76.

ghettos, and later became the notorious commander of Płaszów *Arbeitslager* in Krakow.[20]

The headquarters of *Aktion Reinhardt* was located in the Julius Schreck Barracks (Julius Schreck Kaserne) at Litauer Straße 11, in a former Polish school close to the city centre in Lublin, where Höfle not only worked but lived in a small apartment on the second floor. Also located in Lublin were the buildings in which the belongings and valuables seized from the Jews were stored: the former Catholic Action (*Katolische Aktion*) building on Chopin Straße and in pre-war aircraft hangers on the Old Airfield (*Alter Flugplatz*) on the southeastern outskirts of Lublin.[21]

The most notorious and fearsome member of *Aktion Reinhardt* was *SS-Obersturmführer / Kriminalinspektor* Christian Wirth, the first commandant of Bełżec death camp and later Inspector of the *SS-Sonderkommandos* of *Aktion Reinhardt*. Before his transfer to Poland, Wirth had been a leading figure in *Aktion T4*—the extermination of the mentally and physically disabled in six so-called "euthanasia" killing centers in the Third Reich.

The role of the T4 euthanasia program was fundamental to the execution of *Aktion Reinhardt*, the great majority of the staff in the death camps served their "apprenticeships" in mass murder at the euthanasia institutes of Bernburg, Brandenburg, Grafeneck, Hadamar, Hartheim, and Pirna-Sonnenstein, where the victims had been murdered in gas chambers using CO gas from steel cylinders. The senior officers in both *Aktion T4* and *Aktion Reinhardt* were all police officers with equivalent SS ranks, and, with Himmler's approval, SS NCOs had emptied the gas chambers and cremated the bodies of the victims in portable furnaces. The SS-men performed this work wearing civilian clothes because Himmler did not want the possibility to arise of the public becoming aware of the participation of the SS in the killing. During *Aktion Reinhardt*, the SS authorities also supplemented the forces guarding the death camps by employing former Red Army troops

---

20 Poprzeczny, *Hitler's Man*, op. cit., p. 95

21 Reitlinger, *The Final Solution*, op. cit., p. 314.

who had been captured or had surrendered to the Germans, mostly ethnic Germans (*Volksdeutsche*) from the Ukraine, the Baltic states and the Volga region of Russia, who were trained in an SS camp in the village of Trawniki, 25 kilometers southeast of Lublin. The majority were already anti-Semitic—equating Bolsheviks with Jews—and were ideally suited to the persecution and extermination of Jews.

On November 1, 1941, construction of the first *Aktion Reinhardt* death camp began near the village of Bełżec, 125 kilometers southeast of Lublin, and became operational in mid-March 1942. Construction of the second camp, at Sobibor, between the cities of Włodawa and Chełm on the River Bug, northeast of Lublin, came into operation at the end of April 1942. The third and last of these camps was located near the train station Treblinka,[22] about 100 kilometers northeast of Warsaw. All three camps shared some common vital facts: They were all situated on or close to main railway lines for the speedy delivery of the victims to their deaths and they were located in sparsely-populated regions. The true fate of the Jews was initially hidden from them by announcing that they were being "transported to the east for resettlement and work." The *Aktion Reinhardt* death camps were very similar in layout, each camp being an improvement on its predecessor, and the "conveyor-belt" extermination process developed at Belzec by Christian Wirth was implemented, improved, and refined at the other two camps.

The personnel assigned to *Aktion Reinhardt* came from a number of sources, SS and policemen who served under Globocnik's command in the Lublin district, other SS-men and civilians drafted into the *Aktion* and members of the T4 euthanasia program.[23] Yitzhak Arad quotes in his book *Belzec, Sobibor, Treblinka* that a total of 450 men were assigned to *Aktion*

---

22 The village of Treblinka was in fact situated further from the camp than village of Poniatowo which was the closest village to the extermination camp.

23 Y. Arad, *Belzec, Sobibor, Treblinka—The Aktion Reinhard Death Camps*, Indiana University Press, Bloomington and Indianapolis, 1987, p. 17.

Reinhardt included 92 men from the T4 euthanasia program. However, more recent research by another author has identified a slightly higher total of 103 men, of whom 38 are known to have served at Belzec at one time or another.[24]

The Old Lublin Airfield was also used throughout *Aktion Reinhardt* as a mustering center for personnel transferred from the T4 euthanasia institutions in the Reich, to the extermination of the Jews in the *Generalgouvernement*. The SS-men, police, and civilians thus transferred were usually met at the airfield by Wirth personally, on occasions accompanied by the death camp commandants Reichleitner, from Sobibor, and Stangl, from Treblinka. According to witnesses, at these selections of personnel, all three wore *Schutzpolizei* uniforms and none of them mentioned anything about their future employment or where they would be based. At the airfield depot the newcomers received *Waffen-SS* uniforms, provided by the SS garrison administration (*SS-Standortverwaltung*) in Lublin, but without the SS runes on the right-hand collar patches. The civilian employees from T4, especially the male psychiatric nurses among them, were sent first to the SS training camp at Trawniki, for a two week basic military training course.[25]

The men selected in Lublin and distributed to the three *Aktion Reinhardt* death camps were augmented by a company-sized unit of about 120 black-uniformed auxiliary guards who had also been trained at the SS training camp in Trawniki—the so-called Trawniki-men (*Trawnikimänner*)—usually referred to as "Ukrainians" because they were the majority.

Those who spoke fluent German were appointed platoon or senior platoon leaders—*Zugführers* or *Oberzugführers*. The rest were known as *Wachmänner*. A select few of the *Trawnikimänner* were given other, special duties, including the maintenance and

---

24 S. Berger: *Experten der Vernichtung: das T4 Reinhardt- Netzwerk in das Lagern Belzec , Sobibor und Treblinka*, Hamburger Institut fur Sozialforschung, Hamburg, 2013, pp. 401-415.

25 M. Tregenza, Prvate Report Altoting 1972, Michael Tregenza Lublin Collection.

operation of the engines that pumped their poisonous exhaust fumes into the gas chambers. Among them were the infamous Ivan Marchenko (Ivan the Terrible) and Nikolay Shalayev, at the Treblinka death camp.[26]

In the course of *Aktion Reinhardt*, approximately 1.6 million Jews were murdered in the death camps at Belzec, Sobibor and Treblinka. Jewish property to the value of 178,045,960 *Reichsmark* (RM) was seized by the SS, which represents the minimum known amount. Through the theft of large amounts of cash and valuables by Globocnik, SS-men, policemen and guards, the true total will never be known.

The *Aktion Reinhardt* extermination operation ended officially in November 1943, and Himmler ordered Globocnik, who was by then the Higher SS and Police Leader for the Adriatic coastal region based in Trieste, to produce a detailed "balance sheet" for the murder program. Globocnik produced the requsted financial accounts and suggested that certain SS officers should be suitably rewarded for their "invaluable contribution" to *Aktion Reinhardt*. Globocnik received Himmler's thanks for his "services to the German people," but made no mention of medals for any of Globocnik's subordinates.[27]

After completion of the extermination work in the *Generalgouvernement*, most of the men who had served in *Aktion Reinhardt* were transferred to northern Italy, where their headquarters was in a disused rice mill in the San Sabba suburb of the Adriatic port of Trieste (*Risiera di San Sabba*). Divided into three SS units—RI, R-II and R-III—they operated under the code designation *Einsatz R* (Operation R), still under the command of Christian Wirth. Their primary task was the round-up and deportation to Auschwitz-Birkenau of the surviving Italian Jews, and confiscation of their property and valuables. *Einsatz R* was simply a smaller version of *Aktion Reinhardt*. Additionally, Italian-Jewish mental patients were removed from their hospitals and sent

---

26 Arad, *Belzec, Sobibor, Treblinka*, p. 22.

27 *Ibid.*,op. cit., p. 375.

to the T4 euthanasia institution at Schloss Hartheim in Austria for gassing. The units not engaged in these operations were assigned to security and anti-partisan patrols on the Istrian peninsula.

Wirth turned San Sabba into an interrogation and execution center where not only Jews, but also Italian and Yugoslav partisans were tortured, beaten to death, or simply shot and their bodies cremated in a specially installed furnace in the courtyard.[28] The human ashes were dumped in the Adriatic Sea. There is also evidence that a gas van was used in San Sabba.

The key members of *Aktion Reinhardt* mostly escaped justice, Globocnik and Höfle both committed suicide, whilst Wirth and Reichleitner (the second commandant of Sobibor death camp) were killed by partisans in northern Italy in 1944. Amon Göth was tried and sentenced to death for crimes committed in the Płaszów concentration camp (today a suburb of Krakow) in September 1946. Dr. Irmfried Eberl, the first commandant of Treblinka death camp, committed suicide in a West German prison in 1948 while awaiting trial. Only Franz Stangl[29] (the first commandant of Sobibor and second commandant of Treblinka) and Kurt Franz (the last commandant of Treblinka) were brought to trial. Both were found guilty of crimes against humanity and sentenced to life imprisonment. Gottlieb Hering, the second commandant of Belzec death camp, and commandant of Poniatowa Jewish labor camp died on October 9, 1945, in unknown circumstances in the waiting room at the Katherinen hospital in Stetten im Remstal, Württemberg, Germany.

As for members of the SS garrisons at the three death camps, a number of major figures like Karl Frenzel, from Sobibor, and Heinrich Arthur Matthes, August Miete, and Willy Mentz received life sentences, whist many others received prison terms of less than 10 years, but the vast majority of the SS-men and Ukrainians who

---

[28] *Ibid.*, op. cit., p. 399.

[29] It should be noted that many of the key members in the death camps' garrison were of Austrian nationality! Eberl was Austrian as well as Reichleitner and Stangl.

served within the framework of *Aktion Reinhardt* were never brought to justice. Only Josef Oberhauser was found guilty of war crimes at the Belzec trial in Munich during the 1960s.

Chapter II
The Labor Camps In the Belzec Area

The village of Belzec, in southeastern Poland, first appeared in records during the Middle Ages, and show the village as a settlement of animal breeders. At the beginning of the 17th century, the Lipski family—proprietors of Belzec—endeavoured to acquire a municipal charter, but this attempt failed because of the proximity of major towns such as Tomaszow Lubelski and Florianow, now re-named Narol.[30]

Two hundred years later, in the 19th century, Belzec lay on the border between Galicia and the Kingdom of Poland, with a railway border crossing to that part of Poland under the Tsarist Russian occupation. The location ensured business flourished and this attracted an influx of Jewish settlers, and, just prior to the First World War, over one hundred Jewish families made a living here on cross-border trade. Most of the Jewish settlers came from Rawa Ruska and Jaroslaw. Jewish culture flourished in Belzec, and it had its own house of prayer and a traditional elementary school—a cheder.[31]

During the First World War Belzec was occupied by Austrian troops and a part of the village was burnt down by Russian soldiers as a reprisal for the murder of a Russian officer by locals. During 1915, Belzec was liberated from Austrian occupation and six years later the village was incorporated into the new Republic of Poland.[32]

The Jewish population declined during the interwar years, and on September 13, 1939, the German Army occupied the village. A

---

30 R. Kuwalek, *From Lublin to Belzec*, Ad Rem, 2006, p. 29.

31 *Ibid.*, op. cit, p. 29.

32 M. Tregenza, *Belzec—The Unknown Death Camp of the Holocaust* (rev. 2006). Originally published Fritz Bauer Institut Jahrbuch, 2000, p. 3.

number of the Poles and Ukrainians registered as *Volksdeutsche*—ethnic Germans—and some volunteered for war work in the Reich. History repeated itself when Belzec once again became a border post, this time between the *Generalgouvernement* and the Soviet Union.[33]

From the end of May 1940 until August 1940, the Germans established a number of labor camps in and around the village of Belzec. These housed workers building the so-called "Otto Line"—a series of fortifications along the border with the Soviet Union. The Germans forced Jews from Lublin, Radom, and Warsaw districts to slave on this project, and Gypsies from the Reich and other parts of Poland were also used. The Jews were housed at three sites in Belzec: the Manor, which housed 1,000 people; Kessler's Mill, which housed 500 people; and Locomotive Sheds, which housed 1,500 people.

Outside Belzec village other workers were housed in Cieszanow in two barracks and Plaszow—not to be confused with the notorious Plaszow *Arbeitslager* in Krakow—in two houses and in Lipsko near Narol.[34]

The labor camps were established in abandoned synagogues, warehouses or barns, a total of some 35 camps were created with over 10,000 workers employed on building fortifications, roads and regulating rivers.

The commander of the labor camps complex was *SS-Sturmbannführer* Hermann Dolp, who had also been the commandant of the Lipowa Street Camp in Lublin and during 1941—after the Nazi invasion of the Soviet Union—had served in the "SS Strongpoints in the East" construction program based in Minsk.[35] His deputy was *SS-Hauptscharführer* Franz Bartetzko, who later went on to manage the Jewish forced labor camp at Trawniki, from the spring of 1942.[36] Another more famous SS

---

33 *Ibid.*, op. cit, p. 3.

34 Report *Judenlager an der Grenze*—dated September 24, 1940—YVA Jerusalem.

35 National Archives Kew HW16/32.

36 Helge Grabitz & Wolfgang Scheffler, *Letzte Spuren*, Hentrich Edition 1993, p. 211.

officer, Oskar Dirlewanger, who was the commander of the notorious *SS-Sonderkommando Dirlewanger*, which was made up of petty criminals and cut-throats. They were resoponsible for the orgy of killing of the population during the Warsaw uprising in 1944. Prior to this, Dirlewanger was the commander of a Jewish labor camp at Dzikow, one of the camps in the Belzec area.[37]

The working conditions in the labor camps were truly awful, with workers beaten and tortured, and forced to perform heavy labor on starvation rations. Adam Czerniakow, the chairman of the *Judenrat* (Jewish Council) in the Warsaw ghetto, wrote about the Belzec labor camp conditions several times in his diary. His entry on August 29, 1940, is as follows:

> Word from the Belzec camp, poor food etc. I arranged for two conferences, one with participation of Neustadt. I authorised the *Obmann* (Chairman) from Zamosc to engage doctors at our expense for Belzec. Tomorrow I will try to obtain a loan for the camp.[38]

Another entry in his diary, recorded on September 3, 1940, stated that "Zabludowski, Faust and Furstenburg left for Lublin with the gifts for the workers including 10,000 zloty for the camp. Lambrecht made a demand for twenty doctors for the camp." [39]

Though the labor camps were controlled by the SS, the supply of food, clothes, and the administration was managed by the Lublin *Judenrat*. In Belzec, the Germans established a so-called Jewish *Gremium*, which was responsible for the camp's organization. All costs connected with the existence of the prisoners were paid by the *Judenrat* of the towns from where the prisoners came. It was the *Gremium* who decided the allocation of food to the workers. After August 1940, the *Gremium* was renamed the Central Camps Council and was led by Leon Zylberajch from Lublin.

---

37 Oskar Dirlewanger—Personal File—Letter from Globocnik dated August 5, 1941—Yad Vashem Archive, File 0.68 569.

38 Adam Czerniakow: *The Warsaw Diary of Adam Czerniakow*—Editors Raul Hilberg, Stanislaw Staron and Josef Kermisz, Ivan R Dee, Chicago, 1999, p. 191.

39 *Ibid.*, op. cit, p. 193

The labor camps in Belzec and those located in the area were closed down in October 1940, and this "Eastern Rampart" was only some 40 kilometers in length, 2.5 meters deep and 7.5 meters wide, between Belzec and Dzikow Stary village. Some of the Jewish workers were released prior to the final liquidation of the labor camps, because they were unfit for work; the last transport of workers released went to Hrubieszow in late October 1940.

No account of these terrible working conditions in the Belzec labor camps is complete without mentioning the fate of the Gypsies who were deported from the Reich and were incarcerated on a farm at Belzec Manor. As with the Jews, the Gypsies were also employed in digging fortifications on starvation rations and many succumbed to illnesses such as typhus and dysentery.

One of these Gypsies, Martha W.—a Sinti woman, born in Kiel, Germany, in 1921—was deported to Belzec together with her two children, her mother, and her brother. After the war she recounted her story in an interview with Karin Guth, which is incredibly moving and heart-rending:

> In May, I think it was 16 May 1940, they came for us and brought us to the *Fruchtschuppen* (Fruit Warehouse) in the harbour of Hamburg. My memory is not that good anymore. I only know that a lot of people were in the warehouse. It was like being in an ant-hill, so many people were running around.
>
> We were registered and those above the age of fourteen received a number on the arm, this was not tattooed, as was later the case in Auschwitz, but stamped in ink. The number faded after a few days. I cannot remember how many days we were in the warehouse. Not many perhaps three days. Quite nearby, only some steps away, we were ordered to enter goods wagons at the *Hannoverscher* Station.
>
> There was an awful confusion, there being hundreds of people. We were told we were being transported to Poland, where we would receive a nice little house. And they told me that my father was already there, but we were deceived.
>
> When we arrived at our destination SS surrounded the train. They were there at our arrival and drove us out of the wagons.

Policeman had accompanied us, two to a wagon (probably within the brakers cabin at the rear of some wagons).

We naturally did not travel without a guard. They knew we would have otherwise simply left the train and escaped. We would have done this had we had the chance. The policemen, who had escorted us, appeared thoroughly sheepish, when they saw the SS and heard the SS commandant, a small man standing there with a whip in his hand; immediately shouting, 'if you don't obey the orders!' Oh dear and the rest he said. He called us dogs and we were treated as such. That was so awful. The policemen from Hamburg stood there speechless. I presume they hadn't known what we were to experience in Belzec.

Then we had to walk to a large barn, that was more a very large shed. There was only old straw on the floor. We had to enter this shed , SS guards were posted outside. Today I no longer remember how long we were in that Belzec camp. It was summer when we arrived. I think we were there for some weeks . It was awful there. One could not wash oneself, there were no toilets. We were all crammed together.

We were immediately set to work in a work column. We had to dig tank ditches. There were many Jews in Belzec too. They were housed in the same shed as us and also worked in the column. They usually only remained for some weeks, then they were transported from Belzec to somewhere else.

The food was awful. A Roma was detailed to cook for us all. The SS shot crows and ravens and simply threw them into the large pot. The man didn't want to cook the birds without first plucking the feathers. They beat him so badly that the blood ran out the bottom of his trousers.

One day those of us with children had to line up because the children were to receive something special to eat. I had two children. My daughter was two and my son was one-year old. Each was given a bowl containing milk with bread crumbled in it. Or so it appeared.

This was especially for the children. Well, one child after the other died over the following days. There was such lamenting, lamenting and crying. Shortly after having eaten the children were unable to breathe anymore, they asphyxiated. My little boy died first.

Someone woke me in the morning. I was woken because the chid had kicked and the person wanted to cover him again. So I awoke and went to pick him up. He was already quite stiff.

I was devastated with grief and I didn't know what to do. My cousin, the sister of Mrs B. lifted him and a big clot of pus came out of his throat. All the children experienced this. My two year old daughter died in the same way the next day. They had been poisoned.

One day we had to enter cattle wagons again, in Belzec. There was just a bare floor. There were no windows, only air slits, high up. There were no toilet facilities. We had to enter that train, not knowing what to expect. Nobody told us anything.

We were taken to Krychow. We travelled through the night in this cattle wagon. When we arrived at the station, horse-drawn vehicles awaited us that took us to the camp. It was a former Polish prison, far away from the station. We were guarded by men wearing a black uniform. They were *Volksdeutsche*. These *Volksdeutsche* and SS were everywhere.[40]

[40] Martha W., Interview with Karin Guth, 2005, www.deathcamps.org.

Chapter III
Construction of the Death Camp November 1941–February 1942

The Belzec death camp was built by the *SS Zentralbauverwaltung* (Central Building Administration) in the Lublin district. Work commenced on November 1, 1941, under the stewardship of *SS-Oberscharführer* Josef Oberhauser. A number of local villagers were employed in the construction of the death camp, and after the war provided statements about its genesis. One of these was Edward Ferens, a 36-year-old locksmith, who testified on March 20, 1946, in Belzec:

> In the autumn of 1941 I worked for seven weeks on the construction of the barracks in Belzec which, it later transpired were used in the exterminiation of the Jews. I worked as an ordinary labourer and was forced into this work by the municipal office in Belzec.
>
> During this time six barracks were built. Later more barracks were put up, but by then I was no longer employed on their construction. I remember that we put up a barracks which was especially big, beside a much smaller one; the two were connected by a corridor. This small barracks was well-built and a narrow-gauge railway laid which ran from this barracks across the field.
>
> When we asked the Germans what this barracks was for, they only laughed and said nothing. I remember that the building of the camp was directed by a young German; he was about twenty years old, slim, blond, and allegedlly came from the Kattowitz area. This German had the building plans and often went around with them among the labourers working in the camp area. I asked him what these barracks were being built for? As an answer, the German only laughed ... he only spoke weak Polish. Besides this young German,

> there were no other German specialists involved in the building work.[41]

Stanislaw Kozak, another Polish local worker, provided another key eyewitness account of the building of the death camp. He testified in Belzec on October 14, 1945, and his detailed statement on the first gassing facilities should be viewed as the definitive account:

> There arrived in Belzec in October 1941, 3 SS men who demanded 20 workers from the Belzec community. The municipal office appointed 20 inhabitants of Belzec as workers—I was one of them. The Germans selected the area to the South-East of the railway station where a siding ended.
>
> Alongside the siding ran the railway to Lemberg. We began work on 1 November 1941 with the building of barracks at the end of the siding. One barrack—which stood right next to the siding—was 50 metres long and 12.5 metres wide. It was a waiting room for the Jews. The second barrack 25 metres long and 12.5 metres wide—was for the Jews appointed to bathe in.
>
> Near this barracks we had built a third barracks which was 12 metres long and 8 metres wide. This barrack was divided into three parts by wooden walls—each part being 4 metres wide and 8 metres long. The height of each section was 2 metres. The inner walls of this barracks were so constructed that we nailed planks to them and filled the empty space between them with sand. The interior walls of this barrack were covered with pasteboard, and the floors and walls—to a height of 1.10 metres—were covered with zinc sheeting.
>
> From the first barracks to the second barracks, about which I have already spoken, there led an alleyway 3 metres wide of barbed-wire fencing 3 metres high. The side of the fence nearest the siding was specially covered with pine and fir branches, so that nothing was visible from the siding. From the second barracks a covered passage 2 metres wide, 2 metres high and about 10 metres long—led to the third barracks. Through this passage one arrived at the

41 Edward Ferens Testimony, March 20, 1946. Copy, Holocaust Historical Society UK.

corridor of the third barrack which led through three doors into the three parts of the barracks.

Kozak continued his detailed description:

> Each part of this barracks had on its northern side a door—about 1.80 metres high and 1.10 metres wide. These doors, as well as the ones in the corridor, were sealed with rubber. All the doors in this barrack opened outwards. The doors were very strong—constructed of planks 75mm thick and fastened from the outside by a wooden bar which fitted into two iron hooks.
>
> In each of the three parts of this barrack there was fixed at a height of 10cms from the floor, a waterpipe. The waterpipe branched from each corner along the western wall of each part of this barrack to the middle of the wall, and ended in an opening at a height of 1 metre from the floor. These waterpipes were joined to a main pipe at a junction under the floor.
>
> In each of the three parts of the above—mentioned barracks were placed stoves weighing 250 kilos. One must surmise that the waterpipes were later connected to these stoves. The stoves were 1.10 metres high, 55 cm wide and 55 cm long. Out of curiosity, I glanced into the stove through the open door. I did not see any grate there. The interior of the stove was—so it seemed—lined with firebrick. I could not ascertain what the other stoves were like. The stove opening was oval, with a diameter of about 25cm, and about 50cm above the floor.
>
> Along the northern side of this barrack a 1 metres high ramp made of planks was errected and along this ramp a narrow- gauge railway track was laid which led to the grave right in the noth east corner which had been dug by the 'Blacks.' This grave was dug by 70 'Blacks' ..... it was 6 metres deep, 20 metres wide and 50 metres long. This was the first grave in which the Jews killed in the death camp were buried. The 'Blacks' dug this grave in 6 weeks, during the time we were building the barracks. This grave was later extended to the middle of the northern boundary.
>
> The first of these barracks I mentioned lay 20 metres from the siding and 100 metres from the southern boundary. At that time, when we Poles were building these barracks, the 'Blacks' erected the fencing around the death camp, which consisted of wooden posts between which was strung barbed-wire.

After we had built the aforementioned three barracks, the Germans released us from our work on 22 December 1941. As far as I remember, in January or February 1942, the Germans built three watchtowers around the camp. Further building work in the camp was carried out by Jews under German supervision.

The western, northern and eastern borders of the camp were planted with big fir trees and pines to hide the interior of the camp. The camp was divided—from east to west—in three parts. In the first part were the Jews employed in burying the corpses of the murdered Jews; in the second part—the sorting of the clothing and other belongings of the Jews; and the third part—those employed in working in the camp (even outside the camp).

I know that the Germans baked 500 loaves of bread a day, sometimes more—for the Jews employed in the camp. These Jews were employed in the camp the whole time it was in operation. At the moment of the disbandment of the camp these Jews were taken away by train in the direction of Rejowiec.

Before the New Year of 1942, the Germans brought about 70 Jews in lorries from Lubycza (Krolewska) and Mosty. The 'Blacks' explained that these Jews had worked for two weeks and then been killed in the camp without saying how. [42] [43]

Belzec death camp was tiny, when compared to other extermination centres like Auschwitz-Birkenau, the north, west, and east sides each measuring 275 meters, and the south side 265 meters. It was built on a partly forested sandy ridge known as Kozielsk Hill. Three watchtowers were built at the corners of the camp, two on the east side, and a third at the southwest corner.

A railroad spur originally laid by the *Oberschlesische Holzindustrie* (Upper Silesian Timber Company) entered the camp area at the northwest corner via a sturdy wooden gate and a nearby wooden guard house. Belzec was in fact divided into two: Camp I, in the northern and western part was the reception area, included

---

42 Stanislaw Kozak Testimony, October 14, 1945. Copy, Holocaust Historical Society UK.

43 Authors Note: "Blacks" refer to the Ukrainian *Trawnikimänner* who were captured Red Army volunteers working for the SS, who wore black coloured uniforms and were trained at the Trawniki camp in the Lublin district.

the ramp that could hold twenty cattle wagons, the assembly square for the Jewish deportees, and the undressing and storage barracks. Camp I also housed the administration area, which had two barracks that housed the Jewish prisoners. This area also included the roll-call square and the laundry, kitchen, and other barracks for storage. To the left of the entrance gate already mentioned was the *Trawnikimänner* area, which included their living quarters, a kitchen, plus their clinic, dentist, and barber.

Camp II, the so-called extermination area, included the three gas chambers and the mass graves, which were in the east and northeast areas of the camp. The gas chambers were surrounded by trees, and a camouflage net was placed over the roof to prevent observation from low-flying aeroplanes. As time went by, two barracks were erected in this area for the Jewish work brigades' living quarters and kitchen. Camp II was segregated off from Camp I by barbed wire fences with a heavily guarded entrance gate.[44]

The undressing barracks in Camp I was connected to the extermination area by the so-called *Schlauch* (tube), some 2-meters-wide and 100-meters-long passageway enclosed on both sides by camouflaged barbed wire fences. The naked, doomed Jews passed through this passage way which led directly to the gas chamber facility.

The three gas chambers were etremely primitive, as have been described above, each chamber measuring 6 by 4 meters, and had a maximum capacity of 240 people in each chamber. The three chambers was constructed on concrete foundations and, after the gassing had taken place, the bodies were unloaded through the three doors at the rear of the chambers and transferred to the mass graves, using a narrow-gauge railway with tip-up trucks, though this method was later discarded.[45]

In Belzec village, two well-built stone houses near the station on Tomaszowska Street, were requisitioned from the *Ostbahn* (Eastern Railways), one of which served as Christian Wirth's

---

44 Arad, *Belzec, Sobibor, Treblinka*, pp. 27, 28.

45 Tregenza, *Belzec*, p. 3.

Kommandantur—his office and living quarters—while the other house served as the living quarters for a number of the SS garrison. A third building, a peasants cottage adjacent to the *Kommandantur*, was requisitioned as the death camps general office. Next to the cottage, at the rear of the *Kommandantur* was an armoury. At the rear of the building that housed the SS garrison was a small stable. The complex was surrounded by a wooden fence and barbed-wire, with the exception of the roadside area, which was manned round-the clock by armed sentries.[46]

Some historical accounts claim that Richard Thomalla, from the *Waffen-SS Bauleitung* Zamosc, at General Drescher Straße 34, who built the *Aktion Reinhardt* camps at Sobibor and Treblinka, was involved at the commencement of construction in Belzec on November 1, 1941. However, this is unlikely as he was in Russia during this time as part of the constructing "SS Strongpoints in the East" program, which was under the control of Odilo Globocnik in Lublin. The British Intelligence Service at Bletchley Park intercepted and decoded German police messages using a replica Enigma machine, provided to them by the Poles.[47] Messages sent to Thomalla at Zwiahel on November 21, 1941, would seem to exclude him from overseeing the early stages of the construction of the death camp in Belzec. Of some note is that other key members of Globocnik's staff, such as Hermann Dolp and Kurt Claasen in Minsk, Hermann Höfle in Minsk and Mogilev, and Georg Michalsen in Riga, were also employed on the "Strongpoints in the East" construction projects.[48]

On his return to Lublin in early 1942, he was involved in the latter stages of construction at Belzec, and there can be no doubt he supervised from the start the construction of the other two death camps that formed part of *Aktion Reinhardt,* Sobibor, and Treblinka.

---

46 Interview at Belzec in July 2002 with two local villagers who lived through the occupation.

47 Stephen Tyas, British Intelligence Service, Decoded Radio Messages from the General Gouvernement, 2004.

48 National Archives Kew HW16/32.

Chapter IV Recruitment into Aktion Reinhardt: T4 & Trawniki

T4 was the name of a secret organization, named after its address in Berlin, Tiergartenstraße 4, and this organization was part of the Führer's Chancellery. The T4 organization established several institutions throughout the Reich that murdered mentally ill and disabled men, women, and children by means of gassing by carbon monoxide and lethal injections.[49]

Kurt Hubert Franz was a member of T4, as well as serving as a concentration camp guard at Buchenwald, and during his interrogation in Düsseldorf on December 30, 1959, he provided a detailed account of the T4 recruitment process, and subsequent service in the death camps of *Aktion Reinhardt.* This account has not been altered:

> I was raised in Dusseldorf, and here I went to the primary school. Then I first worked as an errand boy at the firm Peter Holters, Factory of Fine Food. Then I completed a 3 year long apprenticeship as a cook at the *Wittelsbacher Hof.* The apprenticeship time began at one *Hirschquelle* Bar, which had to close after approximately one year, meaning I had to stop, because the owner changed.
>
> After working for a short time as a young cook in Dusseldorf, I came to a working service camp in Ratingen, organized by the *Stahlhelm* on a voluntary basis. There I first worked in the kitchen, but later I also fulfilled normal work service. At the end I was *Gruppenführer*. I was not only in Ratingen in the working service, but also in Heiligenhaus and Honnef. At the last camp this was

49 Raul Hilberg, *The Destruction of the European Jews*, Holmes & Meier, New York, London, 1985, p. 226.

already a *Reichsarbeitdienst* of the time. From 1932 to 1934 I was busy for about two years at the working service.

In 1934 and 1935 I was a volunteer with the butcher–master Martin Stollmann in Oberkassel. In 1935, in autumn, I was drafted to the *Wehrmacht.* I fulfilled my military obligation at the Artillery Regiment 6 in Minden / Westfalen. Towards the end of September 1937 I was discharged with the service degree of *Oberkanonier.*

In October 1937 I then entered the *Waffen-SS.* I came to the *Totenkopfverband-Standarte 'Thüringen.'* This unit was later called, *'Totenkopf-Standarte Thüringen.'* The training period was for 6 weeks, but I want to point out that I myself was immediately designated as a trainer. At the end of 1937, my unit came to the concentration camp Buchenwald, which at the time was being built. My unit was designated for guard service in Buchenwald. The service consisted in that we performed guard duties on watchtowers, and that we were divided as guards, when work had to be performed by inmates outside the camp proper. The inmates were accompanied by members of the guard units, when they marched from the camp gate to their work places, and when they returned after work. During the work, the total object was surrounded by a guarding chain. In Buchenwald I was named a *Sturmann* and then a *Rottenführer.*

At this point Franz explains his recruitment into the T4 organization:

At the end of the year 1939 I was ordered to Berlin. I had to report at the *Führer's* office in the Voss Street, at the Reich's medical leader *SS-Standartenführer* Brandt. Other than myself there were other SS members present, who had to report at the same time. Two of them also came from Buchenwald. Their names were Fritz Jirmann and Herbert Floss. According to my memory there were three SS members from Dachau present, and they were Gottfried Schwarz, one Niemann, called Jonny and one Oberhauser, called with first name Sepp. These names I can remember because we six were first quartered together in Berlin, and because in the time following we met here and there during our service.

At the service station in the Voss Street were present other than the Reichs Medical Leader other persons, but of which I can only recall a certain Blankenburg, who as much as I know had the uniform of an *SA-Standartenführer*. The others present had civilian clothing. Then we were shown a film, which was probably taken in several madhouses, and which contained pictures of mentally ill people with horrible body deformations. Mainly Brandt explained then, that these ill people were a burden for the German people. Brandt or someone else said that it was best to eliminate these ill people.

After this film and the explainations, we 6 SS members from Buchenwald and Dachau had to sign a red certificate, whereby we committed ourselves to keep quiet about everything we had heard and seen. We were told it was a secret Reich matter. This appeared in writing also on the red certificate. Then we were dismissed. If I remember well, there remained the civilians, and I suppose they were probably doctors. They too had to sign the red certificate. They might have been 10 or 12 gentlemen.

After, we left the room, we were approached by a gentleman who might have belonged to the service station or the *Führer's* office. He was more than 1.90 tall and must have been a movie star, which became obvious from the later relation with him. The name could have been Schwennice, or something like that. He made an appointment with us for the next day, in order to buy civilian clothing for us. We then went with him to a department store, where for us six persons only one outfit of civilian clothings was brought for us, and paid by our escort.

On behalf of the *Führer's* office we had been accommodated at a *Pension* at the *Hallesche Ufer*. We were also told about a place called *Lukullus,* where we had to eat. We were told we would receive notice when we were needed. Then it took a few weeks—it could also have been 2 or 3 months—until we heard something further. To my knowledge I was the first to be put to service.

Kurt Franz recalled his service in various T4 institutions:

I had to go to Grafeneck, which was nearby Munsingen in Württenberg. There was an institution in the stage of being established. The first thing I had to do was buy the mobile inventory for the kitchen. In the following time I, as kitchen chief had to take care of the feeding of 60–80 people, meaning for the doctors, nurses, female nurses, administration personnel etc.

> Somewhat aside from the main building, barracks and ovens were erected. There later the sick people were killed and burned, which were brought by buses. How the killing process had been carried out I cannot say, I had nothing to do with it. I have only seen, that these chimneys of the cremation ovens smoked heavily. I would like to correct myself, there was only one chimney, but there were probably several ovens.
>
> From Grafeneck I was then transferred to Aschach, by Linz, at the Danube. There on one of the properties of *Fürst Starhemberg* was also established an elimination institution. There the buses with the sick people went into an inner courtyard, so that one saw even less than in Grafeneck of what happened there. I myself worked there again as a kitchen chief. After training a cook there, I was further transferred to Sonnenstein by Pirna, where there was also an elimination institution. There too I worked as a kitchen chief.
>
> For a very short time I was also at the madhouse in Brandenburg, where there too, sick people were eliminated. I cannot say, I was probably supposed to work there too as a cook. But according to my memory there I laid down ill, having a tumor in my nose. From Pirna, during the late summer of 1941 I was ordered to Berlin. In the *Wilhelmstrasse 40* or *43* I managed a kitchen, in which ate some members of the *Führer's* office and the service station of *Tiergartenstrasse 4*. I think that according to my memory in the *Tiergartenstrasse* there was the 'Common Foundation for Institutional Care.' I suppose there was some kind of connection and that the service station *Tiergartenstrasse 4* was the central place for the carrying out of the total action.

Franz recalled his time in Poland, serving at Belzec and Treblinka death camp, as part of *Aktion Reinhardt*:

> About March 1942 I received a marching order of the *Waffen-SS (Führungshauptamt)* and had to go to Lublin. I was told that I would there be put to work as a cook. In Lublin I had to report to the Higher SS– and Police Leader. After reporting in Lublin at the service station of the Higher SS- and Police Leader Globocnik, I had to march to Belzec. There a camp was being established. I heard that this was a camp, in which Jews were to be eliminated. This camp was indeed operated, while I was still there, as an elimination camp. The killing of the Jews was done by means of a gassing car. The cars looked like the vehicles of the parcel post.

While I was still in Belzec, gas chambers were built. I was informed, that for these gas chambers there were engine rooms. They had allegedly left the engines running and then by means of gas pipes the gas was led to the gas chambers. I think that the Jews killed in Belzec were from Poland itself.

I was in Belzec until the end of 1942.* In Belzec—I had become in the meantime a *SS-Scharführer*—I first trained the members of the personnel militarily, since they had no knowledge about weapons at all. These people had some SS and some police uniforms. I recall that one of them told me that he had been a nurse. These people trained by myself had to participate at the carrying out of the elimination, by receiving the transports. At this the then camp commander *SS-Sturmbannführer* Christian Wirth was really always present. These people trained by myself had to make sure that the arriving Jews reached the gas chambers. For the servicing of the gas chambers there were some kind of specialists who had a special knowledge in engines.

After the arrival of the Ukrainian guard units, Wirth named me to lead them. They might have been about 40 guards. I trained these guards militarily and proceeded to organize their duties. The German commanding orders were known to the guards. Also among them were *Volksdeutsche* from Russia. The guards had to stand guard around the elimination camp. On some occasions they were used against Partisans.

When transports arrived in Belzec, the train went all the way into the camp. In the camp itself were the large pits, in which dead people were thrown in. The following jobs like opening the pits and taking out or in of the bodies, were performed by Jewish working commando's. These working commando's inside the camp were not guarded particularly. They received their orders from SS members who served inside of the camp. While the transports were arriving, and the killing action was performed, the camp was surrounded by guards.

In the beginning of 1943 I was transferred from Belzec to Treblinka.** Treblinka was a liquidation camp that was operating already for some time, when I arrived there. Treblinka was considerably larger than Belzec................ [50] [51]

In the case of the *Trawnikimänner*, their recruitment and role at the Aktion Reinhardt death camps is important to understand. One of the Ukrainian guards was Nikolai Petrovich Malagon, who was interrogated on October 2, 1979, in the city of Vinnitsa. His detailed account will adequately serve to illustrate the historical sequence of events:

> During the Great Patriotic War, I participated with my military unit in the defence of the city of Kiev. In August 1941 I was wounded in the head and taken prisoner by the Germans, together with other soldiers from my unit. While a prisoner, I was first held in a POW camp in the city of Zhitomir. We were later transferred to a camp in the city of Rovno, and a day later we were transferred in railroad cars to a POW camp in the city of Chelm (Poland).
>
> We were held in this camp, for approximately two months. In roughly October or November 1941 we, the POW's were assembled near the barracks and some man, unknown to me, wearing civilian clothes began to select prisoners for work. He selected a total of roughly 60–70 POW's, including myself. This man did not tell us what kind of work we would be doing or where we would do it.
>
> The selected POW's and myself were hauled in three trucks to the village of Trawniki (Poland) and we were told that in this training camp, we would be trained as SS guards. When we arrived at the Trawniki training camp, there were already other POW's there, as well as the camp administration. There was a total of approximately 300 trainees in the camp; these were organized into four companies. Three companies consisted of Ukrainian POW's and one company consisted of Russian POW's. I was in the 3rd Company. The commander of my company was Mayevskiy (I do not remember his first name and patronymic). He was Polish or

---

50 Kurt Franz Interrogation Statement 30, December 1959, NARA, Washington DC.

51 Kurt Franz admitted in other interrogations that he left Belzec for Treblinka in mid-summer or early autumn 1942. As above, there are many eyewitness testimonies from survivors and former camp personnel that state Franz was in Treblinka in August 1942. Why he should state this later date is unknown.

German by nationality, since he spoke these languages well. His fate is unknown to me.

Our platoon leader was Komarkin or Komarik—I do not remember his precise name, a German by nationality, who died roughly in the spring of 1942 from heart disease. The squad leader was Broft, whose first name and patronymic I do not remember. He was a teacher by profession and was a Volga German. His later fate is unknown to me.

Two or three weeks after our arrival at the Trawniki camp, we took an oath of loyalty to Germany and were issued Belgian military uniforms. In January of 1942 the Germans selected 10 men from among the trainees, myself included, and sent us to the city of Zamosc (Poland), where we guarded an estate. Mayevskiy was the senior officer among us. We guarded this estate until the spring of 1942, and then we returned to the Trawniki training camp, where we finished our training course within 2–3 weeks. After this we were awarded the title of SS guards and issued identification. Our identification was printed on heavy paper (I do not remember the colour) and folded double. My photograph was attached to my identification and it had a text in German.

A short time later, as part of a group of guards consisting of 20–25 men whose names I do not remember, I was sent to the Lublin camp. We worked cleaning up the area at this camp and stayed there 5–6 days. From the Lublin camp we were sent to the city of Warsaw, where we stayed approximately three days. During these three days I once guarded the Jewish ghetto.

From Warsaw we, the guards, escorted a train filled with Jewish civilians to the Treblinka death camp. We were all armed with rifles and live ammunition. When we arrived at the Treblinka camp together with the prisoners, we handed them over to the camp guard. When we arrived at the camp, there were other guards there from the Trawniki school.

While at the Treblinka death camp, I met the guard Nikolai Marchenko (Authors Note: This should be Ivan Marchenko) who drove a gas chamber van (this is also incorect—Marchenko operated the engines in the static gas chambers), I do not know where he is at present. In the same camp I met the guard Ivan Demjanjuk. This guard was of average height and heavy build, spoke Ukrainian and had light brown hair. His speech was pure; he pronounced everything well. I did not know where he was from, since I did not talk to him about this. While I was at the Treblinka death camp, he worked there as a cook, preparing food for the guards. I could identify the guard whom I have named as Demjanjuk from photographs.

> In February 1943 approximately 15 of us, the guards, were transferred to the Belzec camp (Poland). Ivan Demjanjuk remained at Treblinka. We were at Belzec for approximately five days and, since some of the guards escaped, we were once again returned to Trawniki, where we were given special insignia and then we were sent to the Auschwitz death camp. I served in this camp from March to April 1943. Then we were transferred to the Buchenwald death camp, where I served as a guard from April of 1943 through February of 1945.[52]

Returning to the German forces and the crucial role played by the T4 personnel, Viktor Brack, who was Philipp Bouhler's deputy and Chief of Section II in the Führer's Chancellery responsible for the T4 management of the euthanasia program testified at his post war trial about the transfer of T4 personnel to *Aktion Reinhardt*:

> In 1941, I received an order to discontinue the euthanasia programme, in order to retain the personnel that had been relieved of these duties and in order to be able to start a new euthanasia programme, after the war, Bouhler asked me—I think after a conference with Himmler—to send this personnel to Lublin, and place it at the disposal of SS-*Brigadeführer* Globocnik.[53]

One of the SS members of the Belzec garrison, *SS-Scharführer* Erich Fuchs testified after the war about the transfer of T4 personnel to the Belzec camp:

> *Polizeihauptmann* Christian Wirth conducted the *Aktionen* in Bernburg. Subordinate to him were the burners, disinfectors and drivers. He also supervised the transportation of the mentally ill and of the corpses. One day in the winter of 1941 Wirth arranged a transport of euthanasia personnel to Poland. I was picked together with about eight or ten other men and transferred to Belzec.

---

52 Nikolai Malagon Interrogation, October 2, 1979, Vinnitsa. Copy, Holocaust Historical Society UK.

53 Arad, *Belzec, Sobibor, Treblinka*, p. 17.

> I don't remember the names of the others. Upon our arrival in Belzec, we met Friedel Schwarz and the other SS men, whose names I cannot remember. They supervised the construction of barracks that would serve as a gas chamber. Wirth told us that in Belzec 'all the Jews will be struck down.' For this purpose barracks were built as gas chambers. I installed shower heads in the gas chambers. The nozzles were not connected to any water pipes; they would serve as camouflage for the gas chamber. For the Jews who were gassed it would seem as if they were being taken to baths and for disinfection.[54]

In late December 1941, Christian Wirth was appointed commandant of Belzec, and Josef Oberhauser, who was in charge of constructing the death camp, was appointed to the post of Wirth's adjutant. The scene was set for a period of trial and error, where Wirth would perfect the process where industrialized mass murder became the deadly norm.

---

54 *Ibid.*, p. 24.

Chapter V
Descent into Mass Murder: The First Phase March-June 1942

The primitive gas chambers were ready for use by the end of February 1942, after Christian Wirth had experimented with bottled carbon monoxide and the use of a converted parcel carrier to a gas van had all proved unequal to the task. *SS-Scharführer* Erich Fuchs testified that "A chemist, a civilian from Berlin, was brought in during the construction. He told me that he had once served with the navy. I admit he may have been known by the name of Dr. Blaurock."[55]

This chemist from T4 was Dr. Helmut Kallmayer—Dr. Blaurock was a pseudonym—and his role in Belzec was to observe the various gasing experiments conducted by Christian Wirth, and to provide advice. Dr. Kallmayer also provided advice on the gassing facilities at the Sobibor death camp.

Mieczyslaw Kudyba, a Polish resident of Belzec, testified about the first experimental killing by gas in Belzec:

> The Germans took out a group of Jews from Lubycze-Krolewska and brought them by car to the Belzec camp. One Jew from that group told me that he had been in the camp some time cutting pine trees. One day all the Jews were driven into a barrack. This Jew was able to hide and later to escape. While in hiding, he heard long screams from the barrack in which the Jews had been locked and then silence. This was the first experimental killing in Belzec. I heard that this Jew who escaped was later caught by the Germans and killed.[56]

At his trial in Jerusalem, Adolf Eichmann, the head of IV B4—the Jewish section of the Reich Main Security Office

---

55 J. Schelvis, *Sobibor, A History of a Nazi Death Camp*, Berg, Oxford, New York, 2007, p. 99.

56 Arad, *Belzec, Sobibor, Treblinka*, p. 26.

Reichssicherheitshauptamt (RSHA)—testified that he visited Belzec and saw the gassing barrack under construction, but near completion. This would indicate the visit took place between January and February 1942, probably after the Wannsee Conference in Berlin on January 20, 1942, which was held to co-ordinate the various agencies in the quest to achieve the "Final Solution to the Jewish Question in Europe."

To achieve the mass killing by gas, the exhaust from a captured Soviet tank engine was connected to the pipe system under the floor of the gas chambers, which had an outlet inside each of the three chambers. The gas pipes and gas outlets were manufactured in the workshop owned by the Czerniak brothers at Saint Tekla Street (now Kopernik Street) in Tomaszow Lubelski.[57]

Michal Kusmierczak, a railway engine driver from Belzec, testified on October 16, 1945, about an experimental gassing that took place in February 1942:

> The camp at Belzec was surrounded by wire and a hedge of fir trees and pines. At first, the gas chambers were built inside one of the barracks, later they had another barracks there. The first experiment at exterminating the Jews in the extermination camp was carried out on the Jews from Lubycza Krolewska. That was in February 1942. At that time about 50 Jews were killed.
>
> One of the 'Blacks' explained to me that the Jews were killed by the exhaust fumes produced by a 250hp engine, or rather were suffocated; the engine was 30m from the gas chamber and hidden about 3m deep in the ground. A pipe led from the engine to the gas chambers. The exhaust pipe was 7 inches in diameter and from this there led 2 and a half inch diameter pipes. As soon as a transport arrived at the station, the engine was started up.[58]

An important document has survived, written by Dr. Richard Turk, the head of the Department of Population Affairs and Welfare in the Lublin district. Its main points were:

---

57 Information supplied by Tomasz Hanejko, Belzec Museum Director, March 2014.

58 Michal Kusmierczak Testimony, October 16, 1945. Copy, Holocaust Historical Society UK.

On March 7 I received a telephone call from the government in Krakow, from Major Regger, in which I was strictly requested, in connection with the resettlement of the Jews from Mielec to the Lublin distrct, to reach an agreement with the SS and Police Leader, and it stressed the highest importance of this agreement.

I arranged a conference with *Hauptsturmführer* Höfle for Monday, March 16 1942, and it took place at 17.30. In the course of this conference, Höfle outlined the following, which of course disguised the true meaning of Belzec:

It would be appropriate if the transport of Jews that arrive in the Lublin district were split in the departure stations into those who are able to work and those who are not. If this division is impossible in the departure stations, eventually it should be considered to divide the transport in Lublin, according to the aforementioned point of view.

All the Jews incapable of work would arrive in Belzec, the final border station in the Zamosc region.

Hauptsturmführer Höfle is preparing the erection of a big camp, where the Jews capable of work will be held and divided according to their professions and from where they will be requested for work.

Piaski will be cleared of Polish Jews and will become a concentration point for Jews arriving from the Reich.

In the meantime Trawniki will not be populated by Jews. The *Hauptsturmführer* asks whether on the train section Deblin-Trawniki 60,000 Jews can be disembarked. After having been informed about the transports of Jews dispatched by us, Höfle announced that out of the 500 Jews who arrived from Suziec, those unable to work can be sorted out and sent to Belzec.

In conclusion, he announced that every day he can receive four to five transports with 1,000 Jews each for the destination of Belzec station. These Jews would cross the border (of the occupied territories of the Soviet Union) and never return to the *General-Gouvernement*.[59]

---

59 Arad, *Belzec, Sobibor, Treblinka*, pp. 44–45.

This same day, March 16, 1942, saw the first deportation within the framework of *Aktion Reinhardt* from the Lublin ghetto at Podzamcze to the Belzec death camp. On the night of March 16, 1942, the Germans commenced the liquidation of the Lublin ghetto. Those unfit for work—on average 1,500 per day—were sent to the collection point at the Marashal-shul Synagogue, and then subsequently to the *Umschlagplatz*, (collection-point)—the loading ramp of the Municipal Abattoir in Turytyczna Street.[60]

Daily, the deportations trains departed for the Belzec death camp, and, during the period from mid-March to mid-April 1942, approximately 26,000 Jews were deported, whilst approximately 1,500 Jews were shot on the spot.

Alojzy Berezowski, the Polish station-master of Belzec testified on November 5, 1945, in Belzec, regarding the first transport of Jews to arrive in Belzec:

> The first transport of Jews arrived towards evening sometime in March 1942. It consisted of about 15 wagons. This train was taken on to the siding. Later during the evening of the same day, at about 9 o'clock, I heard from outside my house—which was in the station—the dreadful screaming of children, women and men, mingled with occasional rifle fire and machine-gun fire.
>
> How many people arrived on this transport, I cannot specify, only that with my own eyes I calculated that in each wagon there were about 40 people. They were covered wagons.[61]

Victor Skowronek—another local—testified in Belzec on October 16, 1945, although it would appear the date of the first transport to arrive at Belzec death camp was March 17, 1942, which was the official start of *Aktion Reinhardt*: "The first transport—16 March 1942, in the evening, one heard howls and screams and sporadic shooting."[62]

---

60 Kuwalek, *From Lublin to Belzec*, Ad Rem, 2006, p. 4.

61 Alojzy Berezowski Testimony, November 5, 1945 in Belzec. Copy, Holocaust Historical Society UK.

62 Viktor Skowronek Testimony, October 16, 1945, in Belzec. Copy, Holocaust Historical Society UK.

SS-Unterscharführer Karl Alfred Schluch, who had served at the T4 institutions at Grafeneck and Hadamar was in Belzec when the mass killings commenced, and he described the process in some detail:

> In the morning or noon time we were informed by Wirth, Schwarz or by Oberhauser that a transport with Jews should arrive soon. The disembarkation from the freight cars was carried out by a group of Jewish prisoners under the command of their *Kapos*. Two or three Germans from the camp staff supervised this action. It was my obligation to carry out such supervision.
>
> After the disembarkation, the Jews were taken to the assembly square. During the disembarkation, the Jews were told that they had come here for transfer and they should go to the baths and disinfection. This announcement was made by Wirth and translated by a Jewish *Kapo*. Afterwards the Jews were taken to the undressing barracks.[63]

Another member of the SS garrison, Kurt Franz, who was responsible for training the *Trawnikimänner* at Belzec, testified:

> I heard with my own ears how Wirth, in quite convincing voice, explained to the Jews that they would have to be deported further and before that, for hygenic reasons, they must bathe themselves and their clothes would have to be disinfected. Inside the undressing barrack was a counter for the deposit of valuables. It was made clear to the Jews that after the bath their valuables would be returned to them. I can still hear today, how the Jews applauded Wirth after his speech. This behaviour of the Jews convinces me that the Jews believed Wirth.[64]

The Jewish deportees were told to leave their luggage in the yard next to the siding and strip naked, the men in the open and the women inside the undressing barrack. After undressing, the men were taken through the "tube" to the gas chambers first and, after the women had their hair shaven off, they and the children were also led through the "tube" and murdered in the gas

---

63 Arad, *Belzec, Sobibor, Treblinka*, p. 70.
64 *Ibid.*, op. cit, p. 70.

chambers. *SS-Unterscharführer* Karl Alfred Schluch testified at his post-war trial what happened next:

> My post in the 'tube' was close to the undressing barrack. Wirth briefed me that while I was there I should influence the Jews to behave calmly. After leaving the undressing barracks, I had to show the Jews the way to the gas chambers. I believe that when I showed the Jews the way they were convinced that they were really going to the baths. After the Jews entered the gas chambers, the doors were closed by Hackenholt himself or by the Ukrainians subordinate to him.
>
> Then Hackenholt switched on the engine which supplied the gas. After five or seven minutes—and this is only an estimate—someone looked through the small window into the gas chamber to verify whether all inside were dead. Only then were the outside doors opened and the gas chambers ventilated. After the ventilation of the gas chambers, a Jewish working group under the command of their *Kapos* entered and removed the bodies from the chambers. Occasionally, I had to supervise at this place; therefore, I can describe the whole process, which I saw and witnessed personally.
>
> The Jews inside the gas chambers were densely packed. This is the reason that the corpses were not lying on the floor but were mixed up in disorder in all directions, some of them kneeling, according to the amount of space they had. The corpses were besmirched with mud, and urine or with spit. I could see that the lips and tips of the noses were a bluish color. Some of them had their eyes closed, others' eyes rolled.The bodies were dragged out of the gas chambers and inspected by a dentist, who removed finger-rings and gold teeth. After this procedure, the corpses were thrown into a big pit.[65]

The Jews that were unable to proceed to the gas chambers were taken directly to the mass graves and there they were shot. *SS-Unterscharführer* Robert Juhrs, who had served in the T4 institution in Hadamar, was one of the SS garrison who took part in such shootings, testified:

---

65 Arad, *Belzec, Sobibor, Treblinka*, pp. 70–71.

> I had to carry out the shooting of Jews once. In that transport the cars were overloaded; some of the Jews were unable to walk. Maybe, in that confusion, some of the Jews had been pushed down and had been crushed underfoot. Therefore, there were Jews that, by no means, could cover the way to the undressing barrack.
>
> Gottlieb Hering gave me an order to shoot these Jews. He told me verbally: "Juhrs, take these Jews to Camp II immediately and shoot them there." These Jews were taken to the gate of Camp II by a Jewish working group, and from there they were taken to the pits by other working Jews. As I remember, there were seven Jews, men and women, who were taken inside the pit.
>
> It is hard to describe the condition these people were in, after their long journey in the unimaginly packed freight cars. I regarded the killing of these people in this way as a mercy and redemption. I shot these Jews with a machine-gun as they stood on the edge of the pit. I aimed directly at their heads so that everyone died instantly. I am absolutely sure that nobody felt any torment.[66]

These first transports of Jews to the death camp from the Lublin ghetto saw approximately 30,000 murdered between March 1942 and mid-April. Other transports from within the Lublin district, from Zamosc, and the transit ghettos of Izbica and Piaski, followed.

On either March 25 or 26, 1942, the first transports to the Belzec death camp came from the Lvov district, namely Zolkiew, quickly followed by mass deportations from Lvov itself, and other places such as Kolomea and Stanislawow.

It was from a transport from Zolkiew that two women, Mina Astman and Malka Talenfeld, escaped from Belzec at the end of March 1942. They managed to record their story on their return to Zolkiew:

> In closed wagons they were brought into the Belzec camp. They were ordered to undress. The people became scared. One of them asked the SS man who was close to him: "What's the reason that we should undress?" Afterward the women were ordered to enter the barrack.... Exploiting the disorder and noise and lack of

66 *Ibid.*, op. cit, pp. 71–72.

> experience of the Germans Astman and Talenfeld jumped into a nearby ditch and sat there undiscovered until dark. Under cover of darkness they escaped from the camp and after a few days returned home.[67]

During the height of these killings, Franz Stangl, the commandant of the Sobibor death camp, was ordered by Odilo Globocnik to report to Christian Wirth in Belzec. Stangl told the author, Gitta Sereny, that Globocnik had written to Stangl, and that Wirth had been appointed as inspector of camps. But Wirth was not appointed to this post until August 1942, and this visit took place in April 1942. In one of his interviews with Gitta Sereny, in a Düsseldorf prison, Stangl explained:

> I went there by car. As one arrived, one first reached Belzec railway station, on the left side of the road. The camp was on the same side, but up a hill. The *Kommandantur* was 200 metres away on the other side of the road. It was a one-storey building. The smell... oh God, the smell. It was everywhere.
>
> Wirth wasnt in his office. I remember, they took me to him... he was standing on a hill, next to the pits..... the pits... full.... they were full. I can't tell you; not hundreds, thousands, thousands of corpses... oh God. That's where Wirth told me—he said that was what Sobibor was for. And that he was putting me officially in charge.[68]

Gitta Sereny, in her book *Into That Darkness*, which recorded her interviews with Stangl, stated that he gave a slightly different version of the same event:

> Wirth wasn't in his office; they said he was up in the camp. I asked whether I should go up there and they said, "I wouldn't if I were you—he's mad with fury. It isn't healthy to go near him." I asked what was the matter. The man I was talking to said that one of the pits had overflowed. They had put too many corpses in it and putrefaction had progressed too fast, so that the liquid underneath had pushed the bodies on top and over and the corpses had rolled down the hill. I saw some of them—oh God, it was awful. A bit

---

67 *Ibid.*, op. cit, p. 264.
68 Gitta Sereny, *Into That Darkness*, Pimlico London 1974, p. 111.

> later Wirth came down. And that is when he told me. I said to Wirth "I couldn't do it", he said, "I simply wasnt up to such an assignment. There wasn't any argument or discussion. Wirth just said my reply would be reported to HQ and I was to go back to Sobibor.[69]

Josef Oberhauser recalled that in late April / early May 1942, Wirth, Schwarz, and almost the entire German personnel left Belzec:

> Before Wirth left his last official duty was to shoot or gas the fifty or so work-Jews of the camp including the *Kapos*. When Wirth and his staff left, I was in Lublin, where I was organizing the transport of a large amount of material. When I came back to Belzec there was no one left apart from about twenty Ukrainians guarding the place. The Ukrainian guards were under the supervision of *SS-Scharführer* Feix.
>
> Curiously, even *SS- und Polizeiführer* Globocnik did not know anything about Wirth and his staff's departure. When he found out that Wirth had disaapeared, he sent me to Belzec to find out where he had gone. I found out that he had travelled to Berlin, via Lemberg and Krakow without informing Globocnik of his departure.
>
> At the beginning of May 1942 *SS-Oberführer* Brack from the *Führer* Chancellery suddenly came to Lublin. With Globocnik he discussed resuming the extermination of the Jews. Globocnik said he had too few people to carry out this programme. Brack stated that the Euthanasia programme had stopped and that the people from T4 would from now on be detailed to him on a regular basis so that the decisions taken at the Wannsee conference could be implemented....... About a week after Brack had come to Globocnik, Wirth and his staff returned to Belzec.[70]

Wirth arrived back in Belzec by mid-May 1942. In the last week of May 1942, two transports from two small ghettos near Zamosc-Laszczow and Komarow arrived at the camp. Then, on June 1, 1942,

---

69 *Ibid.*, op. cit, p. 112.

70 E. Klee, W. Dressen, V. Riess, *Those Were the Days—The Holocaust As Seen By The Perpetrators and Bystanders*, Hamish Hamilton, London, 1991, pp. 228–230.

the Germans organized the first deportation of the Jews from Krakow to the Belzec death camp. This *Aktion* lasted until June 8, 1942, with some 10,000 Jews deported and murdered in Belzec. From his pharmacy in Plac Zgody, Tadeusz Pankiewicz watched the deportations on the evening of June 4, 1942:

> By the following morning, seven thousand had been assembled. There they were kept throughout the hot summer morning, then driven to the railway station and sent off to an unknown destination. The round-up was repeated the following day, the sixth of June. The sorching sun was merciless; the heat makes for unbearable thirst, dries out the throats. The crowd was standing and sitting; all waiting, frozen with fright and uncertainty. Armed Germans arrived, shooting at random into the crowd. The deportees were driven out of the square, amid constant screaming of the Germans mercilessly.[71]

Christian Wirth realized that, with the large scale deportations from Krakow taking place and further large scale deportations from the Lvov and Lublin districts, the three current primitive gas chambers in Belzec could not cope. The deportations to Belzec were halted in the middle of June 1942, and thus the first phase of operation at Belzec had come to an end, with the destruction of approximately 93,000 innocent Jewish men, women, and children.[72]

---

71 Robin O'Neil, *Oskar Schindler, Stepping Stone to Life*, susaneking.com, 2010, p. 84.

72 Arad, *Belzec, Sobibor, Treblinka*, p. 73.

Chapter VI
Construction of the New Gas Chambers—Camp Expansion: Second Phase, June-July 1942

With the realization that the primitive gassing facilities could not cope with the expected large transports from Krakow, Lvov, and the Lublin district the old wooden gas chambers were dismantled, and a new gassing facility of bricks and concrete was constructed during June 1942.

When the old gas chambers were replaced at Treblinka by a larger facility in August 1942, the Germans used bricks from dismantled buildings in Warsaw to be taken from the *Umschlagplatz* and connected to the rear of each daily transport. In the book *Letzte Spuren*, there is a *Waren-Passierschein* (goods permit) Nr. 00667 for driver Fichtner, authorized by *SS-Hauptscharführer* Bartetzko for a trip on June 8, 1942, to collect bricks from the *Transferstelle-Warschau*, who controlled the area where the *Umschlagplatz* was located. In all probability, it would seem logical to assume that these bricks were used in the construction of the new gas chambers in Belzec, as Fichtner was the camp quartermaster there.[73]

The new gas chambers were not located at the same site as the first gas chambers, but were moved to the eastern part of the camp and a watchtower was built close by. Rudolf Reder, who was deported from Lvov in August 1942, provided a detailed description of the gas chambers and the immediate area in his book, *Belzec*:

> After a time I knew all the terrain well. It lay in the middle of a young pine forest. The forest cover was heavy, and to reduce the penetration of light further, one tree was lashed to another in order to double the density of the greenery around the place where the

[73] Grabitz & Scheffler, *Letzte Spuren*, p. 11.

> chambers were. Beyond them was the sandy road where the corpses were dragged.
>
> The Germans had stretched a roof made of smooth wire overhead, and foliage was laid on the wire. The idea was to secure the terrain from observation from airplanes. That part of the camp under the roof of leaves was shaded. From the gate, you entered a huge yard. The large barracks where the women's hair was shaved off stood in the yard. Next to that barracks was a small yard surrounded by a fence made of boards nailed tightly together, without the slightest crack, three metres high. That fence, made of gray boards led straight to the chambers. This way no-one could see what was happening on the other side of the fence.

Reder now describes the gas chamber building itself:

> The building containing the chambers was low, long and wide, gray concrete, with a flat roof covered in tar paper, and above that another roof of netting covered with foliage. From the yard, three steps a meter wide and without railings led up to this building. A big vase full of different-colored flowers stood in front of the building. On the wall it was clearly and legibly written: '*Bade und Inhalationsraume*.' The stairs led to a dark corridor, a meter and a half wide but very long. It was completely empty, four concrete walls. The doors to the chambers opened to the left and the right. The doors made of wood, a meter wide, were slid open with wooden handles.
>
> The chambers were completely dark, with no windows, and completely empty. A round opening the size of an electrical socket could be seen in each chamber. The walls and floors of the chambers were concrete . The corridor and chambers were lower than a normal room, not more than two meters high. On the far wall of each chamber there were also sliding doors two meters wide. After asphyxiation the corpses of the people were thrown out through them.
>
> Outside the building was a small shed, perhaps two meters square, where the 'machine' was, a gasoline-driven motor. The chambers were a metre and a half above the ground, and at the same level as

the chambers wa a ramp at the doors, from which the bodies were thrown to the ground.[74]

SS-Unterscharführer Karl Alfred Schluch recalled the Belzec gas chambers interior:

> I can relate that I saw the gas chambers in the euthanasia institutions, and I was shown the gas chambers in Belzec. These were about 4 x 8 metres. They had a friendly, bright appearance. Whether the color was yellow or grey, I don't remember. Maybe the walls were painted with oil colors.
>
> In any case, the floor and part of the walls were made so that the cleaning would be easy. The newly arriving Jews must not guess the purpose the room served, and they should believe that it was a bath. Vaguely I remember that there were shower-heads on the ceiling.[75]

Rudolf Reder testified in Krakow on December 29, 1945, before the Main Commision for the Investigation of Nazi Crimes in Poland, providing some further details on the gas chamber:

> From the entrance a corridor which had three solid and tightly sealed single doors on either side, ran the length of the building. These doors led into windowless chambers, which at the far end wall, adjoining the loading ramps I described earlier, had double sliding doors. On the other side of the building, i.e. behind the wall at the far end of the corridor, there was a small room where the engines were.
>
> I myself saw that in that small room there was a petrol-driven engine that looked very complicated. I remember the engine had a flywheel, but I could not make out any other specific construction or technical features. Two technicians, Russians from the armed camp staff, always operated the engine. I know only that the engine used up 4 cans of petrol each day, because that is how much petrol was brought to the camp every day. It was when the petrol was delivered to the engine room that I briefly had the opportunity to look inside the room........

74 Rudolf Reder, *Belzec,* Judaica Foundation, Auschwitz-Birkenau State Museum, Krakow, 1999, pp. 122–124.

75 Arad, *Belzec, Sobibor, Treblinka,* p. 74.

> The chambers were so crammed full of people that even after they had died, they were still upright. As soon as all the chambers had been crammed full, the doors were locked, the outside doors were closed by wedging them together, then the engine was started. Prisoner Moniek, a coach driver from Krakow, supervised the operation of the engine.
>
> The engine would always run for precisely 20 minutes, after which Moniek would signal to one of the operators to switch it off. After it had been switched off, Moniek ordered other prisoners to open all the doors wide and drag the bodies out, two at a time, using belts tied around their wrists. The bodies were then taken to the mass graves that had been dug with machines some time earlier. On the way from the ramp to the grave, near the chamber, dentists extracted the gold teeth from the bodies.[76]

On June 13, 1942, the Polish Underground reported that the Jewish work brigade revolted in the extermination area. This will be covered in the section that deals with reports by the Polish Underground, later in the book.

During July 1942, the SS garrison was re-inforced by additional personnel from T4 and additional quarters for them was provided for them in a barracks next to the administration office in the SS compound. In addition to this, the *Trawnikimänner* contingent was expanded to cope with the increased number of transports. The death camp was enlarged, several more barracks were constructed, among them adjacent undressing barracks for men and women, as well as a "barbers" barracks. A second railway track was laid into the camp, to increase the capacity of handling more transports and the unloading ramp area was enlarged.[77]

Reichsführer-SS Heinrich Himmler issued an order on July 19, 1942, to Friedrich-Wilhelm Krüger, Higher SS Police Leader East, to complete the "resettlement" of the Jewish population of the *Generalgouvernement* within the framework of *Aktion Reinhardt* by the end of that year. Transportation difficulties became acute during the German offensive on the Eastern Front.

---

76 Schelvis, *Sobibor*, p. 105.

77 Tregenza, *Belzec*, pp. 7–8.

Himmler ordered *SS-Obergruppenführer* Karl Wolf, his chief of personnel staff to contact the secretary of state of the Ministry of Transport, Dr. Theodor Ganzenmuller, and resolve the problems. On July 28, 1942, Dr. Ganzenmuller replied to Karl Wolf at the Prinz Albrecht Straße 8, in Berlin:

> Since July 22, a train load of 5,000 Jews has departed daily from Warsaw via Malkinia to Treblinka, and in addition a train load of 5,000 Jews has left Przemysl twice a week for Belzec.
>
> *GEDOB* (*Generaldirecktor der Ostbahn*) is in constant contact with the Security Police in Krakow. It has been agreed that the transports from Warsaw through Lublin to Sobibor be suspended for as long as the reconstruction works on that section make those transports impossible (approximately until October 1942). These trains have been agreed upon with the commander of the Security Police in the *General Gouvernement*, and *SS Brigadeführer* Globocnik has been advised.[78]

---

[78] Arad, *Belzec, Sobibor, Treblinka*, p. 51.

Chapter VII
The Killing Frenzy
Visit of Kurt Gerstein and Wilhelm Pfannenstiel & The Deportations from Lvov—August 1942

On August 1, 1942, major changes took place at Belzec death camp. Commandant Christian Wirth was appointed to the post of *Inspekteur der SS-Sonderkommandos-Abteilung Reinhard* (Inspector of *SS-Sonderkommandos*) and set up a temporary office at the Julius Schreck *Kaserne* on *Litauer Straße* in Lublin, before moving to a permanent headquarters—a two-storey villa on Chelmska Street on the *Alter Flugplatz* (Old Airfield) camp. The ground floor rooms were used as offices, staffed by Wirth, Oberhauser—who came with Wirth from Belzec—and Willi Häusler, who came from Berlin and was responsible for salaries and administration, and a couple of secretaries. On the first floor was located a first-class dining room and living quarters for Wirth and his staff. The old airfield camp served as the main sorting depot for the clothing and belongings taken from the victims of Belzec, Sobibor, and Treblinka, in three old hangers.[79]

SS-Obersturmführer Gottlieb Hering replaced Wirth as the commandant of Belzec. He was well-known to Wirth, as he had served in the Stuttgart C.I.D. (Criminal Invesigations Department) with Wirth as well as in a number of T4 institutions throughout the Reich.

SS-Obersturmführer Kurt Gerstein, the chief disinfection officer in the Main Hygienic Office of the *Waffen-SS*, and *SS-*

79 M. Tregenza, *Christian Wirth: Inspekteur des SS Sonderkommandos Aktion Reinhard*, Zeszyty Majdanka Vol XV, Panstwowe Muzeum na Majdanka Lublinm, 1993, pp. 2, 14–15.

Obersturmbannführer Wilhelm Pfannenstiel—professor and director of the Hygienic Institute at the University of Marburg / Lahn—travelled to Lublin to advise on disinfection issues and to see whether *Zyklon B* could be used to improve the killing capacity.

Gerstein wrote a very detailed report of their visit to Belzec in August 1942 on May 4, 1945, in Rottweil, in southwestern part of Germany. Gerstein committed suicide before he could face trial, in his prison cell in Cherche-Midi in Paris, on July 25, 1945. His report and extracts of the testimony by Wilhelm Pfannenstiel follow, providing an almost unique description of Belzec death camp by non-members of the guard personnel:

> The next day we went to Belzec. A small station had been built especially for this purpose on a hill just north of the Lublin—Lemberg Chaussee in the left corner of the demarcation line. South of the road some houses with the notice '*Sonderkommando der Waffen-SS*'. As *Polizeihauptman* Wirth, the actual head of the whole killing installations was not yet there, Globocnik introduced me to SS-*Hauptsturmführer* Obermeyer (from Pirmasens).[80] The latter only let me see that afternoon what he had to show me. I did not see any dead that day, but in the hot August weather the whole place smelt like the plague and there were millions of flies everywhere.
>
> Right by the small two-track station there was a large shed, the so-called cloakroom with a large counter where valuables were handed over. Then there was a room containing about 100 chairs—the barbers room. Then an outdoor path under birch-trees, with a double barbed-wire fence on the left and right, with the sign 'To the inhalation and bathrooms'. In front of us a sort of bath-house with geraniums, then a few steps, and then three rooms each on the right and left 5 x 5 metres, 1.9 metres high, with wooden doors like garages. In the rear wall, hardly visible in the darkness, large sliding doors. On the roof, as a 'witty little joke' the Star of David.

80 Many historical accounts assume this to be Oberhauser not Obermeyer. But Josef Obermeyer was in charge of the sorting operation and disinfection of clothing at the Old Airfield Camp in Lublin, which had a direct connection with Gerstein and Pfannenstiel. Oberhauser was not from Pirmasens—he was born in Munich—and was a *SS-Hauptscharführer* in rank. Wheras Obermeyer was a *SS- Hauptsturmführer*.

In front of the building a notice: 'Hackenholt Institute'. More than that I was not able to see that afternoon.

Shortly before seven the next morning I was informed: "The first transport is coming in ten minutes!" The first train from Lemberg did in fact arrive in a few minutes. Forty-five wagons containing 6,700 people, of whom 1,450 were already dead on arrival. Children were looking out from behind the barred windows, their faces dreadfully pale and frightened, their eyes filled with the fear of death, besides men and women. The train came into the station: 200 Ukrainians tore open the doors and drove people out of the wagons with their leather whips. A big loudspeaker gave further instructions: undress completely, take off artificial limbs, spectacles etc. Give up valuables at the counter without credit notes or receipts. Tie shoes together carefully, otherwise in the pile of shoes, which was a good 25 metres high, no-one could have found a pair that matched. Then the women and children went to the barber who cut off all their hair with two or three chops with the scissors and stuffed it into potato sacks. "That is put to some special use in U-boats—for caulking or something like that," the SS Corporal on duty told me.

Then the procession started to move. With a lovely young girl at the front, they all walked along the path, all naked, men, women and children, without their artificial limbs. I stood with *Hauptmann* Wirth up on the ramp between the chambers. Mothers with their babies at the breast came up, hesitated and entered the death chambers. A sturdy SS man stood in the corner and told the wretched people in a clerical tone of voice: "Nothing at all is going to happen to you! You must take a deep breath in the chambers. That expands the lungs. This inhalation is necessary because of illnesses and infection." When asked what was going to happen to them, he answered: "Well of course, the men must work, building houses and roads , but the women don't have to work. Only if they want to, they can help with the housework or in the kitchen." This gave some of these poor people a glimmer of hope that lasted long enough for them to take the few steps into the chambers without resisting.

The majority realized—the smell told them what their fate was to be! So they climbed the steps and then they saw everything. Mothers with babies at the breast, naked little children, adults, men, women—all naked. They hesitated, but they went into the gas chamber, pushed on by those behind them, or driven in by the leather whips of the SS. Most of them without saying a word. A Jewess of about 40, with eyes blazing, called down upon the heads of the murderers the blood being spilt here. *Hauptmann* Wirth personally gave her five or six lashes in the face with his riding-whip. Then she too disappeared into the chamber.

Many people were praying. I prayed with rhem. I pressed myself into a corner and cried aloud to my God and theirs. How gladly I would have gone with them into the chambers. How gladly I would have their death with them. Then they would have found a uniformed SS officer in their chambers. The matter would have been treated as a case of death by misadventure and dealt with: missing presumed dead, unheralded and unsung. But I could not do that yet. First I had to make known what I had seen here!

The chambers filled. Cram them well in—*Hauptmann* Wirth had ordered. Pepole were standing on each other's feet. 700–800 on 25 square metres, in 45 cubic metres! The SS forced as many in together as was physically possible. The doors closed. Meanwhile the others were waiting outside in the open air, naked.... Now at last I understood why the whole installation was called the Hackenholt Institute. Hackenholt was the driver of the diesel engine—a minor technician who was also the builder of this installation. The people were to be killed with diesel exhaust fumes.

Gerstein recalled what happened next:

But the diesel did not work! *Hauptmann* Wirth came. He was obviously embarrassed that this had to happen on the very day that I was there. Yes I saw everything! And I waited. My stop-watch had recorded it all well. 50 minutes-70 minutes—the diesel did not start! The people were waiting in the gas chambers . In vain! We heard them weeping, sobbing.... *Hauptmann* Wirth struck the Ukrainian who was supposed to be helping *Unterscharführer* Hackenholt mend the diesel. The whip hit him in the face 13 or 14 times. After 2 hours 49 minutes—the stop-watch had recorded it all well—the diesel started.

Up till then people were alive in these four chambers, four times 750 people in four times 45 cubic metres. Another 25 minutes went by. True, many were now dead. One could see that through the little glass window through which the electric light lit up the chamber for a moment. After 28 minutes only a few were still alive. At last, after 32 minutes everyone was dead! Men of the work squad opened the wooden doors from the other side. They—Jews themselves—had been promised their freedom and a certain percentage of all valuables found in payment for the ghastly duty they performed.

The dead were standing upright like basalt pillars, pressed together in the chambers. There would not have been room to fall down or even to bend over. One could tell the families, even in death. They were still holding hands, stiffened in death, so that it was difficult to tear them apart in order to clear the chamber for the next load. The corpses were thrown out—wet with sweat and urine, soiled with excrement, menstrual blood on their legs. Children's bodies flew through the air. There was no time to lose. The whips of the Ukrainians whistled down on the backs of the work squad. Two dozen dentists opened the mouths with hooks and looked for gold. Gold on the right, without gold on the left. Other dentists used pliers and hammers to break gold teeth and crowns out of the Jews.

The naked corpses were carried in wooden barrows just a few metres away to pits of 100 by 20 by 12 metres. After some days the putrefying bodies swelled up and then, a short time later, collapsed violently so that a new batch could be thrown on top of them. Then 10 centimetres of sand was strewn over it so that only a few single heads and arms stuck out. In one of these spots I saw Jews clambering about on the corpses in the pits and working. I was told by an oversight those who were already dead when the transport arrived had not been undressed. Because of the textiles and valuables, which they would otherwise have taken with them to the grave, this had of course to be rectified. Nobody took any trouble either in Belzec or in Treblinka to record or count those who had been killed. The figures were only estimates based on the capacity of the wagons.

The next day—the 19th August 1942—we went in *Hauptmann* Wirth's car to Treblinka, 120 km, NNE of Warsaw. The installations was somewhat similar to that in Belzec except that it was larger. Eight gas chambers and veritable mountains of cases, textiles and underclothes. A banquet in the dining-hall was laid on in our honour in typical Himmlerite Old German style. The meal was simple, but there were masses of everything. Himmler himself had ordered that the men of these Kommandos should receive as much meat, butter and other things, particularly alcohol, as they wanted.

We then went by car to Warsaw............[81]

Some historians have questioned the veracity of Kurt Gerstein's account, but if you compare what he recounted with the testimony of Wilhem Pfannenstiel regarding Belzec, there are clear similarities. His testimony given on April 25, 1960, supports a great deal of what Kurt Gerstein wrote:

> When I am asked about executions of Jews I must confirm that on 19 August 1942 I witnessed an execution of Jews at Belzec extermination camp..... during this first visit I was taken around by a certain *Polizeihauptmann* named Wirth, who also showed and explained to me the extermination installations in the camp. He told me that the following morning a new transport of about 500 Jews would be arriving at the camp, who would be channeled through these extermination chambers. He asked me whether I would like to watch one of these extermination actions, to which, after a great deal of reflection, I consented. I planned to submit a report to the *Reichsarzt-SS* about these extermination actions. In order to write a report I had however, first to observe an action with my own eyes. I remained in the camp, spent the night there and was witness to the following events the next morning.[82]
>
> A goods train travelled directly into the camp of Belzec, the freight cars were opened and Jews whom I believe were from the area of Romania or Hungary were unloaded. The cars were crammed fairly full. There were men, women and children of every age. They were ordered to get into line and then had to proceed to an assembly area and take off their shoes. I stood a little to the side of this line and watched the proceedings together with *Polizeihauptmann* Wirth and *Obersturmführer* Gerstein.
>
> The SS escorts took up guard positions outside the camp and Jewish functionaries from the camp gave the arriving transports to understand that they would now be examined and instructed them to undress so that they could be deloused and take a bath. They

81 G. Schoenberner, *The Yellow Star*, Corgi Books, London, 1978, pp. 134–135.

82 Josef Oberhauser testified that Wirth, Globocnik, and himself were in Treblinka on August 19, 1942, which indicate that this date is incorrect. See below.

also told them they had to inhale in a certain room to prevent them passing on any illnesses through their respiratory tracts. I could not understand what the Jewish camp functionaries were saying but *Herr* Wirth explained it to me.

After the Jews had removed their shoes they were separated by sex. The women went together with the children into a hut. There their hair was shorn and then they had to get undressed. The men went into another hut, where they received the same treatment. I saw what happened in the women's hut with my own eyes. After they had undressed, the whole procedure went fairly quickly. They ran naked from the hut through a hedge into the actual extermination centre. The whole extermination centre looked just like a normal delousing institution. In front of the building there were pots of geraniums and a sign saying 'Hackenholt Foundation', above which there was a Star of David. The building was brightly and pleasantly painted so as not to suggest that people would be killed here. From what I saw, I do not believe that the people who had just arrived, had any idea of what would happen to them.

Pfannenstiel then recalled what happened next:

Inside the building, the Jews had to enter chambers into which was channeled the exhaust of a 100?—HP engine, located in the same building. In it there were six such extermination chambers. They were windowless, had electric lights and two doors. One door led outside so that the bodies could be removed. People were led from a corridor into the chambers through an ordinary air-tight door with bolts. There was a glass peep-hole, as I recall, next to the door in the wall. Through this window one could watch what was happening inside the room but only when it was not too full of people. After a short time the glass became steamed up.

When the people had been locked up in the room the motor was switched on and then I suppose the stop-valves or vents to the chambers opened. Whether they were stop-valves or vents I would not like to say. It is possible that the pipe led directly to the chambers. Once the engine was running, the light in the chambers was switched off. This was followed by palpable disquiet in the chamber. In my view it was only then that the people sensed something else was in store for them. It seemed to me that behind the thick walls and door they were praying and shouting for help.

> After about twelve minutes it became silent in the chambers. The Jewish personnel then opened the doors leading outside and pulled the bodies out of the chambers with long hooks. To do this they had to put these hooks in the mouths of the bodies. In front of the building they were once again thoroughly examined and the bodily orifices were searched for valuables. Gold teeth were ripped out and collected in tins. These activities were carried out by the Jewishcamp personnel.
>
> The bodies were taken from the searching area directly and thrown into deep mass graves which were situated near the extermination institute. When the grave was fairly full, petrol—it may have been some other flammable liquid—was poured over the bodies and they were then set alight. I had barely established that the bodies were not completely burned when a layer of earth was thrown over them and then more bodies were put into the same grave. During the disposal of the bodies I also established that the whole procedure was not entirely satisfactory from the point of view of hygiene.[83]

What is questionable is the date of the visit as recalled by Wilhelm Pfannenstiel—the trip to Treblinka on August 19, 1942. From the testimony by Josef Oberhauser, Wirth went to Treblinka with Odilo Globocnik to see for himself the chaos that Dr. Irmfried Eberl had allowed to develop. Oberhauser accompanied Wirth and Globocnik, supporting Wirth in his new role as *Inspekteur der SS-Sonderkommandos Abteilung Reinhard*. Another extremely important flaw in Kurt Gerstein's account is that he saw a gassing facility with eight chambers. At that time there was only the three chamber gassing facility in August 1942; the new gas chambers construction was only started when Wirth and Stangl were at Treblinka.

This would either indicate that either Gerstein and Pfannenstiel made more than one trip to the extermination camps, or the visit was later, either September or October 1942. It is known that Pfannenstiel was indeed in Lublin in September 1942. A German police message decoded by the British Intelligence Service at

---

83 Klee, Dressen, Riess, *Those Were the Days*, pp. 239–244.

Bletchley Park revealed that Ernst Lerch, Globocnik's adjutant, had to provide a car for him on September 30, 1942.[84]

*

At virtually the same time as the visit of Kurt Gerstein and Wilhem Pfannenstiel in one of the transports from Lvov (*Lemberg*), one of the few survivors from the Belzec death camp, Rudolf Reder, arrived at the camp. We owe a great debt to Reder for writing down his experiences of Belzec—almost a unique account of what life and death was like in this man-made hell. During the month of August 1942, the killings reached a frenzied peak, with 50,000 Jews murdered at Belzec between August 10–23, 1942. Mass deportations from Krakow between August 25–30, 1942, saw 14,000 Jews murdered. Other large scale deportions from Drohobycz, Przemysl, Tarnopol, and Krakow district added to the death toll. So to provide the clearest picture of what happened to all the transports during August 1942 and beyond, we will use extracts from Rudolf Reder book *Belzec* to cover his transportation, arrival, and initial stay in the death camp:

Reder recalls the start of the deportation from the Janowska camp in Lvov:

> At six in the morning they ordered us to get up off the damp grass and form up in fours, and the long rows of the doomed marched to the Kleparow station. Gestapo and Ukrainians surrounded us in tight ranks. Not a single person could escape. They herded us onto the ramp at the station. A long freight train was already waiting just pass the ramp. There were fifty cars. They began loading us. The doors of the freight cars had been slid open and Gestapo stood on both sides, two on each side with whips in their hands beating everyone on the face and head on the way in.[85]

The convoy of death reached Belzec:

> About noon the train reached the Belzec station. It was a small station. Little houses stood around it. The Gestapo lived in these little houses. Belzec was on the Lublin-Tomaszow line, fifteen

84 HW 16/32, National Archives Kew.
85 Reder, *Belzec*, p. 117.

> kilometres from Rawa Ruska. At the Belzec station the train reversed from the main line onto a spur that ran another kilometer, straight through the gate of the death camp. Ukrainian railroad workers also lived near the Belzec station, and there was a small post office. An old German with a thick black mustache got into the locomotive at Belzec—I do not know his name but I would recognise him in an instant—he looked like a hangman.[86] He took command of the train and drove it right to the camp. It took two minutes to get to the camp. The German who had driven the train to the camp got down and 'helped'. Shouting and lashing out, he drove the people from the train. He himself went into each car and checked whether someone remained there. He knew all the tricks. When the train was empty and checked, he signalled with his flag and drove the train out of the camp.[87]

The *Reichsbahn* official was Rudolf Gockel. Teo Pansera, a Polish *Volksdeutscher* who worked for the *Ostbahn* in Belzec, recalled in an interview on July 12, 2000, that the German station master Gockel attended his wedding uninvited, "sitting like a lord" on the first cart, with his pressed uniform and his handle-bar mustache—a sight to behold.[88]

Rudolf Reder remembered the first moments at the death camp:

> The train pulled into a yard about a kilometer long and wide, surrounded by barbed wire and iron fencing, one atop the other, two meters high. The wire was not electrified. You drove into that yard through a wide, wooden gate topped with barbed wire. Next to the gate stood a hut where a sentry sat with a telephone. In front of the hut stood several SS-men with dogs. When a train had passed through the gate, the sentry closed it and went inside the hut.[89]

Now the SS-men took control of the transport:

> Several dozen SS-men opened the cars, screaming "los!" They drove people out of the cars with whips and rifle butts. The cars had

86 Rudolf Gockel, Reichsbahn Official.

87 Reder, *Belzec*, pp. 118–119.

88 Interview with Teo Pansera in Belzec, Michael Tregenza, Chris Webb, July 12, 2000 (Unpublished Journal).

89 Reder, *Belzec*, p. 119.

doors a meter above the ground, and all those being herded out, young and old, had to jump. They broke arms and legs during this, having to jump to the ground...... Aside from the SS, the so-called *'Zugsführers'* were on duty. These were the supervisors of the permanent Jewish death crew in the camp, dressed normally without camp insignia.

The sick, the old and the small children, all the ones who could not walk on their own, were placed on stretchers and set down at the edge of enormous dug graves. Gestapo-man Jirmann[90] shot them there, and then pushed them into the grave with the rifle butt.[91]

The next part of the process was where the SS announced to the new arrivals that they needed to take a bath, all done to allay fears and stop resistance from occurring:

Jirmann spoke very loudly and distinctly. *"Ihr gehts jetzt baden, nachher werdet ihr zur Arbeit geschickt"* (Now you are going for a bath and afterwards you will be sent to work). That was all. Everybody cheered up and was happy that they were going to work after all. They applauded.....

The whole crowd moved on in silence, the men straight through the yard to a building on which it was written in large letters: '*Bade und Inhalationsraume*' (Baths and Inhalation Room). The women went some twenty meters further to a large barracks, thirty meters by fifteen. The women and girls had their hair shaved off in that barracks..... later on I saw that only a few minutes later when they were given wooden stools and lined up across the barracks, when they were ordered to sit, and eight Jewish barbers, robots silent as the grave, approached them to shave their hair down to the scalp with clippers.[92]

Now the doomed women and children took their final journey:

I stood off to the side, in the yard, together with the group picked out to dig graves, watching my brothers, sisters, acquaintances and friends being driven to their death. While the women were being herded forward, naked and shaved, whipped like cattle to the slaughter, without being counted, faster, faster,—the men had

90 Reder said his name was Irrmann, this is incorrect, it is Fritz Jirmann.
91 Reder, *Belzec*, p. 119.
92 *Ibid.*, op. cit, p. 120.

> already died in the chambers. It took more or less two hours to shave the women, which is also how long it took to prepare for the murder and the murder itself.
>
> Several dozen SS-men used whips and sharp bayonets to drive the women to the building with the chambers and up three steps to the gangway, where the askars counted 750 people into each chamber.... I heard the doors closing, the moans and the screams; I heard the desperate cries in Polish and Yiddish, the bloodcurdling laments of the children and the women, and then one joined, terrifying cry..... That lasted fifteen minutes. The machine ran for twenty minutes and after twenty minutes it was very quiet, the *askars* opened the doors from the outside, and I together with the other workers—picked out like me from previous transports, without any tattoos or insignia—we went to work. We dragged the bodies of people who had still been alive not long ago; we used leather straps to drag them to the huge, waiting mass graves and the orchestra played during this, it played from morning to evening.[93]

Rudolf Reder was able, through his book, to shed some light on the social activities of the camp staff, once the daily tasks of exterminating thousands of innocent men, women, and children was concluded for the day:

> No one from the families ever came, and none of them lived with a woman. They raised whole flocks of geese and ducks. People said that in the spring they were sent whole baskets of cherries. Crates of vodka and wine were brought daily...... Each Sunday evening they summoned the camp orchestra and held a drunken party. Only the Gestapo got together, they gorged themselves and drank. They threw scraps of leftovers to the musicians.[94]

The *Trawnikimänner* also enjoyed socializing, and they had a recreation center—a small bar called the Komadowski Bar—on the same side of the road as the *Kommandantur* and SS NCO living quarters on Tomaszowska Steet.

---

93 *Ibid.*, op. cit, pp. 121–122.

94 *Ibid.*,op. cit, p. 137–138n.

Chapter VIII
Jewish Work Brigades

Unlike Auschwitz-Birkenau, with its massive slave-labor force, the Jews selected to live and work were a small fraction of those deported to the death camp. In the first phase of the camp's existence, the Jewish work brigade consisted of 100–150 men. In the second phase, a total of 500 prisoners in Camps I and II were utilized, the vast majority of this number employed on removing corpses from the gas chambers and burying them. There was also a small orchestra.

From the initial transports, Christian Wirth selected between 100 to 150 Jewish men to form various work brigades; they were used to unload people from the cattle cars, collect together their luggage, another work brigade to drag the bodies out of the gas chambers, then throwing them into the tip-up trucks, in the early phase, and bury them in mass graves.

Another work brigade took the collected luggage and belongings of the victims to an abandoned locomotive shed near the Belzec station. In this building, everything was sorted and stored prior to shipment to the main *Aktion Reinhardt* depot on the *Alter Flugplatz* in Lublin, which was near the Lublin concentration camp.

Once a transport arrived at Belzec, it was met by SS guards, *Trawnikimänner,* and Jewish workers under the supervision of the so-called *Zugsführers*—these were the Jewish supervisors of the permanent Jewish work brigades. Jewish prisoners helped with the undressing, and eight barbers were employed to shave the women's and girls' hair before they were gassed in the chambers. The men had been gassed first. A small team of dentists, armed with pincers, extracted gold teeth from the corpses.

Rudolf Reder recalled the living quarters for the work brigades:

> In the camp there were two barracks for the death crew, one for general workers and the second for the so-called skilled workers. Each barrack held 250 workers. The bunks were two-level. Both barracks were the same. The bunks were bare planks with a small tilted board under the head. Not far from the barracks stood the kitchen, and further on the warehouse, administration laundry, stitching workshop, and finally the elegant barracks for the *askars* (*Trawnikimänner*).[95]

Chaim Hirszmann, deported with his family from Zaklikow in early November 1942, recalled how he was selected to work as a barber, and among those who emptied the gas chambers; he testified before the Jewish Historical District Commision in Lublin on March 19, 1946:

> The train entered the camp. Other SS men took us off the train. They led us all together—women, men, children—to a barrack. We were told to undress before we go to the bath. I understood immediately what that meant. After undressing we were told to form two groups, one of men and the other of women with children. An SS man, with the strike of a horsewhip, sent the men to the right or to the left, to death—to work. I was selected to death, I didn't know it then. Anyway, I believed that both sides meant the same—death. But, when I jumped in the indicated direction, an SS man called me and said, "*Du bist ein Militärmensch, dich können wir brauchen*" ("You have a military bearing, we could use you.")
>
> We, who were selected to work, were told to dress. I and some other men were appointed to take people to the kiln. I was sent with the women. The Ukrainian Schmidt, an Ethnic German, was standing at the entrance to the gas chamber and hitting with a knout every entering woman. Before the door was closed, he fired a few shots from his revolver and then the door closed automatically and forty minutes later we went in and carried the bodies out to a special ramp. We shaved the hair of the bodies, which were afterwards packed into sacks and taken away by Germans.
>
> The children were thrown into the chamber simply on the women's heads. In one of the 'transports' taken out of the gas chamber, I

95 Reder, *Belzec*, p. 124.

found the body of my wife and I had to shave her hair. The bodies were not buried on the spot, the Germans waited until more bodies were gathered. So that day we did not bury.[96]

Rudolf Reder recalled how the money and valuables were collected and sent on from the death camp:

> Valuables, money and dollars were taken out of the storehouse each day. The SS-men collected it themselves and put it into suitcases which workers carried to Belzec, to the headquarters. A Gestapo officer went first, with Jewish workers carrying the suitcases. It was not far, only a twenty-minute walk, to the Belzec station. The camp in Belzec, that is, the torture chamber in Belzec, was under this headquarters. Jews working in administration said that the whole shipment of gold, valuables and money was sent to Lublin, where the main headquarters was, with authority over the Belzec headquarters.[97]

Reder continued his account:

> The torn clothes of the unfortunate Jewish victims were collected by workers and carried to the warehouse. There were ten workers there, who had to unstitch every piece of clothing very carefully, under the supervision and whips of the SS, who between themselves divided up the money found.... The Jewish workers sorting and unstitching the clothing couldn't misappropriate anything, and didn't want to.[98]

Chaim Hirszmann told his second wife Pola about his experiences at Belzec, and she later recalled:

> The prisoners were constantly beaten and every day many of the workers from the regular staff were killed. Typhus was prevailing, but one had to avoid admitting the disease. The sick were murdered on the spot. Getting medical treatment or lying down was out of the question. Sick with typhus and with a fever of 40 degree Celsius, my husband worked and somehow managed to conceal his conditions from the Germans..........

---

96 M. Gilbert, *The Holocaust—The Jewish Tragedy*, William Collins, London, 1987, p. 304.

97 Reder, *Belzec*, p. 129.

98 *Ibid.*,op. cit, p. 129.

> Two Czechoslovak Jewesses were working in the camp office. They too, had never entered the camp. They even enjoyed a certain freedom of movement. They often went with the SS men to town to arrange different matters. One day they were told that they would visit the camp. The SS men showed them around the camp and in a certain moment they led the women to the gas chamber and when they were inside, the door closed behind them. They finished with them in spite of the promise that they would live.
>
> The Germans ordered the prisoners to set up a football team and on Sundays games were being played. Jews played with SS men, the same ones who tortured and murdered them. The SS men treated this as a matter of sport, and when they lost a game, they had no complaints....... There were also women employed in the camp, but their number was much smaller than the number of men. There were no children at all. Women worked. They were selected from the transports.[99]

Reder described the workers who toiled in the extermination area of Camp II:

> I belonged to the permanent death crew. There were five hundred of us all together. Only 250 were 'skilled' workers, but of these 200 worked at jobs for which they didn't have to be specialists: digging graves and dragging corpses. We dug the pits, the enormous mass graves, and dragged the bodies. Besides doing their work, the skilled workers also had to take part in this. We dug with shovels and there was also a machine that loaded sand and lifted it above ground level. The machine threw the sand out at the side of the grave. A sandpile formed, which was used to cover the graves, when they were filled with corpses. About 450 people were always occupied with the graves. It took one week to dig one grave.

Reder remembered the brutal guard Heini Schmidt, a *Volksdeutsche,* who supervised the grave diggers:

> We were watched all the time we worked by a thug named Schmidt, who beat and kicked. If someone was not—in his opinion—working quick enough, he would order him to lie down and give him twenty-five lashes with the whip. He ordered him to count, and if he miscounted he gave him fifty instead of twenty-

99 Gilbert, *The Holocaust*, pp. 305–306.

> five. Fifty was too much for any tormented man to bear; the victim usually dragged himself to the barracks and died the next morning. This happened several times a day.
>
> Also thirty to forty workers were shot each day. The physician usually submitted a list of those who were exhausted, or else the so-called *Oberzugsführer,* the main foreman of the prisoners, produced a list of 'offenders' so that thirty or forty died each day. They were led out to a grave at dinnertime and shot.[100]

He also recalled the tasks of the work brigade who had to remove the dead bodies from the gas chambers:

> Aside from digging graves, it was the task of the death crew to pull the corpses out of the chambers, throw them into a high pile, and then drag them all the way to the graves. The ground was sandy. It took two workers to drag one corpse away. We had leather straps with buckles. We put the straps over the arms of the corpses and pulled. The heads often got caught in the sand. We were ordered to sling the corpses of small children over our shoulders two at a time and carry them that way. We left off digging graves when we dragged the corpses..... we had to work that way from early morning until dusk. Dusk ended the working day, because the 'work' was done only by daylight.[101]

Reder continued by describing how a typical working day started and continued:

> At three-thirty in the morning, the askar sentry who walked around the barracks at night was already pounding on the door and shouting *'Auf Heraus!'*—before we could get out of bed, the thug Schmidt burst in and chased us out of the barracks with his riding crop. We ran out holding one shoe in our hands or barefoot. We usually hadn't undressed, and we even slept in our shoes because we couldn't have managed to get dressed in the morning.
>
> At twelve noon we received a meal. We filed past two small windows. At the first one we got mugs, and at the second a half a litre of barley

---

100 Reder, *Belzec*, pp. 130–131.

101 *Ibid.*, p. 131.

> soup, in other words water, sometimes with a potato. Before dinner we had to sing songs; we also had to sing before the evening coffee.[102]

A typical working day ended thus:

> In the evening the lights burned for half an hour. Then they were turned off. The *Oberzugsführer* prowled around the barracks with a whip and didn't allow people to talk. We spoke very quietly with our neighbours. The crew was mostly made up of people whose wives, children and parents had been gassed. Many had managed to get a tallith and tefillin from the warehouse, and when the barracks was locked for the night, in the bunks we heard the murmur of the Kaddish prayer. We were saying prayers for the dead. Then it was quiet.[103]

He recalled how women workers were treated in Belzec:

> In October a transport of Czech Jewish women arrived from Zamosc. There were several dozen women whose husbands worked in the death crew. A decision had been made to keep several dozen women from that last transport.
>
> Forty were assigned to work in the kitchen, laundry and stitching workshop. They were not allowed any contact with their husbands. In the kitchen they peeled potatoes, washed pots and carried water. I don't know what became of them. They surely shared the common fate. These were all educated women. They'd arrived with luggage. Some of them had portions of butter with them, they gave us whatever they had.
>
> And they helped everyone who worked in the kitchen or near the kitchen. They lived in a small separate barracks and had a *Zugsführerka* over them. During work—I fixed stoves everywhere and went all around the camp—I saw how these women spoke with each other. They were not as mistreated as we were. Their work ended at dusk and they lined up in twos for soup and coffee. Like us they'd not had their own clothing taken away or been given striped uniforms.[104]

---

102 *Ibid.*, op. cit, pp. 131–132.

103 *Ibid.*, op. cit, p. 132.

104 *Ibid.*, op. cit, pp. 133–134.

Chapter IX
Transports of Death: Eyewitness Accounts

In this chapter, a number of people from all sides of the story will give their accounts. From one of the Polish locomotive drivers, to German railroad personnel, from Jews who escaped from the death trains, *Wehrmacht* officers and members of the *Schutzpolizei*, who guarded the transports and Jews fleeing Nazi persecution, and others who witnessed the transports to the Belzec death camp.

Stefan Kirsz, a Polish locomotive driver for the *Ostbahn,* who lived in Belzec testified after the war:

> As a co-driver of a locomotive, I led the Jewish transports from the station of Rawa Ruska to Belzec many times. These transports were divided in Belzec into three parts. Each part, which consisted of twenty freight cars pushed by the locomotive, and stopped near the former border wall of 1939 / 40.
>
> Immediately after the freight cars stopped inside the camp, they were emptied of the Jews. Within 3–5 minutes the twenty cars were empty of Jews and their luggage. I saw that in addition to the living, corpses were taken out. The Germans did not allow us to watch the camp, but I was able to see it when I approached the camp and deceptively pretended that I must put the coal closer to the entrance gate.[105]

Mieczyslaw Kudyba testified on October 14, 1945, in Belzec:

> The Germans also took about 30 people to the death camp in a big black vehicle. Some of the Jews of Tomaszow Lubelski were taken to the death camp in this vehicle. According to my reckoning, about 450 people could be put into the gas chambers which we had built near the railway siding.
>
> The transports were lined up on the siding and then shunted into the area of the death camp. In March 1942, when I was going along

[105] Arad, *Belzec, Sobibor, Treblinka*, p. 69.

> the road from Lubycza to Belzec, I saw that the Jews brought in were already undressed and that each one was carrying the clothing to the wagons. At that time about 5 cm of snow lay on the ground.
>
> The undressed children, women and men were screaming. I had a good view of this through the camouflaged trellis of branches, at the moment the wagons were rolled back from the siding. The 2nd and 3rd barracks, of which I spoke at the beginning of my statement, were about 50 metres from the siding. During the time the camp was in operation the Germans built a whole row of barracks on the part of the camp near the siding. There could have been about 30 barracks.[106]

Georg Hölzel, deputy station master at Zwierzyniec station in the Lublin district, was frequently at the Belzec station, and had this to say about the Belzec and transports to the death camp in his interrogation in 1962:

> In Belzec the SS-men lived in small farm houses directly opposite the station. I in no way had any point of contact with the SS-men. During my duty in Belzec I came across one SS-man in particular who always went around with a riding-whip. I noticed that he definitely wore four stars on his collar. I am not familiar with SS ranks.
>
> I once saw how a transport of Jews was shunted into the Belzec camp. It happened like this: that in the station area the engine was changed from the front to the rear of the train, and then shunted it into the camp. The engine was then uncoupled and eventually the camp was locked. At this point the train personnel had to leave the station. Whether the trains were then handled exclusively by German personnel, I cannot say. To my knowledge Polish personnel were used.
>
> I know only from heresay that in the critical times three transports a day rolled into Belzec. These trains also ran on Sundays. I remember such transports. I cannot give numbers. One experience made an impression on me. It was one Sunday afternoon about 1:30 p.m. A transport of Jews was reported from Zawada.

---

106 Mieczyslaw Kudyba Testimony, October 14, 1945. Copy, Holocaust Historical Society UK.

> At our station in Zwierzyniec, engines took on water. This happened also with the above mentioned train. A little Jewish girl was squeezed out of the stationary train who I estimate was ten-twelve years old. She came to me clutching a 5 mark note in her hand—for water. I gave my Polish station master instructions that he could take my water tumbler and hand the girl some water.
>
> I told the girl that she should put her money away. While the girl was drinking, the SS transport leader, who wore four stars as badges of rank appeared suddenly behind me. He then knocked the glass out of the girl's hand with his riding-whip and then dealt the child several more blows. The girl's father squeezed out of the wagon and on his knees begged the SS-Officer to leave her alone.
>
> The SS-Officer drew his pistol and shot the father in the back of the neck. The girl was thrown back into the wagon. The same happened with the dead man. The SS-Officer told me it was a disgrace and not worthy of a German official to be a Jew's slave. When in this connection I am asked the name of this SS-Officer, I can only say that he presumably came from Lublin.
>
> In my opinion, the management of Belzec station came under Zwierzyniec, *SS-Rottenführer* Schuette belonged to this management. To my knowledge he came from the area of Gelsenkirchen or Hamm.[107]

Oskar Diegelmann, a *Reichsbahn Oberinspektor* (Senior Inspector) based in Lublin recalled:

> As a controller I was responsible for ensuring the track was in good condition and in particular that the trains ran smoothly. During a visit to the station at Belzec the supervisor, a Secretary or Senior Secretary from Thüringen, informed me that he was having a lot of problems with the SS, who were stationed near the wood.
>
> Some time later I myself saw and had a word with a number of SS people in the waiting-room at Belzec. When I inquired, they told me that they were not members of the SS but they had merely been given these uniforms. As they described it, most of them came from lunatic asylums or nursing homes in the Reich, where they had been involved in the killing of the mentally ill.

---

107 Georg Hölzel Interrogation 10 January 1962. Zentralle Stelle Ludwigsburg 208/ AR-Z 268/59.

> I would like to say that one day the full significance of Belzec camp became clear to me when I saw mountains of clothes of all types behind our locomotive shed. There was also a large number of shoes there, as well as jewellery and other valuables. The SS had piled these things up there. Petrol was poured over items of clothing that were no longer wearable and they were then burnt.
>
> There were a lot of rumours that valuable items were trafficked by the camp staff in the surrounding area. So it was not surprising that women of easy virtue, in particular, were attracted to the area surrounding Belzec, where they set themselves up in business. There were apparently a lot of orgies at that time.[108]

Fajga Kanner made a statement regarding early transports of Jews to Belzec:

> On March 25, 1942, the transports from Rawa Ruska to Belzec began. At first we were still not aware what Belzec was but, afraid of deportation, we never undressed from March 1942 to January 1943, to be prepared to flee at any moment. We built bunkers.
>
> Transports of Jews, 70 or 80 railroad cars, passed all summer, twice a day. We could hear the moans and crying of smothered children from the cars. The majority did not know where they were headed; they were sure that they were being sent to work. Later transports already knew that they were on their way to the gas. Some jumped from the trains and others were so dispirited that they did not take advantage of possible opportunities to save themselves. Heaps of the corpses of those who had jumped unsuccessfully lay near the tracks and embankments.[109]

Maria Daniel, who lived next to the railway line near Belzec station, testified on October 16, 1945, in Belzec:

> What happened inside the death camp I do not know. I can only state that after the arrival of the wagons inside the camp terrible human cries could be heard, like; "People if you believe in God, rescue us!" This lasted about 5–10 minutes, then silence prevailed.
>
> The empty wagons came out of the camp again and the next lot was shunted in. Then the screams were repeated afresh from inside

---

108 Klee, Dressen, Riess, *Those Were the Days*, p. 234.

109 Reder, *Belzec*, p. 91.

> the camp. Several times I saw naked Jews inside the wagons being conveyed into the camp.
>
> In the summer of 1942 I was a witness when a naked woman lept out of a wagon; she was immediately caught by the 'Blacks' and, naked, taken into the camp.... in 1942, as I travelled on the road from Rawa Ruska to Belzec, I saw Germans bringing 2 lorries full of gypsies; the gypsies were on their knees, pleading to be released.[110]

On August 30, 1942, a *Wehrmacht* Non Commissioned Officer (NCO) Wilhelm Cornides was in Rzeszow on his way to Cholm (Chelm) in the *Generalgouvernement* by train. In his diary, he recorded that a railway policeman in Rzeszow had told him that a marble plaque with golden letters was to be erected on September 1, because by then the city would be free of Jews.

The railway policemen also told him: "That trains filled with Jews pass almost daily through the shunting yards, are dispatched immediately on their way and return swept clean most often the same evening. Some 6,000 Jews from Jaroslaw were recently killed in one day."

Wilhelm Cornides then took the regular passenger train from Rzeszow to Cholm, reaching Rawa Ruska, an important rail junction, on August 31. Cornides stayed in the *Deutsches Haus* (German House), which was located in the Sokol prewar building in the centre of Rawa Ruska. He recorded what he saw in his diary:

> At ten minutes past noon I saw a transport train run into the station. On the roof and running boards sat guards with rifles. One could see from a distance that the cars were jammed full of people. I turned and walked along the whole train. It consisted of thirty – five cattle cars and one passenger car.
>
> In each of the cars there were at least sixty Jews—in the case of the enlisted men's or prisoner transports these wagons would hold forty men, however, the benches had been removed and one could see that those who were locked in here had to stand pressed together. Some of the doors were opened a crack, the windows criss-crossed with barbed-wire. Among the people locked in there were a few men and most of them were old, everyone else was

110 Maria Daniel, October 16, 1945. Copy, Holocaust Historical Society UK.

women, girls and children. Many children crowded at the windows and the narrow door openings. The youngest were surely not more than two years old.

As soon as the train halted, the Jews attempted to pass out bottles in order to get water. The train, ain however, was surrounded by SS guards, so that no-one could come near. At that moment a train arrived from the direction of Jaroslaw, the travellers streamed toward the exit without bothering about the transport. A few Jews who were busy loading a car for the armed forces waved their caps to the people locked in.

I talked to a policeman on duty at the railway station. Upon my question as to where the Jews came from he answered; "Those are probably the last ones from Lvov. That has been going on now for three weeks without interruption. In Jaroslaw they only let eight remain, no-one knows why".

I asked; "How far are they going?" Then he said; "To Belzec". And then? "Poison. I asked, "Gas". He shrugged his shoulders, then he said; "At the beginning they always shot them I believe.

Here in the *Deutsches Haus* I just talked with two soldiers from the front-line Prisoner of War Camp 325. They said these transports had lately passed through every day, mostly at night. Yesterday a 70-car one is supposed to have gone through.

From Rawa Ruska Cornides took the afternoon train to Cholm. The things he learned on this journey were so extraordinary that he made three separate entries in his diary within an hour. The first entry was at five-thirty p.m.

When we boarded at Four-Forty p.m. an empty transport had just arrived. I walked along the train twice and counted fifty-six cars. On the doors had been written in chalk sixty, seventy, once ninety, occasionally forty—obviously the number of Jews inside the cattle cars.

In my compartment I spoke with a railway policenan's wife who was visiting her husband here. She says these transports are now passing through daily; sometimes also with German Jews. Yesterday six children's bodies were found along the tracks. The woman thinks that the Jews themselves had killed these children—but they must have succumbed during the trip. The railway policeman who was escorting the train joined us in our compartment. He confirmed the woman's statement about the children's bodies which were found along the track yesterday. I asked, "Do the Jews know what is happening to them?"

The woman answered; "Those who come from far wont know anything, but here in the vicinity they know already. They attempt to run away, if they notice that someone is coming for them. So for example, most recently in Cholm, three were shot on their way through the city. In the railway documents these trains run under the name of resettlement transports, remarked the railway policeman. He then said; "That after the murder of Reinhard Heydrich, several transports containing Czechs had passed through."

Cornides continued his account:

Camp Belzec is supposed to be located right on the railway line and the woman promised to show it to me , when we pass it. Five -forty p.m.—a short halt. Opposite us a transport again stops. I speak with the policeman in front of the compartment we ride in. I ask; "Are you going back home to the Reich?" Grinning he says, "You probably know where we are coming from. Well for us the work is never finished." Then the transport opposite us moves away, thiry-five empty and cleaned wagons. In all probability this was the train that I had seen at One p.m. in Rawa Ruska station.

Six-twenty p.m.—we passed Camp Belzec. Before then, we travelled for some time through a tall pine forest. When the woman called, "Now it comes." One could see a high hedge of fir trees. A strong sweetish odour could be made out distinctly. "But they are stinking already," says the woman. "Oh nonsense, its only the gas," the railway policeman said laughing. Meanwhile we had gone about 200 meters—the sweetish odour was transformed into a strong smell of something burning. "That is from the crematory," said the policeman.

A short distance further on the fence stopped. In front of it one could see a guard house with an SS post. A double track led into the camp. One track branched off from the main line over a turntable from the camp to a row of sheds some 250 meters away. A freight car happened to stand on the turntable. Several Jews were busy turning the turntable—SS guards, rifles under their arms stood by. One of the sheds was open, one could distinctly see that it was filled to the ceiling with bundles of clothes.

> As we went on, I looked back one more time—the fence was too high to see anything at all. The woman says, "That sometimes, while going by one could see smoke rising from the camp," but I did not notice anything of the sort. My estimate is that the camp measures about 800 meters by 400 meters.

In his diary, Cornides recorded conversations he had with other witnesses. A policeman in the town hall restaurant in Cholm on September 1, 1942, said:

> The policemen who escort the Jewish trains are not allowed into the camp. The only ones who get in are the SS and the Ukrainian Special Services. But these people are doing a good business over there. Recently a Ukrainian visited us, and he had a whole stack of money in notes and watches and gold and all kinds of things. They find all of that when they put together the clohing and load it.
>
> Upon the question, as to how these Jews were actually being killed, the policeman answered, "They are told that they must get rid of their lice, and then they must take off their clothes and then they come into a room, where first off they get a hot blast of air, which is already mixed with a small dose of gas. That is enough to make them unconscious. The rest comes after, and then they are burned immediately.[111]

A member of the *Schutzpolizei* in Lvov, Josef Jacklein—a *Zugwachtmeister*—wrote a report concerning a transport from Kolomea to Belzec dated September 14, 1942:

> On 9 September 1942 I received orders to take over command of the Jewish resettlement train which was leaving Kolomea for Belzec on 10 September 1942. On 10 September 1942 at 19.30 hours in accordance with my orders, I took over command of the train together with an escort unit consisting of one officer and nine men at the railway yard in Kolomea. The resettlement train was handed over to me by the *Schutzpolizei Hauptwachtmeister* Zitzmann. When it was handed over to me the train was already in a highly

---

111 M. Gilbert, *The Final Journey*, George Allen & Unwin Ltd, London, 1979, pp. 92–95.

unsatisfactory state. *Hptw.* Zitzmann had informed me of this fact when he handed it over to me.

As the train had to depart to schedule and there was no other person who could take responsibility for loading on the Jews, there was nothing left for me to do but to take charge of the transport train in its unsatisfactory state. The condition of the train notwithstanding, the insufficient number of guards—i.e. one officer to nine men in the escort unit—would have been reason enough for me to refuse to take over command of the train. However, in accordance with my orders, I had to take over the train with the escort manpower I had. *Hptw.* Zitzmann stayed at the station with his guard unit until the train departed. Both units had their hands full preventing Jews escaping from the cars, since it had meanwhile become so dark that it was not possible to see the next car properly. It was not possible to establish how many Jews escaped from the train before its departure alone, however, it is probable that almost all were eliminated during their escape attempts.

At 20.50 the train departed from Kolomea on schedule. Shortly before its departure I divided up my escort squad, as had been planned beforehand, putting five men at the front and five men at the rear of the train. As the train was, however, very long—fifty-one cars with a total load of 8, 200 Jews—this distribution of manpower turned out to be wrong and the next time we stopped I ordered the guards to post themselves right along the length of the train. The guards had to stay on the brake housing for the entire journey. We had only been travelling a short time when the Jews attempted to break out of the wagons on both sides and even through the roof. Some of them succeeded in doing so, with the result that five sations before Stanislau I phoned the stationmaster in Stanislau and asked him to have nails and boards ready, so that we could board up the damaged cars temporarily and to put some of his *Bahnschutz* (Track guards) at my disposal to guard the train.

When the train reached Stanislau the workers from Stanislau station as well as the *Bahnschutz* were at the station waiting for our train. As soon as the train stopped, work began. An hour and a half later I considered it adequately repaired and ordered its departure. However, all of this was of very little help, for only a few stations later when the train was stationary I established that a number of very large holes had been made and all the barbed wire on the ventilation windows had been ripped out. As the train was departing I even established that in one of the cars someone was using a hammer and pliers. When these Jews were questioned as to why they had these tools in their possession they informed me that they had been told that they might well be of use at their next place of work. I immediately took away the tools. I then had to have the train boarded up at each station at which it stopped, otherwise it would not have been possible to continue the journey at all.

At 11.15 hours the train arrived in *Lemberg*. As there was no replacement escort squad, my squad had to continue guarding the train until Belzec. After a short stop at Lemberg station the train went to the suburban station of Kleparow, where I handed over nine wagons to *SS-Obersturmführer* Schulze which had been marked with an 'L' and had been designated for *Lemberg* compulsory labor camp. *SS-Obersturmführer* Schulze then loaded on about 1,000 more Jews and at about 13.30 hours the transport departed again.

At *Lemberg* the engine was replaced and an old engine was attached which was not powerful enough for the weight of the train. The train driver never managed to reach top speed with his engine so that the train, particularly when travelling uphill, moved so slowly that the Jews could jump off without any risk of injury. I ordered the train driver on numerous occasions to drive faster but this was impossible. It was particularly unfortunate that the train frequently stopped in open country.

The escort squad had meanwhile used up all the ammunition that had been brought with us as well as an extra 200 bullets that I had obtained from some soldiers, with the result that we had to rely on stones when the train was moving and fixed bayonets when the train was stationary. The ever-increasing panic among the Jews, caused by the intense heat, the overcrowding in the wagons, the stink of the dead bodies—when the wagons were unloaded there were about 2,000 dead in the train—made the transport almost impossible.

At 18.45 the transport arrived in Belzec and I handed it over to the *SS-Obersturmführer* and head of the camp at 19.30 hours. Towards 22.00 hours the transport was unloaded. I had to be present during

> unloading. I was not able to establish the number of Jews that had escaped.[112]

Thomas Toivi Blatt, a Jew who lived in Izbiza, a typical shtetl in southeastern Poland, tried to escape Nazi persecution to Hungary. In his book, *From the Ashes of Sobibor*, he recounts his journey, which took him past Belzec on his way to Lvov:

> It was one in the morning, time to get ready for the train. Slowly one after another, we departed. The date is etched on my memory: 26 October 1942..... Suddenly a kind of subdued anxiety spread among the passengers. They closed the windows; some lit cigarettes. What had happened? Why did the talk turn to whispers? I caught scraps of sentences. "They gas..... fat for soap." Despite the closed windows, the odor of rotting flesh seeped through.
>
> Belzec! Of course. I grew numb with shock. We were passing near one of the rumoured death factories. My heart pounding I looked out of the window. There were scarce woods, then in the distance I saw flames—now fading, now shooting higher into the sky. This was the destiny I was trying to escape. The smell receded as the train raced on, but I could still see the reflection of fire in the sky.[113]

Janett Margolies, a Jewish woman, was deported from the Tarnopol ghetto, in eastern Galicia, on November 8, 1942, and escaped from one of the death convoys en route to Belzec. She recalled:

> On the way, a policeman came close to me, whispering quietly into my ear to join the younger ladies in the wagon. When we arrived at the railroad station, the men were separated, and we were pushed toward the railroad cars. I did observe where the young were concentrated, joining them in the wagon, which was closed and sealed.
>
> We were eighty women. The small windows were high up, with bars and thorny wire. Once inside, we found out that somebody had smuggled in a file to cut bars. I started to organize a crew.

112 Klee, Dressen, Riess, *Those Were the Days*, pp. 232–235.

113 Thomas Toivi Blatt, *From the Ashes of Sobibor*, Northwestern University Press, Evanston, Illinois, 1997, pp. 46–47.

Standing on top of the others, we started to work. The train continued to run. When the job was finished, and the bars cut, each candidate, legs through the window, then hold on with their hands, later with only one hand, and with a strong swing, jump into the direction of the running train.

I stood watching the jumping. Most of them were killed on the spot. Some were killed by trains coming from the opposite direction. Others were shot by Gestapo watchmen. Those who succeeded were later caught by special railroad watchmen. Of all the Tarnopol train jumpers, I think that I was the only left alive.

I took quite a while to decide to jump, or not to jump. I realized fully, how hopeless the situation looked.... I decided to jump. Already hanging outside the wagon, I got tangled up in the thorny wire. Being scared, I cried out loudly, feeling that I was falling down. A shot was heard over my head, it was a watchman. Luckily he missed. At the same moment I noticed a locomotive running straight toward me. With my last strength, I rolled over downwards into a depression. All this lasted just a few seconds. I was saved, but badly injured, bleeding from my head and hands. I tore out a little frozen grass, putting it on my wounds. I succeeded in stopping the bleeding. Later I wiped it off my face, bringing myself to order.[114]

114 Janett Margolies, Escapes from Belzec Transports, www.deathcamps.org.

Chapter X
The End of the Slaughter

During the months between September 1942 until December 1942, the transports continued to roll into Belzec daily and the slaughter continued unabated. From Galicia, the Lublin District, Krakow, and a number of other cities, towns, and villages, the Jews were rounded up and shipped to Belzec. In the month of September, major deportations took place from Bilgoraj, Kolomea, Stanislawow, Stryj, and Sanok, and on October 28, 1942, 7,000 Jews were deported from Krakow, with further deportations from Kolomea, Stryj, and Sandomierz. In November, the last major deportation from Lvov took place over three days from November 18–21, 1942, where between 8,000 to 10,000 Jews were taken to Belzec.

Rudolf Reder witnessed the particularly brutal killing of Azriel Szeps, the vice president of the Zamosc *Judenrat*, during November 1942:

> It was around November 15, when the weather had already turned cold and snow and mud covered the ground. A large transport from Zamosc arrived like many others in the middle of a blizzard. The transport contained the whole *Judenrat* (Jewish Council).[115]
>
> Everyone was standing there naked and, in the normal course of events, the men were driven to the chambers and the women to the barracks where hair was shaved off. But the President of the *Judenrat*[116] was ordered to remain in the yard. As the *Askars* herded the transport to be killed, a whole parade of SS men stood around the President of the *Judenrat*. I do not know his name, I saw a middle-aged man as white as a corpse and completely calm.[117]

---

115 This deportation took place on November 2, 1942, the Zamosc *Judenrat* were first taken to Izbica during October 16–18, 1942, and from there to Belzec death camp.

116 He was vice president of the Zamosc Jewish Council.

117 His name was Azriel Szeps.

The SS-men ordered the orchestra to move into the yard and await orders. The orchestra made up of six musicians usually played in the space between the gas chambers and the graves. They played without a break, on instruments gotten from the murdered. I was working then on some masonry work and saw them all. The SS-men ordered the orchestra to play the tune, '*Es geht alles vorbei*' and '*Drei Lilien, kommt ein Reiter gefahren, bricht der Lilien*.' They played on violins, flutes and an accordion.

This went on for some time. Afterwards they stood the President of the Zamosc *Judenrat* against a wall and beat him with lead-tipped canes, mostly about the head and face, until the blood flowed. Jirmann, the fat Gestapo man Schwarz, Schmidt, and several *Askars* carried out the torture. They ordered their victim to dance and jump to their blows and the music.

After several hours, they brought him a quarter-loaf of bread and forced him with beatings to eat it. He stood there with the blood trickling down, indifferent, serious and I didn't hear a single moan. This man's tribulations continued for seven hours. The SS-men stood laughing: "*Das ist eine hohere Person, Prasident des Judenrates*' (This is a dignitary, the head of the *Judenrat*), they called out with loud, cruel bravado. Not until six p.m. did the Gestapo-man Schmidt push him along to the edge of the grave, shoot him in the head, and kick him onto the heap of gassed corpses.[118]

Reder, at the end of November 1942, was sent under escort to Lvov to collect sheet metal by Fritz Jirmann. Reder recounted what happened next:

I went there, loaded into a truck with four Gestapo-men and a sentry. In Lemberg (Lvov), after a whole day loading sheet metal I was left alone in the truck with one hoodlum guarding me. The rest went off to have a little fun. I sat there for a few hours without thinking or moving. Then I chanced to notice that my guard had dozed off and was snoring. By reflex, without a moments thought, I slipped out of the truck; the thug was still asleep.

I stood on the sidewalk, for a while longer, I pretended to be fussing with something near the sheet metal, and then I moved

118 Reder, *Belzec*, pp. 134–135.

> slowly away. Legionow Street was very busy. I pulled my cap down. The street was dark and no-one saw me. I remembered where my landlady lived, a Polish woman, and made my way there. She hid me.[119]

Right to the end of its operational life the horrors of Belzec continued, and Mieczyslaw Nieduzak testified in Belzec on October 17, 1945, about several instances of brutality:

> During the time of the death camp in Belzec was being built and then in operation, I lived in Rawa Ruska. Towards the end of 1942 I travelled through Belzec station and while waiting there for a train, I began a conversation with the 'Blacks' as I know the Russian language well; the 'Blacks' began to tell me certain things about the death camp.
>
> One of these 'Blacks' boasted to me how he had torn a young Jewish girl from her mother—a young girl who had clung tightly to her mother—seized her by the hair and with all his strength beaten her against a post so that her spine was broken and the girl was killed instantly.
>
> The other told me of the following occurrence; as he drove the Jews into the gas chambers, one of them hit him on the head with a piece of wood; he was forced to shoot this Jew. A third 'Black' told the following story; A Jew who had knocked a 'Black' to the ground was punished in the following way—by being tied to a post and rubbed so hard with a goosefeather floor polisher that his naked bones showed. They only stopped when he lost consciousness. This happened before the eyes of the Jews who were employed in the death camp and had been forced to watch.
>
> When I began to ask questions about how the Jews were killed in the gas chambers, they broke off the conversation with the advice that I should not ask that.[120]

The last transports to arrive at the Belzec death camp came from Rohatyn on December 8, 1942, and Rawa Ruska between

---

119 *Ibid.*, op. cit, pp. 141–142.

120 Mieczyslaw Nieduzak Testimony, October 17, 1945. Copy, Holocaust Historical Society UK.

December 7–11, 1942, where between 2,000 and 2,500 were murdered.

With these final transports Belzec ceased its mass murder function, and for the rest of its existence the death camp staff and prisoners exhumed and burned the Jewish victims that had crossed its threshold. The next chapter will cover in greater detail what happened between November 1942 until March 1943.

Chapter XI
Exhumation and Cremation November 1942–March 1943

Rudolf Reder claims in his book that Heinrich Himmler visited Belzec death camp in October 1942, along with *SS-Gruppenführer* Fritz Katzmann, then *SS-Polizeiführer* for Lvov district, in mid-October 1942. It is possible that this visit triggered the vast exhumation and cremation program that commemced in Belzec in November 1942. That was the case with the Treblinka death camp, following Himmler's visit in February 1943; having found out that the victims had been buried and not burnt, he ordered that cremations should begin immediately.

Heinrich Gley, an *SS-Oberscharführer*, testified after the war:

> As I remember, the gassing stopped at the end of 1942, when snow was already falling. Then the unearthing and cremation of the corpses began. It lasted from November 1942 until March 1943. The cremation was conducted day and night without interruption. At first the burning took place at one site, and later at two. One cremating site had the capacity to burn 2,000 corpses in twenty-four hours.
>
> About four weeks after the beginning of the cremation operation, the second burning site was erected . On the average, during five months, at the first burning site about 300,000 corpses were cremated, and in four months at the second burning site about 240,000 corpses. Naturally, these are average estimates.[121]

Maria Daniel, a Polish woman who lived in the village of Belzec, testified after the war:

> We could see a machine that took out the corpses from the graves and threw them into the fire. There were a few such fires going simultaneously. At that time a dreadful smell dominated the whole

121 Arad, *Belzec, Sobibor, Treblinka* , pp. 172–173.

area, a smell of burned human bones and bodies. From the moment they began burning the corpses, from all directions of the camp came the smell of the corpses. When the Germans completed the burning of the corpses, they dismantled the camp.[122]

Heinrich Gley provided a statement on February 6, 1962, in Münster:

> I was assigned with a big Jewish work brigade to the cremation of the corpses by means of railway lines which served as a grate. About 80–90 Jews then worked under my supervision in three shifts. The cremation site was as long a rail and about 4–5 metres wide. The rails were placed on top of big rocks and narrow-gauge rails served as a cross-mesh. The cremation surface could take about 200 corpses. First, a wood fire was kindled under the iron grate. During the course of the cremation operation the corpses later served as the only fuel. From time to time the badly twisted rails had to be replaced by new ones.[123]

Gisela Gdula, who lived in a house in Belzec village that housed the bakery that served the death camp, was interviewed in the survivng building on 20 July, 2002, and recalled that "The pyres were like a volcano and the villagers scraped human fat off their windows."[124]

Gley testified further:

> When all the bodies had been removed from the graves, a special search commando sifted through the earth and extracted all the leftovers: bone, clumps of hair, etc and threw these remains on the fire. An additional mechanical excavator was brought to accelerate the work. One excavator came from Sobibor and the other from the Warsaw district, which were operated by Hackenholt.[125]

---

[122] *Ibid.*, op. cit, p. 173.

[123] Statement by Heinrich Gley, February 6, 1962, in Münster. File Number 208 AR-Z 268/59.

[124] Interview with Gisela Gdula, Mike Tregenza, and Chris Webb, July 20, 2002, in Belzec.

[125] Robin O'Neil, *Belzec—Stepping Stone to Genocide*, JewishGen, Inc, 2008, p. 180.

Rudolf Reder recalled in his book *Belzec* how he later found out how the evidence of the crimes committed at Belzec was erased:

> And later, the local residents told me, the bones were ground up and the wind had scattered the dust over the fields and forests. A prisoner named Spilke, brought for the purpose from the Janowska Camp to Belzec, set up a machine for grinding human bones. He told me that he found only piles of bones there and that all the buildings had disappeared. Later he managed to escape and save himself. He gave me his account of this right after the liberation of Lvov by the Red Army.[126]

Two of the SS camp personnel died in separate incidents during March 1943; first Fritz Jirmann was accidentally shot and killed by Heinrich Gley, who testified about this incident in 1963:

> One evening, the company commander, Jirmann, ordered me to go with him to a copse near the *Kommandantur* where a bunker was located. I did not know what he intended doing there, but on the way I learned from him that two Ukrainians were locked-up there who, during their guard duty had broken into the valuables room.
>
> As Jirmann opened the bunker door, both Ukrainians lept on him and knocked him to the ground. As he dropped the torch during the incident , I could not see how he—Jirrman—had fallen to the ground as the first Ukrainian came out of the bunker. I assumed it was one of the Ukrainians and fired at him. As a matter of fact, it was Jirmann I had fatally wounded.[127]

Jirmann was buried in the German military cemetery in Tomaszow Lubelski, and his remains were later re-buried in the Przemysl German military cemetery in 1996.

SS-Oberscharführer Erwin Fichtner, the camp quartermaster at Belzec, was killed by Polish partisans on March 29, 1943, near Tarnowatka. He too, like Jirmann, was buried in in the German

---

126 Reder, *Belzec*, pp. 134–135.

126 *Ibid.*, op. cit, pp. 142–143.

127 Tregenza, *Christian Wirth: Inspekteur des SS Sonderkommandos Aktion Reinhard*, p. 48.

military cemetery in Tomaszow Lubelski and was later moved to the German military cemetery in Przemysl.[128]

[128] Michael Tregenza private correspondence with the author 2002.

Chapter XII
The Final Days

With the last of the bodies exhumed and cremated the SS started to dismantle the barracks, destroy the buildings, and plant trees and shrubs to disguise the mass slaughter that had taken place at Belzec.

SS-Scharführer Werner Dubois testified about the dismantling of the camp:

> The transports to Belzec and, consequently, the gassing operations, stopped quite suddenly. As staff members of the Belzec camp, we were informed that the place would be re-built completely. A working group of Jews, whose size I don't remember, was in charge of the demolition work. It is worth mentioning that at that time March–April 1943 the cremation of the corpses was terminated and the graves were levelled.
>
> The camp was emptied entirely and levelled accordingly. I heard that some planting was done there. The Jewish work commando, after accomplishing this work, was taken to Sobibor. I remained in Belzec for two more days, together with some of my colleagues and guards, to carry out the last clearing and loading..... Some time later, when I was in Sobibor, I heard that during the transport of the Jewish work commando from Belzec to Sobibor, some mutiny and shooting took place, which led to some deaths.[129]

Fritz Tauscher testified on December 18, 1963, in a prison in Stadehelm:

> After the cremations had been carried out, Commandant Hering left Belzec. Wirth then assigned me to complete the job of closing down the camp, levelling the ground and planting new shrubs. This was finished by the end of March or early April 1943. To carry out this task we had available: the remainder of the core German

---

129 Arad, *Belzec, Sobibor, Treblinka* , p. 370.

staff including Dubois and Jührs, the Ukrainian guards and 300 to 350 Jewish labourers.

> The latter had been assured by Hering that after Belzec had closed down, they would be taken to a labor camp of their own choice, either Lublin, Trawniki or Budzyn. What happened in fact was that about 14 days before the work was fully completed Wirth, the inspector of the three extermination camps, turned up all of a sudden without warning early one morning. At the same time, a train with eight or nine wagons pulled into the camp. Wirth announced that the Jews were now going to a camp of his choice, and they all had to get into the train.[130]

The destination of this transport was the Sobibor death camp. Edward Luczynski, a local Belzec villager testified about this transport on October 15, 1945, in Belzec:

> During the time of the disbandment of the camp a few transports of completely naked Jews were brought to Belzec, which were then sent on to Sobibor. These Jews came from the direction of Lwow, it was said that they came from the city of Lwow itself. Between Belzec station and Mazily, a small village about 8 kilometres NW of Belzec and the next station along the line, the naked Jews began to leap out of the wagons, but they were shot down by the Germans.
>
> The Jews who had been chosen to work in the death camp in Belzec were, after the disbandment of the camp,put into railway wagons almost naked and brought to Sobibor. From this transport only Sylko Herc from Krakow was able to escape[131]: he came to Belzec and told me how he had saved himself. From here he went to Krakow; whether he is still alive or not, I do not know. I know that he had a wife and children in Krakow who had been hidden by a Catholic priest.[132]

One thing worthy of mention is that whilst the wooden barracks were burnt down, the fences and watch towers taken down, and the gas chambers destroyed, the sturdily built

130 Schelvis, *Sobibor,* p. 145.

131 This is incorrect Chaim Hirszmann also escaped from this transport.

132 Edward Luczynski Testimony, October 15, 1945. Copy, Holocaust Historical Society UK.

Kommandantur and the adjacent house used for the SS camp staff were returned to the *Ostbahn*.[133]

Edward Luczynski testified about the lengths the Germans went to in order to disguise the site:

> After levelling and cleaning the area of the extermination camp, the Germans planted the area with small pines and left. At that moment, the whole area was plucked to pieces by the neighboring population, who were searching for gold and valuables. That's why the whole surface of the camp was covered with human bones, hair, ashes from cremated corpses, dentures, pots and other objects.[134]

A special SS commission inspected the area to ensure that all traces of the mass murder had been eradicated, and the SS finally left Belzec on May 8, 1943. The SS garrison was distributed to a number of camps in the Lublin district, either to Sobibor or Treblinka, or the labor camps at Poniatowa, Dorohucza, Budzyn, or the Old Airfield camp in Lublin, which was the main sorting depot for the clothes of the Jews murdered in Belzec, Sobibor, and Treblinka death camps.[135]

In a number of well-regarded accounts of when the transport of Jewish workers left Belzec for Sobibor, there appears to be much confusion and conflict. Yitzhak Arad states in his book *Belzec, Sobibor, Treblinka*, on page 265, that this transport left in July 1943. Robin O'Neil, in his book *Belzec—Stepping Stone to Genocide*, states on page 183 that Leon Feldhendler, one of the leaders of the revolt in Sobibor, has testified that this transport from Belzec arrived on June 30, 1943, whilst Thomas Toivi Blatt, in his book *Sobibor—The Forgotten Revolt*, writes on page 31 that the transport from Belzec arrived on June 26, 1943.

It seems unlikely that if the SS did leave Belzec on May 8, 1943—and indeed this seems more likely as the demolition and planting work was completed in April 1943—that the Jewish

---

133 Tregenza, *Belzec*, p. 9.

134 Arad, *Belzec, Sobibor, Treblinka* , p. 371.

135 Tregenza, *Belzec*, p. 9.

workers who toiled on this project would have left two months later. It is more logical that this transport left just before the SS left Belzec in May 1943, and indeed the statement of a Sobibor survivor, Moshe Bahir, would seem to support this view:

> One day in the month of May 1943, we were ordered to remain in our huts. We were not taken to work, and this aroused dark forebodings in us. In the afternoon the *Bahnhofkommando* (station / transport reception commando) was summoned to its usual work at the train station. When the men got to the train, a dreadful vision appeared before them. This train had brought the last of the Jews from the Belzec death camp who had been engaged in burning the bodies of those killed in the gas chambers.[136]

Odilo Globocnik, the head of *Aktion Reinhardt,* wrote to Heinrich Himmler proposing that a small farm should be built on the sites of all three death camps, occupied by a guard to ensure that the Polish population did not search for gold and valuables on the sites, and to provide the false perception that these former sites of mass murder were just innocent farmsteds.

A small group of 12 Ukrainians under the command of *SS-Unterscharführer* Karl Schiffner went to Belzec from Treblinka to build the farmhouse, and *SS-Scharführer* Heinrich Unverhau, from Sobibor, also came to Belzec, and testified about this visit after the war:

> A few weeks before the uprising in Sobibor, I and three other SS men and a larger group of Ukrainian auxiliaries were again ordered to go to Belzec. We were doing afforestation work there ..... We had to prevent the Poles from turning the whole area upside down in their searches for gold.[137]

This work was completed at the end of October 1943, the SS vacated the site, and a former Ukrainian *Volksdeutscher* member of the camp personnel settled into the farm with his family.[138]

---

[136] Moshe Bahir Testimony. M. Novitch, *Sobibor Matrydom and Revolt*, Holocaust Library, New York, 1980, p. 159.

[137] Arad, *Belzec, Sobibor, Treblinka*, p. 371.

[138] Tregenza, *Belzec*, p. 9.

Part II
Survivors, Victims, Perpetrators, and the Aftermath

Chapter XIII
Jewish Survivors and Victims

This chapter is an attempt to record some of the names of Jewish survivors and victims who set foot on the living hell that was Belzec death camp. What has been created is not an impersonal statistic, but an attempt to show that these people were flesh and blood, and to honor their memory.

Where possible where surnames and some personal details are known, these have been included but are painfully aware that there are many more names, and many more accounts are unknown, so this roll of remembrance will never be complete. This list does not claim be a definitive one—that will probably never be achieved. The Germans did not make transport lists of names of Polish Jews, but comprehensive records exist in the case of the German Jews deported from the Reich.

We have relied on information according to a number of sources, victims databases on reputed websites, books, survivor accounts, and personal correspondence. This information is respectfully presented, and hopefully the memory has been preserved, in an accurate and fitting manner. Firstly, we will cover the survivors / escapees, and then those who were selected at Belzec to work in other camps, and, finally, the victims. All the names shown are in alphabetical order, surname first then, where known, forenames.

Rudolf Reder, in his book *Belzec*, was able to devote one paragraph to his fellow inmates who endured the hell called Belzec, and he wrote this:

> We moved around like people who had no will anymore. We were one mass. I know a few names, but not many. Who was who and what their names were, in any case, were matters of complete indifference. I know that the physician was a young doctor from somewhere near Przemysl, he was called Jakubowicz. I also met a

merchant from Krakow, Schlüssl, and his son, and a Czech Jew named Ellenbogen, who was said to have a bicycle warehouse, and a chef, Goldschmidt, who'd been well known at the Brüder Hanicka restaurant in Karlsbad. No one took any interest in anyone else. We went mechanically through the motions of that horrible life.[139]

*

Belzec Survivors—this includes those who survived the Holocaust, or escaped from the camp but did not survive:

ASTMAN, Mina. Deported from the Zolkiew ghetto in the Galician district at the end of March 1942. Escaped from the camp along with Malka Talenfeld. They returned to Zolkiew and their story was recorded. Her fate is unknown but it is likely she did not survive.

BACHNER. A dentist from Krakow. Arrived in the camp with the last transports from Krakow at the begining of October 1942. When the transport reached the camp, he succeded in entering a latrine and hid there for a few days. One night he was able to leave the latrine pit and escaped from the camp. He returned to Krakow, but his eventual fate is unknown. He told his story to Tadeusz Pankiewicz in Krakow.

HERC, Sylko. Sylko and his father (first name unknown), were both deported from Krakow to Belzec. A member of the Jewish work brigade that dismantled the camp and was put on a train in May 1943, bound for Sobibor death camp. He escaped along with Chaim Hirszman and returned to Belzec village where he spoke to Edward Luczynski about the escape. He returned to Krakow but his eventual fate is not known.

HIRSZMAN, Chaim. Born on October 24, 1912, in Janow Lubelski. He was a mechanic and metal worker by profession and lived in Janow Lubelski during the occupation. In September 1942 Chaim, his wife, and 6-month-old child went to Zaklikow, from

[139] Reder, *Belzec*, pp. 132–133.

where they were deported to Belzec. They were both murdered on arrival, but Chaim was selected to work.

Chaim was part of the Jewish work brigade who dismantled the camp and put on a train to the Sobibor death camp in May 1943. He escaped from the death train along with Sylko Herc and managed to join a partisan group in the forests near Janow Lubelski. He fought bravely, murdering 29 Germans, and was awarded the Grunwald Cross.

He gave evidence to the Jewish Historical District Commission on March 19, 1946, and that same evening he was murdered by two or three men from the *Narodowe Sily Zbrojne* (NSZ, National Armed Force) group in Lublin. Chaim maried Pola, who also testified after his murder on what he had told her of his experiences in Belzec.

REDER, Rudolf. Born on April 4, 1881, in Lvov. He lived in Lvov and was by profession a chemist in the soap industry. He was deported to Belzec from Lvov on August 16, 1942. He worked in the "death brigade," clearing the gas chambers and digging mass graves.

He managed to escape from Lvov after being sent there by Fritz Jirmann at the end of November 1942, and hid with his landlady until Lvov was liberated by the Red Army.

Reder lived in Krakow and wrote his memoirs in 1946—the only account by a survivor of Belzec, and then emigrated to Toronto, Canada, changing his name to Roman Robak. He attended the Belzec trial of Josef Oberhauser, in Munich; Oberhauser was the only member of the SS garrison to stand trial for the crimes committed at Belzec.

SAND, Jozef. Born in 1924. He was a student of the Jewish Gimnazjum in Lvov. Joseph Rebhun, in his account *Leap for Life*, recalls:

> On a sunny morning in the ghetto, I suddenly encounter someone, Josef Sand, whom I have not seen for years. He adds some

information that is so incredible I do not mention it to anyone in the ghetto, so as not to be considered certifiably crazy. Sand tells me that he ran away from Belzec. I have no clear idea how he escaped. He had been taken there as a member of a small group separated from the one thousand taken from the Janowska camp.

In Belzec, he claimed, he had helped to build showers through which poisonous gas could be piped in for the trapped Jews; the showers kill thousands each day. He swears to me that he is telling the truth, but it is impossible to believe what I hear. He looks normal to me, and yet his story is incredible. I ask him what he intends to do now. To leave the ghetto as soon as possible, he says; he just came to find out about his family. I never see him or hear about him again.

SHAPIRO, Isaac. He was a rabbi from Lvov, who was deported to Belzec in October 1942. He worked in the Jewish "sorting brigade," shifting through the clothes and possessions of the Jews murdered in the gas chambers. He escaped in the cattle wagons taking away the clothes for distribution to the Reich.

SZMIRER. A Jew called Podgorski, a survivor from the Lublin ghetto, met Mr. Szmirer, a 21-year-old man, somewhere on a ghetto street. Szmirer was the son of a well-known furniture merchant from Lublin, and he said he had been deported to Belzec during the *Aktion* in March 1942.

Szmirer informed him that he had escaped from Belzec hidden under the clothes of the gassed victims on a freight train that had returned to Lublin. Back in Lublin, Szmirer had informed some members of the Jewish Council about his experiences, though it would appear that not many people believed him. His eventual fate is unknown, but it is likely he perished during the final liquidation of the Lublin ghetto on November 9, 1942.

Whilst undoubtedly there were more escapes from Belzec, this incredibly low number shows just how efficient at mass murder Belzec was, although it is recognized that it was very primitive in construction. Franz Suchomel, in an interview with Claude Lanzman for his film *Shoah*, had this to say about Belzec:

> Belzec was the laboratory. Wirth was camp commandant. He tried everything imaginable there. He got off on the wrong foot. The pits were overflowing and the cesspool seeped out in front of the SS mess hall. It stank—in front of the mess hall, in front of their barracks.
>
> .... Wirth with his own men—with Franz, with Oberhauser and Hackenholt—he tried everything there. Those three had to put the bodies in the pits themselves, so that Wirth could see how much space he néeded. And when they rebelled—Franz refused—Wirth beat Franz with a whip. He whipped Hackenholt too..... Kurt Franz. That's how Wirth was. Then, with that experience behind him, he came to Treblinka.[140] [141]

*

Victims from Germany—Murdered at Belzec

This is a listing of all the Jews who were deported from the Reich to the Belzec death camp, from the Bundesarchiv Memorial website. Where there is doubt as to the whether the individuals were murdered in Belzec or another camp, such as Sobibor, or Auschwitz, then these people have not been included:

APFELBAUM, Nathan. Born on February 5, 1890, in Rzeszow, Poland. Emigrated from Berlin to Poland. Deported from Rzeszow on July 7, 1942. Perished in Belzec on July 7, 1942.

APFELBAUM, Sara. Born on September 12, 1895, née Kurz, in Blizne, Poland. Emigrated from Berlin to Poland. Deported from Rzeszow on July 7, 1942. Perished in Belzec on July 7, 1942.

BAUM, Johanna. Born on May 11, 1907, in Frei-Laubersheim. Deported from Mainz-Darmstadt on March 25, 1942, to the Piaski transit ghetto in Poland.

---

140 C. Lanzmann, *Shoah*, Pantheon Books, New York, 1985, pp. 62–63.

141 Authors Note: Suchomel is not correct here, the SS barracks were outside the camp area in one of the stone houses belonging to the *Ostbahn*.

BECKER, Joel. Born on January 28, 1932, in Kiel. Expelled to Poland in 1939. Perished in Belzec during September 1942.

BEIN, Malka. Born on March 31,1886, in Gorlice, Poland. A resident of Leipzig, she was expelled to Poland on October 28, 1938.

BERGER, Jenta. Born on October 22, 1889, née Gartner, in Nowy Zmigrod, Poland. Emigrated to Poland on July 24, 1939, from Munich.

BERGER, Josef. Born on August 30, 1887, in Nowy Zmigrod, Poland. Emigrated to Poland on July 24, 1939, from Munich.

BERGER, Lemel. Born on December 10, 1885, in Sokolow, Poland. Expelled to Poland from Nuremburg on October 28, 1938, to the Bentschen internment camp. perished in Belzec in 1942.

BERGER, Sara. Born on June 16, 1888, née Kaufmann, in Nienadowka, Poland. Expelled to Poland from Nuremburg on October 28, 1938, to the Bentschen internment camp. Perished in Belzec in 1942.

BINDER, Aron. Born on September 17, 1897, in Nowy Sacs, Poland. Deported from Berlin.

BRODREICH, Lionel. Born on March 8, 1881, in Einartshausen. Deported from Mainz-Darmstadt on March 25, 1942, to the Piaski transit ghetto in Poland.

BRUCKNER, Adolf. Born on May 7, 1931, in Cologne. Perished in Belzec in June 1942.

BRUCKNER, Regina. Born on May 12, 1890, née Piperberg, in Blazowa, Poland. Deported from Rzeszow, Poland, to Belzec. Perished in Belzec in 1942.

BRUCKNER, Salomon. Born on September 15, 1870, in Sienliawa, Poland. Expelled to the Bentschen internment camp. Deported from Rzeszow, Poland to Belzec.

BUCHSDORF, Golda. Born on January 4, 1884, in Lvov. Expelled from Breslau to Poland in 1938 / 39. Deported from Lvov ghetto to Belzec. Perished in Belzec during 1942.

DECKER, Johanna. Born on January 13, 1895, in Wachenheim. Deported from Mainz-Darmstadt to the Piaski transit ghetto in Poland.

DOMINITZ, Sabina. Born on April 18, 1897, née Unger, in Tuchow, Poland. Expelled to the Bentschen internment camp on October 28, 1938, from Cologne. Deported to Belzec.

DREILINGER, Edith. Born on May 15, 1922, in Vienna, Austria. Lived in Gelsenkirchen. Perished in Belzec during 1942.

DREILINGER, Egon. Born on October 16, 1928, in Gelsenkirchen. Perished in Belzec during 1942.

DREILINGER, Hermann. Born on July 27, 1917, in Stryj, Galizien. Lived in Gelsenkirchen. Perished in Belzec during 1942.

DREILINGER, Klara. Born on November 29, 1924, in Vienna, Austria. Lived in Gelsenkirchen. Perished in Belzec during 1942.

DRESNER, Gretel. Born on July 30, 1896, née Cohn, in Greiz. Emigrated to Poland during August 1939. Deported from the Nowy Sacs ghetto to Belzec, where she perished on August 18, 1942.

EPSTEIN, Wolf. Born in 1895 in Pilzno, Poland. Emigrated from Berlin to Poland. Deported from the Debica ghetto to Belzec.

FISCH, Esther. Born in 1905, née Hubermann, in Warka, Poland. Expelled from Dresden to Poland on August 2, 1939. Deported from the Krakow ghetto to Belzec in 1942.

FISCH, Frieda. Born on August 26, 1911, in Nadworna, Poland. Expelled from Dresden to Poland on October 28, 1938. Deported from Krakow ghetto to Belzec in 1942.

FISCH, Gerson. Born on July 7, 1873, in Nadworna, Poland. Expelled from Dresden to Poland on October 28, 1938. Deported from the Krakow ghetto to Belzec in 1942.

FISCH, Hanni. Born on June 10, 1930, in Dresden. Expelled from Dresden to Poland on August 2, 1939. Deported from the Krakow ghetto to Belzec in 1942.

FISCH, Jakob. Born on June 9, 1904, in Nadworna, Poland. Expelled from Dresden to Poland during 1938–39, to the Bentschen internment camp. Deported from the Krakow ghetto to Belzec in 1942.

FISCH, Jakob. Born on October 11, 1904, in Nadworna, Poland. Expelled from Dresden to Poland on August 2, 1939. Deported from the Krakow ghetto to Belzec in 1942.

FISCH, Rachel. Born on October 17, 1887, in Nadworna, Poland. Expelled from Dresden to Poland on October 28, 1938. Deported from the Krakow ghetto to Belzec in 1942.

FISCH, Rita. Born on December 18, 1931, in Dresden. Expelled from Dresden on August 2, 1939 to Poland. Deported from the Krakow ghetto to Belzec in 1942.

FRIEDMAN, Miriam. Born in 1933 in Frankfurt am Main. Deported to the Tarnow ghetto in Poland. Perished in Belzec 1942.

GERSTNER, Betty. Born on February 25, 1922, in Chemnitz. Expelled to Poland on October 28, 1938. Deported from the Slomniki ghetto to Belzec in September 1942.

GERSTNER, Chawa. Born on December 19, 1895, née Weisberg, in Lodz, Poland. Expelled to Poland on October 28, 1938. Deported from the Slomniki ghetto to Belzec in September 1942.

GERSTNER, Jakob. Born on September 1, 1896, in Krakow, Poland. Expelled to Poland from Chemnitz on October 28, 1938, to the Bentschen internment camp. Deported from the Slomniki ghetto to Belzec in September 1942.

GERSTNER, Sigo. Born on August 18, 1929, in Chemnitz. Expelled to Poland from Chemnitz on October 28, 1938, to the Bentschen internment camp. Deported from the Slomniki ghetto to Belzec in September 1942.

GLASER, Adele. Born on December 15, 1895, in Oswiecim, Poland. Lived in Furth. Perished in Belzec during 1942.

GLASER, Berta. Born on May 18, 1930, in Furth. Perished in Belzec during 1942.

GOLDBERGER, Jenny. Born 1880, in Stargard. Lived in Berlin. Expelled to Poland during October 1938 to the Bentschen internment camp. Perished in Belzec in 1942.

GUTFREUND, Lea. Born on June 13, 1895, in Przeworsk, Poland. Expelled from Leipzig to Poland on October 28, 1938.

HERSCHLAG, Henrietta. Born on April 15, 1910, in Ropczyce, Poland. Emigrated to Poland from Düsseldorf. Deported from the Debica ghetto to Belzec, where she perished.

HERSCHLAG, Tauba. Born on June 25, 1890, née Drexler, in Sobeszice, Poland. Expelled on October 28, 1938, to Bentschen internment camp. Deported from the Debica ghetto to Belzec.

HEUBERGER, Meyer. Born on February 5, 1876, in Krakow, Poland. Expelled from Leipzig on October 28, 1938, to Poland.

HILLMANN, Hersch. Born on April 22, 1890, in Nadworna, Poland. Expelled from Chemnitz on October 28, 1938, to the Bentschen internment camp.

HILLMANN, Klara. Born on November 6, 1896, in Mielec, Poland. Expelled from Chemnitz to Poland. Perished in Belzec during 1942.

HILLMANN, Max. Born on April 18, 1926, in Chemnitz. Expelled from Chemnitz to Poland. Perished in Belzec during 1942.

HILLMANN, Rolf. Born on June 9, 1930, in Chemnitz. Emigrated to Poland on July 29, 1939. Perished in Belzec during 1942.

HOROWITZ, Regine. Born in 1914, née Buchsdorf, in Lvov, Poland. Expelled from Breslau to Poland. Deported from the Lvov ghetto to Belzec.

JOSEPH, Berta. Born on March 14, 1891, née Grunbaum, in Kuppenheim. Deported from Mainz-Darmstadt on March 25, 1942, to the Piaski transit ghetto in Poland.

JOSEPH, Max. Born on September 22, 1882, in Worms. Deported from Mainz-Darmstadt on March 25, 1942, to the Piaski transit ghetto in Poland.

JOSEPH, Theresa. Born on February 16, 1922, in Edingen. Deported from Düsseldorf on April 22, 1942, to the Izbica transit ghetto in Poland. Deported to Belzec in May 1942.

KALLANN, Ernst. Born on February 24, 1922, in Bitburg. Deported from Düsseldorf on April 22, 1942 to the Izbica transit ghetto in Poland. Deported to Belzec in May 1942.

KAPP, Flora. Born on October 8, 1884, in Rulzheim. Deported from Mainz-Darmstadt on March 25, 1942, to the Piaski transit ghetto in Poland.

KATZ, Jenny. Born on December 27, 1877, née Konig, in Felsberg. Deported from Mainz-Darmstadt on March 25, 1942, to the Piaski transit ghetto in Poland.

KATZ, Manuel. Born April 20, 1878, in Erdmannrode. Deported from Mainz-Darmstadt on March 25, 1942, to the Piaski transit ghetto in Poland.

KELLER, Arthur. Born on November 27, 1921, in Gimbsheim. Deported from Mainz-Darmstadt on March 25, 1942, to the Piaski transit ghetto in Poland.

KELLER, Eugen. Born on April 13, 1911, in Gimbsheim. Deported from Mainz-Darmstadt on March 25, 1942, to the Piaski transit ghetto in Poland.

KLEIN, Senta. Born on October 15, 1893, née Minczeles, in Lvov, Poland. Emigrated from Berlin on March 24, 1939, to Poland. Deported from the Lvov ghetto to Belzec.

KLEIN, Stella. Born on May 15, 1920, in Lvov, Poland. Emigrated from Berlin on March 24, 1939, to Poland. Deported from the Lvov ghetto to Belzec.

KLEINZAHLER, Mina. Born on November 7, 1905, née Morgenstern, in Nowy Sacs, Poland. Emigrated to Poland on February 6, 1933.

KOHANE, Kalman. Born June 13, 1888 in Krakow, Poland. Expelled to Poland in 1938 from Berlin. Deported from the Krakow ghetto to Belzec in 1942.

KOHANE, Tina. Born on November 24, 1889, in Bielitz, Poland. Emigrated to Poland in 1939 from Berlin. Deported from the Krakow ghetto to Belzec in 1942.

KOHS, Dora. Born on October 3, 1901, née Fischel, in Bedzin, Poland. Expelled on October 28, 1938, from Leipzig to Poland. Deported from the Dabrowa Tarnowska ghetto to Belzec in 1942.

KORN, Arno. Born on June 2, 1929, in Berlin. Emigrated to Poland. Perished in Belzec during August 1942.

KORN, Cacilie. Born on February 2, 1895, née Straus, in Debica, Poland. Emigrated to Poland from Berlin during 1939. Perished in Belzec on August 15, 1942.

KORN, Jakob. Born on May 11, 1885, in Gorlice, Poland. Expelled to Poland from Berlin on October 28, 1938. Perished in Belzec during August 1942.

KORN, Simon. Born in 1890, in Gorlice, Poland. Emigrated to Poland from Berlin.

KORN, Walter. Born on January 11, 1913, in Worms. Deported from Mainz-Darmstadt on March 25, 1942, to the Piaski transit ghetto in Poland.

KOSCHITZKY, Chaja. Born in 1882, in Checiny, Poland. Emigrated to Poland from Berlin. Perished in Belzec in 1942.

KOSMANN, Alfred. Born on March 12, 1898, in Antwerp, Belgium. Deported from Mainz-Darmstadt on March 25, 1942, to the Piaski transit ghetto in Poland. Perished in Belzec on April 15, 1942.

KOSMANN, Emmy. Born on December 28, 1895, née Hausmann, in Wachenheim. Deported from Mainz-Darmstadt on March 25, 1942, to the Piaski transit ghetto in Poland.

KOSMANN, Lutz. Born on May 8, 1926, in Worms. Deported from Mainz-Darmstadt on March 25, 1942. to the Piaski transit ghetto in Poland.

KOSMANN, Ruth. Born on September 25, 1924, in Worms. Deported from Mainz-Darmstadt on March 25, 1942, to the Piaski transit ghetto in Poland.

KRISTELLER, Hilda. Born on April 13, 1899, née Reinheimer, in Worms. Deported from Mainz-Darmstadt on March 25, 1942, to the Piaski transit ghetto in Poland.

KRISTELLER, Paul. Born on September 14, 1895, in Schwenten. Deported from Mainz-Darmstadt on March 25, 1942, to the Piaski transit ghetto in Poland. Perished in Belzec.

LAMBEK, Hirsch. Born on July 6, 1860, in Siary, Poland. Emigrated to Poland from Leipzig. He was deported from the Gorlice Ghetto to Belzec in August 1942, where he perished.

LEDERBERGER, Aron. Born on January 25, 1892, in Krakow, Poland. Emigrated to Poland from Leipzig on August 28, 1939.

LEDERBERGER, Jetti. Born on January 27, 1894, née Wanderer, in Leipzig. Emigrated to Poland from Leipzig.

LESERKIEWICZ, Lydia. Born on July 31, 1927, in Dusseldorf. Expelled to Poland on October 28, 1938, to Bentschen internment camp. Deported from the Nowy Targ ghetto to Belzec, where she perished in 1942.

LEVY, Josef. Born on September 2, 1892, in Aach. Deported from Düsseldorf on April 22, 1942, to the Izbica transit ghetto in Poland. Deported to Belzec in May 1942.

LEVY, Selma. Born on November 25, 1890, in Aach. Deported from Düsseldorf on April 22, 1942, to the Izbica transit ghetto in Poland. Deported to Belzec in May 1942.

LEVY, Selma. Born on February 19, 1911, née Hirsch, in Neumagen. She was deported to the Izbica ghetto on April 22, 1942. Deported to Belzec in May 1942.

LOEB, Anna. Born on March 25, 1885, née Westheimer, in Hasloch. Deported from Mainz-Darmstadt on March 25, 1942, to the Piaski transit ghetto in Poland. Deported to Belzec, via Chelm.

LOEB, Ernestine. Born on July 21, 1898, in Sprendlingen. Deported from Mainz-Darmstadt on March 25, 1942, to the Piaski transit ghetto in Poland. Deported to Belzec.

LOEB, Hedwig. Born on November 4, 1895, in Sprendlingen. Deported from Mainz-Darmstadt on March 25, 1942, to the Piaski transit ghetto in Poland. Deported to Belzec.

LOEBL, Leo. Born on August 16, 1887, in Bamberg. Deported from Berlin to Belzec.

MAYER, Anna. Born on December 5, 1894, née Strauss, in Niederhofheim. Deported from Mainz-Darmstadt on March 25, 1942, to the Piaski transit ghetto in Poland. Deported to Belzec.

MAYER, August. Born on March 13, 1895, in Frankfurt am Main. Deported from Mainz-Darmstadt on March 25, 1942, to the Piaski transit ghetto in Poland. Deported from there to Belzec.

MAYER, Betty. Born on August 27, 1895, in Westhofen. Deported from Mainz-Darmstadt on March 25, 1942, to the Piaski transit ghetto in Poland. Deported to Belzec.

MAYER, Hermann. Born on October 6, 1879, in Bingen. Deported from Mainz-Darmstadt on March 25, 1942, to the Piaski transit ghetto in Poland. Deported from there to Belzec.

MAYER, Kurt. Born on September 23, 1915, in Worms. Deported from Mainz-Darmstadt on March 25, 1942. to the Piaski transit ghetto in Poland. Deported from there to Belzec.

MAYER, Lisbeth. Born on May 31, 1912, in Worms. Deported from Mainz-Darmstadt on March 25, 1942, to the Piaski transit ghetto in Poland. Deported to Belzec, where she perished on April 7, 1942.

MAYER, Margot. Born on April 15, 1926, in Niederhofheim. Deported from Mainz-Darmstadt on March 25, 1942, to the Piaski transit ghetto in Poland. Deported to Belzec.

MAYER, Moses. Born on March 9, 1884, in Alsheim. Deported from Mainz-Darmstadt on March 25, 1942, to the Piaski transit ghetto in Poland. Deported from there to Belzec, where he perished on June 30, 1942.

MAYER, Rosa. Born on January 28, 1898, née Lovy, in Hesloch. Deported from Mainz-Darmstadt on March 25, 1942, to the Piaski transit ghetto in Poland. Deported to Belzec, where she perished on April 8, 1942.

MAYER, Senta. Born on July 27, 1902, in Maikammer. Deported from Mainz-Darmstadt on March 25, 1942, to the Piaski transit ghetto in Poland. Deported to Belzec.

METZGER, Paula. Born on December 7, 1885, in Kirchheimbolanden. Deported from Mainz-Darmstadt on March 25, 1942, to the Piaski transit ghetto in Poland. Deported to Belzec.

MEYER, Franziska. Born on October 13, 1906, in Worms. Deported from Mainz-Darmstadt on March 25, 1942, to the Piaski transit ghetto in Poland. Deported to Belzec.

MEYER, Gertrude. Born on March 15, 1927, in Worms. Deported from Mainz-Darmstadt on March 25, 1942, to the Piaski transit ghetto in Poland. Deported to Belzec.

MEYER, Lucie. Born on April 7, 1925, in Worms. Deported from Mainz-Darmstadt on March 25, 1942, to the Piaski transit ghetto in Poland. Deported to Belzec.

NEMANN, Wilhelm. Born on May 22, 1888, in Leszno, Poland. He was a resident of Halle. Deported to Belzec.

NEUFELD, Klara. Born in 1920 in Horodenka, Poland. Expelled from Wittichenau on October 28, 1938, to Poland. Deported from the Lvov ghetto to Belzec in 1942.

NEUFELD, Rosa. Born in 1918 in Muhlenbach. Expelled from Wittichenau on October 28, 1938, to Poland. Deported from the Lvov ghetto to Belzec in 1942.

NEUFELD, Rut. Born in 1923. Expelled from Wittichenau on October 28, 1938, to Poland. Deported from the Lvov ghetto to Belzec in 1942.

NEUFELD, Zipora. Born in 1884, née Laster, in Horodenka, Poland. Expelled from Wittichenau on October 28, 1938, to Poland. Deported from the Lvov ghetto to Belzec in 1942.

ORTWEILER, Henny. Born on September 18, 1890, née Muller, in Erfurt. Deported from Weimar-Leipzig on May 10, 1942, to the Belzyce ghetto in Poland. Deported to Belzec.

PESE, Gerda. Born on October 23, 1907, in Weiswasser. Deported from Breslau on April 13, 1942, to the Izbica transit ghetto in Poland. Deported to Belzec.

PESE, Margarete. Born on June 5, 1880, née Rosenberg, in Friedeberg. Deported from Breslau on May 3, 1942, to Lublin. Deported to Belzec.

REICH, Joseph. Born on February 12, 1883, in Rzeszow, Poland. Expelled from Berlin on October 28, 1938, to the Bentschen internment camp. Settled in the Tarnow ghetto in Poland. Deported to Belzec.

REICHSTEIN, Kathe. Born on June 7, 1882, née Ert, in Hannover. Expelled from Hannover to Bentschen internment camp on October 28, 1938. Deported from the Tarnopol ghetto to Belzec in September 1942.

REINMANN, Elsa. Born on September 10, 1903, in Essenheim. Deported from Mainz-Darmstadt on March 25, 1942, to the Piaski transit ghetto in Poland. Deported to Belzec.

ROSEN, Chaim. Born on August 10, 1889, in Turka, Poland. Emigrated from Leipzig on July 15, 1939, to Poland.

ROSENBERG, Adolf. Born on November 11, 1879, in Hildesheim. Deported from Mainz-Darmstadt on March 25, 1942, to the Piaski transit ghetto in Poland. Deported to Belzec.

SALOMON, Ferdinand. Born on May 26, 1904, in Worms. Deported from Mainz-Darmstadt on March 25, 1942, to the Piaski transit ghetto in Poland. Deported to Belzec.

SALOMON, Regina. Born on June 19, 1886, née Lavy, in Aach. Deported from Koblenz on April 30, 1942, to the Krasniczyn Ghetto. Deported to Belzec in May 1942.

SCHENKEL, Moses. Born on December 13, 1894 in Gorlice, Poland. Expelled from Leipzg on October 28, 1938, to Poland.

SCHIFF, Awigdor. Born on January 16, 1940, in Furth. Deported from Nurnberg on March 24, 1942, to the Izbica transit ghetto, Poland. Deported to Belzec death camp.

SCHIFF, Benno. Born on August 24, 1894, in Oberthulba. Deported from Nurnberg on March 24, 1942, to the Izbica transit ghetto, Poland. Deported to Belzec.

SCHIFFMANN, Greta. Born on March 7, 1922, in Dortmund. Expelled from Dortmund to Bentschen on October 28, 1938.

SELINGER, Dyna. Born on August 29, 1886, née Ellend, in Tarnow, Poland. Emigrated to Poland from Leipzig on August 1, 1939.

SELINGER, Hirsch. Born on April 2, 1882 in Rzeszow, Poland. Emigrated to Poland from Leipzig on August 1, 1939.

SONDHEIMER, Felicitas. Born on November 17, 1908, née Rosenstrauch, in Karlsruhe. Deported from Mainz-Darmstadt on March 25, 1942, to the Piaski transit ghetto in Poland. Deported to Belzec, via Chelm.

SONDHEIMER, Josef. Born on November 14, 1889, in Burstadt. Deported from Mainz-Darmstadt on March 25, 1942, to the Piaski transit ghetto in Poland. Deported to Belzec, via Chelm.

SONNENBERGER, Cornelie. Born on July 19, 1891, in Worms. Deported from Mainz-Darmstadt on March 25, 1942, to the Piaski transit ghetto in Poland. Deported to Belzec.

STEIN, Liba. Born in 1890, née Pfenig, in Lesko, Poland. Expelled from Dresden to Poland on October 28, 1938.

STEIN, Wolf. Born on December 21, 1885, in Dynow, Poland. Expelled from Dresden to Poland on October 28, 1938.

STIEFEL, Bertha. Born on April 1, 1878, in Muhlheim. Deported from Mainz-Darmstadt on March 25, 1942, to the Piaski transit ghetto in Poland. Deported to Belzec, via Chelm.

TANZER, Elkan. Born on November 18, 1883, in Podgorze, Krakow, Poland. Emigrated from Leipzig to Poland on May 11, 1938.

TANZER, Ruchel. Born on July 10, 1890, née Lemberger, in Krakow, Poland. Emigrated from Leipzig to Poland on November 9, 1938.

TUTEUER, Hans. Born on March 11, 1932, in Kaiserslautern. Deported from Mainz-Darmstadt on March 25, 1942, to the Piaski transit ghetto in Poland. Deported to Belzec.

TUTEUER, Lina. Born on March 16, 1907, née Mayer, in Worms. Deported from Mainz-Darmstadt on March 25, 1942, to the Piaski transit ghetto in Poland. Deported to Belzec.

WACHENHEIMER, Albrecht. Born on February 24, 1885, in Worms. Deported from Mainz-Darmstadt on March 25, 1942, to the Piaski transit ghetto in Poland. Deported to Belzec, via Chelm.

WEIS, Hillel. Born on November 28, 1939, in Worms. Deported from Mainz-Darmstadt on March 25, 1942, to the Piaski transit ghetto in Poland. Deported to Belzec.

WEISS, Elias. Born on August 5, 1882, in Hamburg. Deported from Koblenz on March 22, 1942, to the Izbica transit ghetto in Poland. Deported to Belzec.

WEISSBERGER, Eva. Born on September 12, 1922, in Zabrze, Poland. Expelled on October 27–28, 1938, to Poland. Deported from Krosno ghetto to Belzec in September 1942.

WEITZ, Amalie. Born on August 31, 1890, née Spielmann, in Ropczyce, Poland.

WEITZ, Minna. Born on July 18, 1886. Resident of Kiel and Leipzig.

WEITZ, Rubin. Born on May 18, 1886, in Rzeszow, Poland.

WERMUTH, Ida. Born on July 26, 1894, née Presser, in Grybow, Poland. Lived in Frankfurt am Main, before emigrating to Poland. Perished in Belzec on August 24, 1942.

WOLF, Gertrud. Born on April 29, 1903, née Levy, in Aach. Deported from Mainz-Darmstadt on March 25, 1942, to the Piaski transit ghetto in Poland. Deported to Belzec, where she perished on March 31, 1942.

WOLF, Marie. Born on January 17, 1928, in Bingen. Deported from Mainz-Darmstadt on March 25, 1942, to the Piaski transit ghetto in Poland. Deported to Belzec.

WOLFF, Gertrud. Born on May 12, 1894, née Aron, in Gorlitz, Poland. Deported from Breslau on April 13, 1942 to the Izbica transit ghetto. Deported to Belzec.

WOLFF, Hans. Born on July 22, 1924, in Hambuch. Perished in Belzec in May 1942.

WOLFF, Simon. Born on January 21, 1888, in Landeshut. Lived in Breslau. Perished in Belzec during 1942.

*

Belzec Victims from other Countries

This is a partial listing, in alphabertical order. This list has been compiled from survivor testimony and from two major websites consulted, which were the Holocaust Historical Society and Yad Vashem Central Shoah database. Where it is listed that an individulal might have died at Belzec or another camp / place, then these entries have been omitted, unless there is compelling evidence that the individual perished in Belzec. Most of the victims listed were born and raised in Poland, but where the birthplace was in a different country, then this is shown. This list will never be complete, but will be updated if re-prints occur.

ADLER, Aba. Born in 1877. He was married to Henia and was a merchant by profession. Deported from Proszowice to Belzec, where he perished during 1942.

ADLER, Ber. Deported from Zamosc to Belzec.

ADLER, David. Born in 1893, in Dukla. He was a businessman who lived in Yaslo. Deported to Belzec.

ADLER, Dwora. Born in 1909, née Beitler, in Narol. Married to Natan. Deported from Rawa Ruska to Belzec, where she perished during 1942.

ADLER, Elka. Born in 1900 in Lubaszow. Married to David. Perished in Belzec during 1942.

ADLER, Ester. Born in 1899, née Nestel, in Strzeliska. Married to Kisiel. Perished in Belzec in 1942.

ADLER, Freude. Born in 1924, in Strzeliska. Perished in Belzec during 1942.

ADLER, Gitel. Deported from Zamosc to Belzec.

ADLER, Golda. Born in 1937, in Kolomea. Perished in Belzec during 1942.

ADLER, Hena. Born in 1897, née Gut, in Wojtkowka.

ADLER, Hersh. Born in Wojtkowka in 1896. Perished in Belzec.

ADLER, Kisiel: Born in 1892. Married to Ester. Deported from Strzeliska to Belzec, where he perished during 1942.

ADLER, Klara. Born in 1886, in Kolomea. Married to Leon. Perished in Belzec during 1942.

ADLER, Leib. Born in 1907, in Krakow. Married to Sala and was a butcher by profession. Deported from Krakow to Belzec.

ADLER, Leibisch. Born in 1905, in Kurdanow. Married to Sara.

ADLER, Malka. Born in 1909, née Muntz, in Zamosc. Married to Yitzhak. Perished in Belzec during 1942.

ADLER, Maurycy. Born in 1892, in Skawina. Deported from Krakow to Belzec.

ADLER, Miriam. Born in 1917, née Oringer, in Kolomea. She was single. Perished in Belzec during 1942.

ADLER, Mordekhai. Born in 1908, in Belz. Married to Khana. Deported from Lubicza Krolewska to Belzec, where he perished during 1942.

ADLER, Moses. Born in 1903, in Wojtkowka. Perished in Belzec during 1942.

ADLER, Mosze. Born in 1896, in Izbica. Married to Feiga. Deported from Izbica to Belzec.

ADLER, Natan. Born in 1940, to Natan and Dvora in Rawa Ruska.

ADLER, Olga. Born on April 3, 1882, née Furth, in Susice, Czechoslovakia. Married to Siegfried. Lived in Vienna, Austria. Perished in Belzec on May 15, 1942.

ADLER, Rivka. Deported from Zamosc to Belzec.

ADLER, Sala. Born in 1916, née Noihof. She was married to Arie and was a housewife. Perished in Belzec.

ADLER, Sarah. Born in 1915. Deported from Zagorze to Belzec, where she perished during 1942.

ADLER, Siegfried. Born on June 26, 1876, in Luka, Czechoslovakia. He was a Textile factory owner and was married to Olga. Perished in Belzec on May 15, 1942.

ALLERHAND, Jozek. Grandson of Maurycy and Salomea Allerhand. Deported with them from Lvov in August 1942 to Belzec.

ALLERHAND, Maurycy. Born in 1862 in Lvov. He was a professor at Lvov University and author of many books about jurisprudence, which are still in use today by students and lawyers in Poland. Before the Second World War, he was a member of the Polish Supreme Court. During 1941–42 he lived in the Lvov ghetto where he wrote a diary. During the "Great Action" in August 1942, he was deported to Belzec, along with his wife Salomea and their grandson Jozek. All three perished in Belzec. The diary he wrote in the Lvov ghetto was found after some time. His second gransdon, Dr. Leszek Allerhand, published the diary in Poland in 2003, under the title *Notes from the Other World*.

ALLERHAND, Salomea. Née Weintraub. The wife of Professor Maurycy Allerhand. Deported to Belzec with him and their grandson Jozek from Lvov in August 1942.

AUERBACH, Herman. Born October 26, 1901, in Tarnopol. He was a famous mathemtician and a professor at Lvov University. Before the Second World War, he published many works about mathematics and geometry, which were translated from Polish into French and German and are still in use today. Whilst he was in the Lvov ghetto during 1941–42, he wrote his last work on geometry, on the reverse side of German documents. On August 17, 1942, during the "Great Action," he was deported to Belzec, where he perished. His last work, written in the Lvov ghetto, was finally published in Polish in 1992.

BACHNER, Moszey. Born in 1904 in Krakow. He was a merchant and single. Deported from Krakow to Belzec.

BAJLER, Abram Icchoc. Born in 1927. Son of Fela and Shimon Hirsh, deported together with his parents to Belzec.

BAJLER, Fela. Born in 1905, "resetted" to Zamosc from the Warthegau. Deported to Belzec together with Szlamek Bajler. She was the sister-in-law of Szlamek, and they were deported from Zamosc, during the "First Action" on April 11, 1942.

BAJLER, Rivka. Born in 1938, the daughter of Fela and Shimon Hirsh. Deported from Zamosc with her parents to Belzec.

BAJLER, Shimon. Born in 1901. He was the brother of Szlamek and husband to Fela. Deported along with other members of his family from Zamosc to Belzec in April 1942.

BAJLER, Szlamek. Lived in the Warthegau until December 1941. Deported to the Chelmno (Kulmhof) death camp, on January 13, 1942, from the town of Izbica Kujawska. Selected for the "death brigade," who worked at emptying the gas vans and digging mass graves. Escaped from Chelmno on January 19, 1942, and for several days lived in the Warsaw ghetto. There he made contact with Emanuel Ringelblum and he informed him of the death camp in Chelmno and how the Germans were murdering the Jews.

He left Warsaw and went to live with his brother and sister-in-law in Zamosc. When the deportations as part of *Aktion Reinhardt* commenced, Szlamek once again made contact with Ringelblum and his *Oneg Shabbat* group, sending a letter informing them that "Belzec is the same as in Kulmhof."

Szlamek was deported from the Zamosc ghetto along with his sister-in-law, brother, and other members of the family on April 11, 1942, to Belzec, where he perished. Their fate was related to Emanuel Ringelblum by Fela Bajler's son. Szlamek's harrowing report about Chelmno is virtually unique, as there were so few survivors .

BALDACHIM. Engineer. From a statement made in 1968 by Panteleon Radunkow, who was a Ukrainian teacher in the Belzec village during the occupation: "Engineer Baldachim came from Rzeszow. He worked in a group of Jewish prisoners who were allowed to work outside the death camp, of course guarded by Ukrainians. Radunkow met Baldachim several times and from him learned many detais about the death camp, including the method of killing. Radunkow sent post cards written by Baldachim to the Rzeszow Ghetto, where his family still lived. According to Radunkow, Engineer Baldachim, was killed in the course of the liquidation of the camp in 1943."

BALDINGER, Sara. Born in 1920, in Biecz. She was a pupil.

BARAN, Jakub. Deported from the Lvov ghetto to Belzec in March 1942.

BAUER, Sosza. Born in 1902, in Drohobycz. She was single. Perished in Belzec during September 1942.

BAUER, Yakob. Born in 1874, in Poland. He was a restaurant owner. Perished in Belzec during 1942.

BAUM, Gitel. Born in 1897, in Tomaszow Lubelski. She was married to Shalom and was a housewife. Perished in Belzec during 1942.

BAUM, Leib. Born in 1916, in Wielopole. He was single. Perished in Belzec during 1942.

BAUM, Naftali. Born in 1915, in Broniszow. He was married to Rivka and was a landowner. Persihed in Belzec during 1942.

BAUM, Zofia. Born in 1894, in Podboz. Married to Beniamin. Deported from Sambor to Belzec.

BECK, Salomea. Born in May 1924, in Zakopane. Deported from Nowy-Targ to Belzec during September 1942.

BEER, Hene. Born on November 1, 1914, née Verner, in Tuchow. She was a clerk by profession and married. Perished in Belzec during September 1942.

BEICZER, Leizor. Born in 1888, in Szczebrzesyn, Poland. Perished in Belzec during 1942.

BEIN, Estera. Born in 1875, in Poland. She was married to Yehuda and was a housewife.

BEKER, Awraham. Born in 1924, in Witkow Nowy. He was single and a pupil. Perished in Belzec during 1942.

BEKERMAN, Reizl. Born in 1910, in Zmudz. She was a clerk by profession and single. Perished in Belzec during 1942.

BEKKER, Henryk. Born on June 6, 1886, in Bialystok. He was an architecht who graduated from the Politechnic High School in Munich. Before the Second World War, he was the leader of the *Folkspartaj* (Jewish People's Party) in Lublin and a member of the Lublin City Council. From 1936, he was the president of the Jewish Community Council, and became the first president of the Lublin *Judenrat* after the Nazi occupation.

On March 31, 1942, he was deported, together with his wife, from Lublin to Belzec. After the selection of the *Judenrat* members, he knew about the fate of the deportees and went to the *Umschlagplatz* in Lublin without suitases, wearing his prayer shawl. Perished in Belzec along with his wife.

BENDLER, Ronia. Born in 1887, in Tomaszow Mazowiecki. She was married to Motel and was a housewife.

BER, Brejndel. Born in 1902, in Lubashov. She was widowed and was a grocer by profession. Perished during 1942 in Belzec.

BERCHARD, Fryda. Born in 1925, in Rawa Ruska.

BERGER, Isak. Born in 1914, in Uhnow. He was a merchant by profession and single. Perished in Belzec during 1942.

BERGER, Mendl. Born in 1914, in Wielopole. He was married and was a merchant by profession. Perished in Belzec during 1942.

BERGER, Nesia. Born in 1889, in Uhnow. She was married and was a housewife. Perished in Belzec during 1942.

BERKOWICZ, Marie. Born in 1871, in Vienna, Austria. Deported from Krakow to Belzec, where she perished during June 1942.

BERKOWICZ, Sara. Born on March 14, 1914, in Krakow. She was a clerk by profession and married. Deported from Krakow to Belzec, where she perished on October 28, 1942.

BERLINSKA, Mala. Born in 1916, in Zywiec. Deported from the Belzyce ghetto to Belzec during 1942.

BERNBLAT, Chaja. Born in 1923, in Tomaszow Lubelski. She was a pupil and single. Perished in Belzec during 1942.

BERNSTEIN, Gitel. Née Boryslaw. She was married to Berl and was a housewife. Deported from Boryslaw to Belzec in 1942.

BILITZ, Frida. Born in 1909, in Krakow.

BINDER, Leib. Born in 1885, in Rozdol. He was married to Lea and was a merchant by profession.

BINDER, Mirl. Born in 1923, in Rozdol. She was single.

BINDER, Mojsze. Born in 1882, in Rozdol. He was married to Frida and was a merchant by profession.

BINDER, Samoil. Born in 1921, in Rozdol. He was a merchant by profession and single.

BINDER, Simcha. Born in 1903, in Rozdol. He was married to Sara and was a merchant by profession.

BIRNBAUM, Rebeka. Born on May 15, 1912, in Rozwaldow. She was married to Shlomo and lived in Dukla. Perished in Belzec during 1942.

BIRNBERG, Rozia. Born in 1902, in Podwoloczyska. She was married and perished in Belzec during 1942.

BLAICHER, Frida. Born in 1916, née Blum, in Proszowice. She was married and a housewife. Deported from Krakow to Belzec in 1942.

BLAJBERG, Mendel. Born in 1901, in Niemirow. He was married. Deported from Niemirow to Belzec.

BLANDE, Icchak. Born in 1882, in Laszczow. He was married and was a merchant by profession. Perished in Belzec during 1942.

BLANDE, Zacharia. Born in 1919, in Laszczow. He was married and was a merchant by profession. Perished in Belzec during 1942.

BLANDER, Faivel. Born in 1907, in Tomaszow Lubelski. He was married and was a merchant by profession. Perished in Belzec during 1942.

BLANDER, Yehoshua. Born in 1882, in Tomaszow Lubelski. He was married and a textile merchant by profession. Perished in Belzec during 1942.

BLANK, Mordko. Born in 1896, in Tomaszow Lubelski. He was married and a hairdresser by profession.

BLANKENHAMER, Hersh. Born in 1910, in Uhnow. He was married. Perished in Belzec during 1942.

BLAT, Hana. Born in 1882. She was married to Lipa and lived in Krasnystaw. Perished in Belzec during 1942.

BLAT, Reizl. Born in 1895, in Izbica.

BLATT, Fela. Born in 1895, in Krakow. She was married and a housewife. Deported from Slominki to Belzec in 1942.

BLATT, Hersz. Born in 1902, in Warsaw. Deported from Krakow to Belzec.

BLATT. Lea. Born in 1895, in Przemysl. Deported from Przemysl to Belzec.

BLATT, Rywka. Born in 1884, in Krakow. She was a housewife and married. She lived in Plaszow. Deported from Krakow to Belzec.

BLAU, Zlata. Born in 1890, in Sanok. Perished in Belzec during 1942.

BLAUTAL, Szajndel. Born in 1900, in Kolomea. She was single and was deported from Kolomea to Belzec.

BLAUTHAL, Chaja. Born in 1910, in Kolomea. Deported from Kolomea to Belzec in 1942.

BLAUTHAL, Jehudit. Born in 1902, in Kolomea. She was single. Deported from Kolomea to Belzec in 1942.

BLAUTHAL, Rachel. Born in 1914, in Buczacz. She was single and was deported from Stanislavov to Belzec during 1942.

BLECH, Chana. Born in 1882. Deported from Zamosc to Belzec during 1942.

BLEIBERG, Gitel. Born in Opatow. She was married to Yehoshua and was a housewife.

BLEIBERG, Hersh. Born in 1922, in Jaworow.

BLEJBERG, Sarah. Born in 1899, in Lubashov. She was married and perished in Belzec during 1942.

BLEM, Dr. Karol. Deported from the Lvov ghetto to Belzec in March 1942.

BLIC, Ichak. Born in 1910, in Krakow. He was married. Perished in Belzec during 1942.

BLITER, Etla. Born in 1914, in Glogow. She was single.

BLITTER, Tauba. Born in 1895, in Sokolow Malopolski. She was married. Deported from Sokolow to Belzec in 1942.

BLITZER, Shendel. Born in 1922, in Sokolow. She was single and perished in Belzec during 1942.

BLOCH, Rysia. Born on January 22, 1898, in Delatyn. She was married and was deported from Lvov to Belzec.

BLONSHTEIN, Rachel. Born in 1908, in Gliniany.

BLUM, Rywka. Born in 1900, in Gorlice. She was married to Elimelekh and was a housewife. Perished in Belzec during 1942.

BLUM, Sara. Born in 1870, in Wodzislaw. Deported from Proszowice to Belzec during 1942.

BLUM, Zeev. Born in 1861, in Wladyslawow. He was a tinsmith by profession and lived in Proshovitza. Perished in Belzec during 1942.

BLUMBERG, Dow. Born in 1914, in Lubaczow. He was single and a lawyer by profession. Perished in Belzec during 1942.

BLUMBERG, Icchak. Born in 1892. He was married to Lea and was a haberdasher by profession. He lived in Lubaszewo. Perished in Belzec during 1942.

BLUMENFELD, Chaja. Born in 1917, in Lubicz. She was married to Moshe. Perished in Belzec during 1942.

BLUMENFELD, Feiwel. Born in 1900, in Oswiecim. He was married and was a rabbi. Deported from Proszowice to Belzec during 1942.

BLUMENFELD, Rakhel. Born in 1898, née Wolosker, in Przemysl. She was married to Arie and was a merchant by profession. Deported from Przemysl to Belzec during 1942.

BLUMENTAL, Eliezer. Born in 1908, in Jagelnica. He was single and a baker by profession.

BLUTH, Ester. Born in 1910, in Ropczyce. She was married. Deported from Ropczyce to Belzec in 1942.

BLUZER, Malka. Born in 1896, in Tomaszow Lubelski. Married to Yisrael. Perished in Belzec during 1942.

BOIM, Jozef. Born in 1890, in Pstragowa. He was married. Deported from Wielopole to Belzec during 1942.

BOJM, Chaja. Born in 1896, in Zamosc. She was a housewife. Deported from Zamosc to Belzec in 1942.

BOSKER, Ester. Born in 1889, in Zamosc. She was a grocer. Deported from Zamosc to Belzec.

BRANDE, Rywka. Born in 1901, in Czortkow. She was married and was housewife. Deported from Radziechow to Belzec.

BRANDL, Malka. Born in 1914, in Trawniki. She was single and was deported from Trawniki to Belzec.

BRAUN, David. Born in 1903, in Zamosc. He was married to Shifra and a factory owner.

BRAUN, Sara. Born in 1906, in Dukla. She was married to Shlomo and was a housewife. Deported from Tarnow to Belzec.

BRAUN, Tonia. Born in 1912. She was single and was deported from Krakow to Belzec.

BRIK, Mindl. Born in 1878, in Debica. She was a widow and a housewife. Perished in Belzec during 1942.

BRIKS, Chana. Born in 1902, in Slupca. She was a housewife.

BRIKS, Ferka. Born in 1867, in Slowce.

BUNDER, Herman. Born in 1906, in Rozdol. He was single and was a merchant by profession.

BURSZTYN, Lejba. Born in 1910, in Szczebrzeszyn. He was a merchant by profession. Deported from Szczebrzeszyn to Belzec.

DACH, Chaim. Born in 1892, in Jozefow. He was a merchant by profession. Deported from Jozefow to Belzec.

DANZIG, Yitzhak. Born in 1910, in Krakow He was a Tailor by profession and married. Deported from Krakow to Belzec in 1942.

DAR, Wolf. Born in 1913, in Dembica. He was single and was a merchant by profession. Deported from Tarnow during 1942 to Belzec.

DELIGACZ, Yoel. Born in 1875, in Trembowla. He was a merchant by profession and married. Perished in Belzec during 1942.

DEMESTI, Wolf. Born in 1910, in Bilgoraj. He was married to Hadasa and was a merchant by profession. Perished in Belzec during 1942.

DEUTSCH, Dr. Deported from the Lvov ghetto to Belzec during the "Small Action" on June 28, 1942, when about 8,000 of Lvov's Jews were resettled from the ghetto to the Janowska camp and then onto Belzec.

DINTER, Leibish. Born in 1901, in Belz. He was married to Tova and was a merchant by profession.

DODYK, Chaya. Née Zaleszczyki. She was a housewife and was deported from Karolowka to Belzec during 1942.

DOMINIK, Sarah. Born in 1875, in Sanok. She was a housewife and perished in Belzec during 1942.

DOMINITZ, Reizl. Born in 1880, née Zilbershtein, in Lubaczow. She was married to Shmuel and was a housewife. Perished in Belzec during 1942.

DORENBUST, Elimelech. Born in 1880, in Bilgoraj. He was married to Dvora and was a butcher by profession. Deported from Bilgoraj to Belzec during 1942.

DORNFELD, Dr. Jakob. Born in 1895, in Boryslaw. He was a physician and married. Deported from Boryslaw to Belzec during 1942.

DRAJER, Sara. Born in 1900, in Skarbiszow. Deported from Krasnystaw to Belzec during 1942.

DREIFACH, Zofia. Deported from the Lvov ghetto to Belzec in March 1942.

DYM, Rachela. Born in 1910, in Rzeszow. She was a lawyer by profession and single. Deported from Rzeszow to Belzec.

ECKSTEIN, Baruch. Born in 1895, in Kolbuszowa. He was married and a merchant by profesion. Perished in Belzec during 1942.

ECKSTEIN, Ilek. Born in 1924, in Drohobycz. He was single. Perished in Belzec during 1942.

EDELSTEIN, Ita. Born in 1880, in Rawa Ruska. She was married to Yehoshua and a housewife. Deported from Rawa Ruska to Belzec.

EDELSTEIN, Sucher. Born in 1872, in Galicia. He was married to Lea. Deported from Sokal in 1942 to Belzec.

EHRLICH, Aszer. Born in 1912. He was a merchant. Perished in Belzec during 1942.

EHRLICH, Benzion. Born in 1910, in Zamosc. He was a merchant by profession in Trawniki. Deported from Trawniki to Belzec in 1942.

EICHENBAUM, Chawe. Born in 1902 in Tarnopol. She married Samuel Naftali Teicholz in Tarnopol and lived in an apartment on Rynek Street. As they had a religious ceremony for the wedding, it was not officially recognized by the Polish government. They had two children, Chaya, born on December 16, 1923, and Malka, born sometime during 1933.

She was a housewife and mother and, on November 8–9, 1942, while living in the Tarnopol Ghetto, the Nazis started an *Aktion* during which her husband and Malka were shot, and she was deported to Belzec. Chaya survived by changing her name to Sonja Tarasowa. She subsequently married J.M.A. van der Horst. Chaya (Sonja) has four children and eight grandchildren. The Hebrew name of one grandchild, Anna, is Chawe, after her great grandmother.

EISNER, Ludwika. Born in 1893, née Weinstock. Deported from the Przemysl ghetto to Belzec during the "First Action" on July 27, 1942.

EKSTEIN, Gitla. Born in Tarnobrzeg, née Ekshtein. She was married and was a hosewife in Kolbuszowa. Perished in Belzec during 1942.

ELENBOGEN, Ischak. Born in 1898, in Rzeszow. He was married and was a merchant by profession.

ELLENBOGEN. A Czech Jew who once owned a bicycle store, as remembered by Rudolf Reder.

ELOWICZ, Riwka. Born in 1885, née Veinberger, in Krukenice. She lived in Nowy Sacz. Perished in Belzec during 1942.

ELTSTER, Josef. Born in 1904, in Krystonopol. He was married to Glika and was a merchant by profession. Deported from Szczewice to Belzec during 1942.

ENGLANDER, Chana. Born in 1905, in Oleszyce. She was married to Shmul and a clerk by profession. Deported from Tarnow to Belzec in June 1942.

EPSTEIN, Cipa. Born in 1901, in Zydaczow. Deported from Skole to Belzec, where she perished on September 7, 1942.

EPSTEIN, Herszel. Born in 1878, in Magerow. He was a widower and a teacher by profession. Deported from Niemirow to Belzec.

EPSTEIN, Malka. Born in 1915, in Mielec. She was single and was deported from Krakow to Belzec.

EPSTEIN, Mindl. Born in 1890, in Wierzbowiec. She was married and was deported from the Trembowla ghetto during 1942 to Belzec.

EPSTEIN, Sara. Born in 1911, in Skalat. She was married to Sheya and was a tailor by profession. Deported in 1942 to Belzec.

EPSZTEJN, Hana. Born in 1897, in Skalat Stary. She was married to Moshe. She lived in Belzyce. Deported to Belzec in 1942.

ERLICH, Abram. Born in 1905, in Bychawa. He was married to Bluma and was a merchant by profession. Perished in Belzec during 1942.

ERLICH, Arie. Born in Laszczow. He was married and was a merchant by profession. Deported to Belzec in 1942.

ERLICH, Bracha. Born in 1875, in Lashchov. She was married and was a housewife. Perished in Belzec during 1942.

ERLICH, Brantche. Born in 1920, in Bichava. She was single. Deported to Belzec.

ERLICH, Eli. Born in 1900, in Chelm. He was a shop-owner. Deported from Chelm to Belzec.

ERLICH, Ester. Born in 1912, in Bichava. She was single. Deported from Bichava to Belzec during 1942.

ERLICH, Hersh. Born in 1898, in Leshtshov. He was married and was a merchant by profession. Perished in Belzec during 1942.

ERLICH, Josef. Born in 1916, in Bichava. He was single and a merchant by profesion.

ERLICH, Rivka. Born in 1878, in Bichava. She was married. Perished in Belzec during 1942.

ERLICH, Rivka. Born in 1914, in Dukla. She was married and was housewife. Perished in Belzec during 1942.

ERLICH, Rywka. Born in 1920, in Laschov. She was single. Perished in Belzec during 1942.

ERLICH, Shmuel. Born in 1900, in Laszczow. He was married and was a merchant by profession. Perished in Belzec during 1942.

FAJERSZTAJN. The family of a dentist from Lublin. They were deported to Belzec during Easter 1942. The family lived in the same house as the family of Dr. Teresa Buk-Szmigielska, at the border of the Lublin ghetto, in the Old Town. They had close and friendly contact with a Polish family. When SS-men evicted them from their flat, Mrs. Fajersztajn said to the mother of the doctor, "Farewell Mrs. Buk, we know they are taking us to our death." Shortly after the war, the mother of Dr. Buk-Szmigielska met a survivor, who told her that the Fajersztajn famiy was deported to Belzec. Dr. Buk-Szmigielska only remembers the surname of the family.

FELDMAN, Aharon. Deported from Zamosc to Belzec.

FELDMAN, Berl. Born in 1900, in Grodzisk. He was married to Rachel and lived in Krakow.

FELDMAN, Chaim. Born in 1922, in Krystynopol. He was single and lived in Witkow.

FELDMAN, Chana. Born in 1910, in Zbaraz. She was married and was a housewife. Perished in Belzec during 1942.

FELDMAN, Elke. Deported from Zamosc to Belzec.

FELDMAN, Ester. Born in 1888, née Tzukermann. She was a housewife and lived in Korzec. Perished in Belzec on August 15, 1942.

FELDMAN, Fejga. Born 1883 in Odessa, Russia. She was married to Dawid. Deported from Lvov to Belzec during 1942.

FELDMAN, Gina. Born in 1923, in Stryj. She was a student and was deported from Stryj to Belzec.

FELDMAN, Helena. Deported from Kochawina to Belzec, where she perished on September 2, 1942.

FELDMAN, Hersh. Deported from Zamosc to Belzec.

FELDMAN, Jehuda. Born in 1882. He was married to Frimet and lived in Wadowice. Perished in Belzec during 1942.

FELDMAN, Mordekhai. Born in 1887, in Krystynopol. He was married to Zlata and was a merchant by profession.

FELDMAN, Pinkhas. Born in 1895, in Probuzhne. He was married to Golda and was a merchant by profession. Perished in Belzec during 1942.

FELDMAN, Zlata. Born in 1887, in Witkow. She was married to Mordekhai and was a housewife.

FRENKEL, Gabriela. Jewish painter and painting teacher in Lvov. Graduated from the Academy of Art in Paris. Deported from the Lvov ghetto to Belzec during March 1942.

FRIESS, Dawid. A well-known butcher from Tarnow, born in 1870. Deported with his son and daughter during the "First Action" to Belzec on June 11, 1942, where they all perished.

GABEL, Abraham. Born in 1872. He was married and lived in Lubaszow. Perished in Belzec during 1942.

GARBAR, Berta. Born in 1897, in Boryslaw. She was married to Yaakov and was a housewife. Perished in Belzec during 1942.

GARFINKEL, Ben. Born in 1911, in Boryslaw. He was single and a metal worker by profession. Perished in Belzec during 1942.

GARFINKEL, Chaja. Born in 1890, in Zamosc. She was married to Yitzhak and a housewife. Perished in Belzec during 1942.

GARFUNKEL, Regina. Born in 1896, née Bindefeld, in Frankfurt, Germany. She was married to Yisrael and was a housewife. Deported from Bochnia to Belzec.

GASTMANN, Fiszel. Born in 1920, in Brzesko. He was single. Perished in Belzec during 1942.

GEISLER, Rivka. Born in 1911, in Czortkow. She was single.

GEISLER, Yeshayahu. Born in 1888, in Laszkowice. He was married and a merchant. Deported from Czortkow to Belzec during 1942.

GELBARD, Regina. Born in 1899, née Kohen, in Korolowka. She was married and was housewife. Deported from Lvov during 1942 to Belzec.

GELEMTER, David. Born in 1895, in Warsaw. He was married to Miriam and was a bookeeper by profession. Perished in Belzec during 1942.

GELER, Josef. Born in 1880, in Nowy Sacs. He was married and was a furrier by profession. Deported from Nowy Sacs to Belzec during 1942.

GELER, Leib. Born in 1900, in Sloboda. He was married to Miriam. Deported from Kolomea to Belzec during 1942.

GELLER, Rachel. Born in 1895, in Bardiov, Czechoslovakia. She was married and was deported from Gorlice to Belzec in 1942.

GELLER, Yakub. Born in 1882, in Gorlice. He was married to Rakhael and was a leather merchant by profession. Deported from Gorlice to Belzec during 1942.

GERSZTENFELD, Ita. Born in 1883, in Miechow. She was a housewife, married to Aharon. Deported from Miechow in 1942 to Belzec.

GLANCMAN, Leja. Born in 1909, in Boryslaw. She was married and was housewife. Deported from Boryslaw to Belzec during 1942.

GLASMAN, Mordechai. Born in 1900, in Mielec. He was married to Sara and was a merchant by profession. Deported from Mielec to Belzec during 1942.

GLAZER, Icek. Born in Lipiny. He was married to Dona and was a merchant by profession. Deported from Zamosc to Belzec, during 1942.

GLEJZER, Mayer. Born in 1922, in Maciejow. He was single and was a merchant by profession.

GLOBIN, Shmuel. Born in 1875, in Chelm. He was married and was a merchant by profession. Perished in Belzec during 1942.

GLOGER, Rosza. Born in Probuzna. Perished in Belzec during 1942.

GOLDBAUM, Marysia. Deported from the Lublin ghetto to Belzec during April 1942.

GOLDBAUM, Sara Rebeka. Deported from the Lublin ghetto to Belzec during April 1942.

GOLDBAUM, Srul. Deported together with his wife Zysia and younger daughter Sara from the Lublin ghetto during April 1942 to Belzec.

GOLDBAUM, Zysia. Deported from the Lublin ghetto to Belzec during April 1942.

GOLDBERG, Chana. Born in 1870, in Lenka. She was married to Yehuda and was a housewife. Deported from Dabrowa to Belzec during 1942.

GOLDBERG, Sara. Born in 1913. Deported from Przemysl to Belzec in 1942.

GOLDBERG, Sara. Born in 1915, in Nowy Sacs. She was single and a clerk by profession. Perished in Belzec during 1942.

GOLDBERG, Sara. Born in 1922, in Mosciska. She was married and was housewife. Perished in Belzec during 1942.

GOLDENBERG, Gizela. Born in 1906, in Lvov. She was single and a clerk by profession.

GOLDGISST, Chaja. Born in 1918, in Chmienik. She was single.

GOLDGRABER, Rywa. Born in 1881, in Szczebrzeszyn. She was married.

GOLDMAN, Chawa. Born in 1902, in Lubaczow. Deported to Belzec during 1942.

GOLDMAN, Dawid. Born in 1925, in Bolin. Deported from Bochnia during 1942 to Belzec.

GOLDMAN, Dwora. Born in Rajowiec. She was single.

GOLDMAN, Resia. Born in 1921, in Bochnia. Perished in Belzec during 1942.

GOLDNER, Leib. Born in 1907, in Snyatin. He was married to Khaia and was a clerk by profession.

GOLDSAND, Sara. Born in 1910, in Majdan Kolbuszowski. She was a housewife and married to Aharon. Deported from Rzeszow to Belzec.

GOLDSCHMIDT. A chef de cuisine who had been well-known at the *Bruder Hanicka* restaurant in Karlsbad, as remembered by Rudolf Reder.

GOLDSTEIN, Chaja. Born in 1893, in Probuzna. She was married to Tzvi. Perished in Belzec during 1942.

GOLDSTEIN, Jozef. Born in Lublin. Married to Rakhel. Deported from Lublin to Belzecin 1942.

GOLDSTEIN, Moshe. Born in 1923, in Zaklikow. He was single and was a merchant by profession. Perished in Belzec during 1942.

GOLDSZTAJN, Abram. Born in 1877. He was married to Malka. Deported from Lublin to Belzec during 1942.

GOLDSZTAJN, Jechiel. Born in 1895. He was married to Sara. Deported from Lublin to Belzec during 1942.

GOMOLINSKI, Ruchcia. Born in 1892, in Piotrkow Trybunalski. She was married and was deported from Piotrkow to Belzec during 1942.

GOMOLINSKI, Tonia. Born in 1920, in Piotrkow Trybunalski. He was a clerk by profession. Deported from Piotrkow to Belzec during 1942.

GONOROV, Szaja. Born in 1877, in Tomaszow Lubelski. He was married to Rakhel and was a merchant by profession. Perished in Belzec during 1942.

GORTLER, Chaja. Born in 1910 in Krasnobrod. She was married to Tzvi.

GOTESMAN, Scheindel. Born in 1912, née Khamudes, in Boryslaw. She was married to Yitzhak.

GOTLIB, Towa. Born in 1920, in Kulikov. She was married and was housewife. Perished in Belzec during 1942.

GOTTLIEB, Hinda. Born in 1904, in Lubaczow. Perished in Belzec during 1942.

GRADA, David. Born in 1900, in Krakow. He was married to Adela and was a clerk by profession. Perished in Belzec during 1942.

GRAF, Chaia. Born in 1900, née Brand, in Krasnik. She was married to Nakhum and was a housewife. Perished in Belzec during 1942.

GREBEL. Born in 1908, in Gliniany. Deported from Przemyslany during 1942 to Belzec.

GREINER, Dwora. Born in 1912, in Kosow Pokucki. She was married and was housewife. Perished in Belzec on September 7, 1942.

GRIN, Beila. Born in 1910, in Dukla. She was married to Eliahu. Deported from Korczyna to Belzec during 1942.

GRIN, Rywka. Born in 1892, in Brzesko. She was married to Moshe and was a housewife. Perished in Belzec during 1942.

GRIN, Yehoszua. Born in 1882, in Korczyna. He was married to Rakhel. Deported from Korczyna to Belzec during 1942.

GRINBERG, Malka. Born in 1888, in Modliborshitz. She was married to Yosef and was a housewife. Perished in Belzec during 1942.

GRINBERG, Rywka. Born in 1874, in Zamch. She was married to Mendel. Perished in Belzec during 1942.

GRINER, Lejba. He was married and a carpenter by profession. Deported from Plonka to Belzec.

GRINFELD, Simon. Born in 1900, in Krakow. He was married to Roza and was a lawyer by profession. Perished in Belzec during 1942.

GRINSZTEIN, Aron. Born in 1919, in Starokonstantinov, Ukraine. He was single and a tailor by profession. Deported from Hrubieszow, Poland, to Belzec, in 1942.

GRINTUCH, Riwka. Born in 1912, in Torbin. She was married to Avraham.

GRIS, Yehoshua. Born in 1913, in Dabrowa. He was married to Itel and was a merchant by profession.

GRISGOT, Mosze. Born in 1878, in Podhajce. He was married to Shprintza and was an agronomist by profession. Perished in Belzec during 1942.

GROSFELD, Jehuda. Born in 1909, in Krakow. He was married and was a merchant by profession.

GROSSER, Jakub. Born in 1898, in Tomaszow Lubelski. He was married to Sima and was a shoemaker by profession. Deported from Komorow to Belzec during 1942.

GRUNER, Golda. Born in 1880, in Brody. She was married to Efraim and was a housewife.

GRYNBERG, Bat, Szewa. Born in Bychawa. She was married to Moshe and was a seemstress by profession. Perished in Belzec during 1942.

GRYNBERG, Mordchaj. Born in 1868, in Zabia Wola. He was married to Ester and was a merchant by profession. Perished in Belzec during 1942.

GRYNBERG, Szmuel. Born in 1917, in Bychawa. He was single. Perished in Belzec during 1942.

GRUENSTEIN, Mendel, Lejb. Rabbi from Tarnow, deported to Belzec on September 12, 1942, during the "Second Action" in the Tarnow ghetto.

GUMPLOWICZ, Taube. Born on August 28, 1868, in Krakow. She lived there until 1941. She was the second wife of Henryk Hersz Gumplowicz, who was the father of Anna Rozalia Imich and Matylda Schneider. Deported from Wieliczka on August 26, 1942, to Belzec.

GURFEIN, Abraham. Born on April 22, 1891, in Sanok. He was married to Sara and was a merchant by profession. Deported from Sanok to Belzec in September 1942.

GURFEIN, Yitzhak. Born on March 21, 1925, in Sanok. He was single and a pupil.

GUTENBERG, Kajla. Born in 1911, née Rafalovitz, in Proszowice. She was married to Moshe and was a housewife. Perished in Belzec during 1942.

GUTMAN, Sophie. Daughter of Markus Gutman.

GUTMAN, Zofia. Deported together with her mother from Zolkiew to Belzec on March 20, 1942. She entered the gas chamber supporting her mother.

GUTTMANN, Eta. Born in 1939, to Miriam and Shlomo, in Kolomea. Perished in Belzec during 1942.

GUZIK, Anna. Born in Sanok. She was a housewife. Perished in Belzec during 1942.

HABER, Herman. Born in 1898, in Podliski. He was married to Tova and was a merchant by profession. Deported from Chodorow to Belzec.

HABER, Tauba. Born in 1898, in Knihynice. She was married.

HABERMAN, Sara. Born in 1872, in Rawa Ruska. She was a widow and a housewife. Deported from Rawa Ruska to Belzec.

HALBERSTADT, Shlomo. He was a member of the Lublin *Judenrat*. Deported to Belzec on March 30, 1942, following the selection of *Judenrat* members.

HALPERN, Leonia. Deported from the Lvov ghetto to Belzec in March 1942.

HALPERN, Meir. Born in 1900, in Brzezany. He was married and was a merchant by profession. Deported from Krakow to Belzec during 1942.

HALPERN, Zalman. Born in 1867. He was a widower and a grain merchant by profession. Perished in Belzec during 1942.

HAMPEL, Dwosia. Born in 1905, née Gertler, in Miechow. She was married to Aharon.

HAROWITZ, Frida. Born in Probuzna. Perished in Belzec during 1942.

HARTMANN, Pesia. Born in 1898, in Chrzanow. She lived in Brzesko and was married to Reuven. Perished in Belzec during 1942.

HARTSTEIN, Dora. Born in 1903, in Stryj. She was a philosopher by profession. Perished in Belzec during September 1942.

HEIBLUM, Ephraim. Born in 1920, in Starachowice. He was single and a butcher by profession. Deported from Starachowice to Belzec.

HEIM, Noach. Born in 1900, in Skawina. He was married and was a merchant by profession. Perished in Belzec during 1942.

HEIZLER, Malka. Born in 1912, née Goldberg, in Moscicka. She was married to Avraham and was a housewife. Deported during 1942 from Moscicka to Belzec.

HELER, Roza. Born in 1891, in Zaklikow. She was married to Barukh and was a housewife. Deported from Zaklikow to Belzec during 1942.

HELFGOTT, Edzia (née Gottlieb) Born during 1907 in Sambor. Deported from Synewodzko Wyzne, near Stryj on October 18,1942 to Belzec, where she perished.

HELLER, Bluma. Born in 1907, in Rozdol. She was married to Kalman and was a housewife.

HELLER, Zejniwl. Born in 1918, in Tomaszow Lubelski. He was single and was deported from Tomaszow Lubelski to Belzec.

HELMAN, Wolf. Born in 1907, in Belz. He was single and a salesman by profession. Perished in Belzec during 1942.

HENIG, Idel. Born in 1917, in Sanok. He was single and was a merchant by profession. Deported from Sanok to Belzec during 1942.

HERBSTMAN, Chaim. Born in 1908, in Brzesko. He was married to Feigel. Deported to Belzec during 1942.

HERBSTMAN, Malka. Born in 1894, in Lubashov. Married to Shlomo. Deported to Belzec in 1942.

HERC. Father of Sylko Herc, deported from Krakow to Belzec. A member of the Jewish work-brigade. He died of natural causes in the camp, and according to Sylko, who escaped, the Germans organized a normal funeral, complete with a coffin.

HERING, Shmuel. Born in Poland, married to Reizl. Deported from Janow Lubelski to Belzec.

HERLICH, Inda. Born in 1919, in Laszczowo. She was married.

HERNHUT, Szaja. Born in 1869, in Zamosc. His well-known family were the owners of a printing-office in Zamosc. Deported to Belzec during 1942.

HERSCHMANN, Kurt. Deported from Prague on June 12–13, 1942, on Transport AaH (*Attentat auf Heydrich*—Assassination of Heydrich), when about 1,000 Jews were sent to the east as a reprisal measure following the death of Reinhard Heydrich. This transport was officially destined for Ujazdow in the Lublin district, but the deportees were gassed at Belzec.

HERSCHMANN, Wilhelmina. Deported from Prague on June 12–13, 1942, on Transport AaH, along with her son.

HILLER, Bela. Born in 1892, in Dzorkow. She was a housewife and was married to Yekhiel.

HILLMANN, Rosa. Born in 1898, in Dolina. She was married and a teacher by profession. Deported from the Lvov ghetto in 1942.

HIMELFARB, Chaim. Born in 1890, in Krasnosielc. He was single and a ritual slaughterer. Perished in Belzec during 1942.

HIROM, Abraham. Born in 1915, in Krakow. He was married and was a merchant by profession.

HIROM, Gitel. Born in 1910, in Krakow. She was single and a seemstress by profession.

HIROM, Lea. Born in 1913, in Kolomea. She was married and was a housewife. Perished in Belzec during 1942.

HIROM, Mordcha. Born in 1882, in Kolomea. He was married and was a merchant by profession. Deported from Krakow to Belzec.

HIRSCHFELD, Chana. Born in 1885, in Iasi, Romania. She was married to David. Deported from Niemirow to Belzec.

HIRSCHFELD, Feiwel. Born in 1915, in Niemirow. He was a single and a clerk by profession.

HIRSCHFELD, Roiza. Born in 1895, in Przemysl. She was married to Tzvi.

HIRSCHFELD, Salomon. Born in 1910, in Lezajsk. He was single and was a merchant by profession.

HIRSHHORN, Sara. Born in 1908. She was married and was a housewife. Perished in Belzec during 1942.

HIRSZHORN, Natan. Born in 1905. He was married to Mindl. Perished in Belzec during 1942.

HISCHHORN, Lea. Born in 1902, in Rawa Ruska. She was married to David. Deported from Rawa Ruska to Belzec.

HISS, Roza. Born in 1887, in Lvov. She was married and was a housewife.

HISS, Wolf. Born in 1880, in Lvov. He was married to Roiza and was a merchant by profession.

HIT, Kalman. Born in 1864, in Zamosc. Perished in Belzec during 1942.

HITELMAN, Awram. Born in 1909, in Kurow. He was married to Khaia and an egg trader by profession. Deported from Kurow to Belzec during 1942.

HOCHMAN, Hersz. Born in Zamosc. Deported from Zamosc to Belzec.

HOCHMAN, Mina. Born in 1880, in Zamosc. She was a housewife. Deported from Zamosc to Belzec in 1942.

HOENIG, Chaya. Born in 1914, in Probuzna. She was married. Perished in Belzec during 1942.

HOENIG, Israel. Born in 1887, in Probuzna. He was married to Khala and was a merchant by profession. Perished in Belzec during 1942.

HOENISCH, Israel. Born in 1892, in Kolomea. He was married to Batsheva and was a merchant by profession. Deported from Kosow to Belzec in 1942.

HOFFMAN, Zysi. Born in 1892, née Kornbrot, in Wolbrom. She was married to Yehoshua. Perished in Belzec on September 4, 1942.

HOFMAN, Sara. Born in 1921, in Piaski. She was single and was deported from Piaski to Belzec.

HOLANDER, Josef. Born in 1920, in Rawa Ruska. He was single. Perished in Belzec during 1942.

HOLCER, Abrahm. Born in 1910, in Nowy Sacs. He was single and was a merchant by profession. Perished in Belzec during 1942.

HOLCER, Ruchel. Born in 1910, in Mielec. She was married to Avraham. Deported from Nowy Sacs to Belzec in 1942.

HOLCER, Slomo. Born in 1883, in Nowy Sacs. He was married and was a merchant by profession. Deported from Nowy Sacs to Belzec in 1942.

HOLCER, Wolf. Born in 1866, in Dabrowa Gornicza. He was married to Gitel and was a merchant by profession. Deported from Dabrowa Gornicza to Belzec in 1942.

HOLDER, Kalman. Born in 1879, in Wisnice. He was married to Reizl and was a merchant by profession. Deported from Krakow to Belzec during 1942.

HOLENDER, Yisrael. Born in 1902, in Rawa Ruska. He was married.

HOLLAENDER, Ana. Born in 1879, in Krakow. She was married to Avraham and was a housewife. Deported from Makow to Belzec.

HOLZER, Gitta. Born in Tuchov. She was married to Nakhum.

HONIG, Jacob. Born in 1864, in Dzikov. He was married to Khana and was a merchant by profession. Deported from Lvov to Belzec during 1942.

HORN, Dr. Bernard. Born on December 16, 1880, in Brody. He was married to Roda and was a lawyer by profession.

HORNUNG, Sala. Born in 1913, in Przemysl. She was a student and single.

HOROVICH, Rabbi Abraham. Born in Probuzna. Deported from Probuzna to Belzec during 1942.

HORWIC, Baruch. Born in 1895, in Tomaszow Lubelski. He was single and was a ritual slaughterer by profession.

HUETTNER, Bronislawa. Born in 1890, in Jaroslaw. She was a housewife.

HUPPERT, Mendel. Born in 1891, in Krakow. He was married to Gitel and was a housepainter by profession. Deported from Krakow to Belzec in 1942.

IMBER, Shmuel, Yankev. Born in 1889, in Jezierna, in eastern Galicia. Shmuel was a nephew of Naftali Herz Imber, who wrote the song "Hatikvah," the national anthem of Israel. He studied in Zloczow and Tarnopol. He became famous for writing Yiddish poems and published literary works. Deported from Zloczow to Belzec on November 3, 1942.

IMICH, Anna. Born on December 24, 1895, née Gumplowicz, in Krakow. She lived there until 1941 and moved to Wieliczka, from where she was deported to Belzec on August 26, 1942. She was deported together with her sister, Matylda Schneider, stepmother Taube Gumplowicz, and other members of the Gumplowicz family.

JAKUBOWICZ. A young physician from somewhere near Przemysl, as remembered by Rudolf Reder.

JUST, Rajzel. Born in 1920, in Rawa Ruska. She was single and a pupil. Perished in Belzec during 1942.

KATZ, Klara. Born in 1893, in Zolkow. She was single and was a clerk by profession. Deported from Zolkow to Belzec during 1942.

KATZ, Lea. Born in 1918, in Zbaraz. She was a pupil and single. Deported from Zbaraz to Belzec during 1942.

KLISKES, Josel. From Zamosc, he was arrested by the SS together with some Czech Jews while waiting for soup at the welfare kitchen in the Zamosc ghetto. Deported to Belzec in 1942.

KOHN, Rivka. Born in 1883, née Ingelman, in Tomaszow Lubelski. She was married to Mordekhai and was a housewife living in Grodzisk. Deported from Grodzisk to Belzec during 1942.

LAUFER, Elja. Born in 1897, in Krakow. She lived in Warsaw. Perished in Belzec during 1942.

LEDERKREJMER, Szulim. Born in 1912, in Tomaszow Lubelski. He was single.

LEDERKREMER, Mirl. Born in 1882, née Brand, in Tomaszow Lubelski. She was married to Eliezer and was a merchant by profession. Deported to Belzec during 1942.

LIBMAN, Zisel. Born in 1919, née Sofer, in Borszczow. She was married and was a seemstress by profession. Deported from Borszczow to Belzec during 1942.

LIEBMAN, Sara. Born in 1898. She lived in Lvov and Borszczow. Perished in Belzec during 1942.

LIPSZYC, Sala. From Radom. She was deported to Belzec and was among other Jewish women who worked in the death camp. Some Polish people from the Belzec village had contact with her, because she was allowed to leave the camp for work at the commandant's office, which was located outside of the death camp. She told some of the Poles details about the gas chambers and the extermination process. She was murdered by the Nazis during the course of the liquidation of the death camp.

LORBER, Etka. Born on November 10, 1893, in Tarnopol. She was married to Shmuel and was deported from Tarnopol to Belzec during August 1942.

LORBER, Malcia. Born in 1902, in Zbaraz. She was married and was housewife. Deported to Belzec during 1942.

LURBER, Menakhem. Born in 1912, in Kolomea.

MANDELSBERG-SZYLDKRAUT, Dr. Bela. She was a doctor of history, who graduated from the University of Warsaw. She published historical works about the Jews in Lublin. Before the Second World War, she was a teacher in Lublin. Deported together with her whole family to Belzec during March 1942.

MARGULES, Dr. Ozjasz. Deported from the Lvov ghetto to Belzec during March 1942.

Mariska. A Jewish girl who worked together with two other Jewish girls in the SS bakery, which was located in the village of Belzec. She was not allowed to speak and had to sleep in the bakery itself, or a nearby hut. The bakery building was guarded by a Ukrainian. One day she was taken away, together with her two Jewish co-workers, and shot by the SS when the camp was closed down in May 1943.

Mawka / Miriam. A Jewish girl who worked together with two other Jewish girls in the SS bakery.

MEZEL, Golda. Deported from the Tarnow Ghetto to Belzec during the "Second Action" on September 12, 1942.

Moniek. Rudolf Reder mentioned a Jewish prisoner from the work-brigade named Moniek, who was a coach driver from Krakow. He supervised the motor room in which the gas was produced. Reder provided this information to the Main Commission of the Investigation of the Nazi Crimes in Poland.

MUNK, Max. A cigarette case belonging to Max Munk, bearing the inscription "Max Munk, Wien 27," was found in 1997 at the former Ramp area, during the archaeological investigations.

NACHTIGAL, Berko. A Jewish *Kapo* photographed holding a stick in front of the workshops in the death camp. He was described by Dr. Janusz Peters at the hospital in Tomaszow Lubelski as being well-built and strong. He was killed in the camp.

NADEL, Genia. Born in Poland, née Tilleman. Married to Avraham. Deported from Drohobycz to Belzec during 1942.

OEHLBERG, Emil. Born in 1913, in Tarnopol. He was married and was an agronomist by profession. Deported from Kolomea to Belzec.

OLENDER. The wife of Abraham Olender and his two children were deported from Krasnik to Belzec on April 12, 1942, during the "First Action." Abraham Olender was incarcerated in the Budzyn labor camp.

PFEFFER, Markus (Maks). Born in 1891, a lawyer by profession. Deported from the Przemysl Ghetto at the begining of the "First Action" on July 27, 1942.

PFEFFER, Sara. Born in 1920. She was a student. Deported from the Przemysl Ghetto at the begining of the "First Action" on July 27, 1942.

PUTER, Shmuel. Born in 1910, in Zamosc. He was married to Beile and was a beverage merchant by profession. Deported from Zamosc to Belzec during April 1942.

RACKER, Yehiel. Born in Gorlice. He was married. Perished in Belzec during 1942.

ROSENFELD, Maksymillana. A well-known pianist from Lvov. Deported from the Lvov ghetto to Belzec during March 1942.

ROZENEL. The wife of Nuchim Rozenel and their three children were deported to Belzec during the "First Action" in the Krasnik ghetto on April 12, 1942. They were killed, but Nuchim was incarcerated in the Jewish Labor camp in Budzyn. He escaped from Budzyn during the evacuation of the camp in July 1944.

Sala / Salomea. A Jewish girl who worked together with two other Jewish girls in the SS bakery, which was located in the village of Belzec. She was not allowed to speak and had to sleep in the bakery itself, or a nearby hut. The bakery building was guarded by a Ukrainian. One day she was taken away, together with her two Jewish co-workers, and shot by the SS when the camp was closed down in May 1943.

SCHLUSSEL. Remembered by Rudolf Reder as a merchant from Krakow. Probably killed in the camp.

SCHNEIDER, Matylda. Born on August 2, 1900 , née Gumplowicz, in Krakow. She lived there until 1941. Deported from Wieliczka to Belzec on August 26, 1942, together with her sister Anna Imich, stepmother Taube Gumplowicz, and other members of the Gumplowicz family.

SCHRAGER, Leon. A Jewish carpenter from the Lvov ghetto. He was deported to Belzec during March 1942. From the railway station in Belzec, he sent a letter to his son Henryk Schrager, stating that he was now in Belzec.

SCHREIBER. Remembered by Rudolf Reder, a Jew from the Sudetenland, a former lawyer who worked in the camp office. He probably perished in the death camp.

SCHREIBER, Rabbi Anshel. A Hassidic rabbi from Lvov. He was a famous religious scholar, a member of the Religious Affairs

Department in the Lvov ghetto. Deported to Belzec during March 1942, although he had a special ID card, showing that he worked for the *Judenrat* administration. The official reason the Nazis gave the for his deportation was that Schreiber was too religious and looked like a typical Orthodox Jew.

SEGEL, Jakub. Deported from Zolkiew, near Lvov, during the "First Action" on March 20, 1942. He said goodbye to his wife in public, in front of the gas chamber building, and the Jews waiting to be gassed started crying.

SIEGFRIED, Erna. Born in 1910. Married to David Siegfried.

SIEGFRIED, Esther. Born in 1920. She was single.

SIEGFRIED-SCHWINGER, Eva. Born in 1907. Married to Efram Schwinger.

SIEGFRIED, Dr. Josef. Born in Radomysl Wielki. He was an economist who graduated from the universities of Vienna and Cologne. Before the war, he was a representative of the Lublin Trade Company. During the occupation, he was a member of the Lublin *Judenrat*, responsible for health affairs. He also co-operated with the *Judisches Soziale Selbshilfe*. Deported to Belzec during April 1942.

SIEGFRIED, Josef. Born in 1903. He was married.

SIEGFRIED, Mina. Born in 1911. Married to Benjamin Siegfried.

SIEGFRIED, Natan. Natan and Regina were the parents of nine chidren and lived at 10 Kazimierza Wielkiego in Jaslo. They were both murdered in Belzec along with other members of their family.

SIEGFRIED, Regina. Natan and Regina were the parents of nine chidren and lived at 10 Kazimierza Wielkiego in Jaslo. They were both murdered in Belzec along with other members of their family.

SIEGFRIED, Szymon. Born in 1910. Married to Rachel, née Kaplan.

SILBER, Regina. Born in 1915, in Krystnoypol. She was married to Khaim and was a housewife. Deported from Witkow to Belzec.

SILBERBERG, Schifra. Born in May 1914, née Shteiner, in Nowy Sacs. She was married and was a housewife. Deported from Nowy Sacs to Belzec.

SILBERMAN, Aron. Born on August 18, 1889, in Ustrzyki Dolne. He was married to Feigl and was a merchant by profession. Deported from Rymanov to Belzec.

SILBERPFENIG, Rivka. Deported from the Tarnow Ghetto to Belzec during the "Second Action" on September 12, 1942.

SILBERSTEIN, Leib. Born in 1904, in Lodz. He was married to Daria and was a merchant by profession. Perished in Belzec during 1942.

SILBIGER, Szymon. Born in 1890, in Brzesko. He was married to Malka and was a merchant by profession. Deported from Brzesko to Belzec during 1942.

SINGER, Henrik. Born in 1894, in Szczucin. He was married to Henia and was a merchant by profession. Deported from Szczucin to Belzec.

SINGER, Reisel. Born in 1918 in Brzesko. She was single. Prished in Belzec during 1942.

SINGER, Salman. Born in 1900 in Zolkiew. He was married to Sara and was a craftsman by profession.

SINGER, Sara. Born in 1892, in Brzesko. She was married to Kalman and was a housewife. Perished in Belzec during 1942.

SOKALER, Dr. Michal. He was a Lawyer and a violinist from Lvov. Deported from the Lvov ghetto to Belzec during the 'Great Action' during August 1942.

SONNENSCHEIN, Mala. Born in 1915, in Krakow. She was married. Perished in Belzec during 1942.

SPODEK, Maria. She was a young Jewish woman from Zamosc. Deported to Belzec and selected on the ramp for work in the camp laundry. She was killed in 1943 when the camp was liquidated. She was remembered by Krystyna Natyna during an investigation organized in 1966 by the Polish Secret Police.

STADLER, Martha. Born on May 14, 1904, née Drucker, in Korycany. She met her husband Otto in Zlin, Moravia, in 1924. After the First World War, they moved to Vienna, Austria. They had two children in Vienna—Harry, in 1925, and Robert, in 1929.

In 1934, the family moved from Vienna to Klatovy, then Czechoslovakia, then to Pilsen and Prague in April-May 1939. From Prague, Martha and Otto were taken to Theresienstadt during February 1942, and in the middle of March 1942 were deported on Transport AB to the Izbica transit ghetto in Poland. She was deported to Belzec along with Otto, where they both perished.

STADLER, Otto. Born on March 22, 1897, in Strazow Na Sumave (Czech Republic). He met his wife Martha in Zlin, Moravia, in 1924.

STYK, Ozjasz. Famous co-painter of "Raclawice's Panorama"—the painting depicts the battle of Raclawice, fought in April 1794, between Russian troops and a Polish peasant army, defending Polish independence. The Poles won the battle, but lost the war. Before the Second World War, the painting was exhibited in Lvov, and today it can be seen in Wroclaw. He was deported from the Lvov ghetto to Belzec in March 1942.

SUSSKIND, Mindla. Born in 1913, in Biecz. Deported from Biecz to Belzec during 1942.

SZEPS, Azriel. Born in 1886, in Zamosc. He was a well-known tailor in Zamosc, a member of the Zionist Organisation, and vice-president of the Zamosc *Judenrat.* Before the Second World War, he was a member of the City Council and the Jewish

Community Council. In October 1942, he was deported with his family and other Jews from Zamosc to Izbica, and in early November from Izbica to the Belzec extermination camp. Rudolf Reder witnessed his death and this is covered in depth in Chapter 10 of his book, *Belzec*.

SZEPS, David. Son of Azriel and Pesa. Deported with his parents from Zamosc to Izbica, and from there to Belzec in early November 1942.

SZEPS, Lea. Daughter of Azriel and Pesa. Deported with her parents from Zamosc to Izbica, and from there to Belzec in early November 1942.

SZEPS, Pesa. Born in 1890. Married to Azriel Szeps. Deported from Zamosc to Izbica, and from there to Belzec in early November 1942.

SZLAM, Frajda. Born in 1890, in Zamosc. Deported from Zamosc to Belzec together with her husband Icek during 1942.

SZLAM, Icek, Dawid. Born in Zamosc. He was married to Frajda and was a merchant by profession. Deported from Zamosc to Belzec during 1942.

TABAK, Rachel. Born in 1888, in Stryj. She was married and was housewife.

TAJTELBAUM, Roza. Born in 1885, in Krakow. Married to Yekhezkel. Deported from Krakow to Belzec during 1942.

TAJTLER, Syma. Born in 1897, née Rozenberg, in Boryslaw. She was married to Moritz and was a housewife. Perished in Belzec during 1942.

TAU, Chawa. Born in 1912, in Chelm. She was married to Fishel and was a housewife. Deported during 1942 from Lublin to Belzec.

TAU, Schlomo. Born in 1892, in Piask. He was married and was a merchant by profession. Deported to Belzec during 1942.

TAUB, Aharon. Born in 1909, in Krakow. He was single. Deported from Wieliczka to Belzec.

TAUCHER, Wolf. Jewish *Kapo*, described by Dr. Janusz Peters, who worked at the hospital in Tomaszow Lubelski, as being well-built and very strong.

TEICHTAL, Josef. Born in 1908, in Brzesko. He was married and was a merchant by profession. He perished in Belzec on 28 October, 1942.

TEITELBAUM, Lieba. Born in 1872, in Rymanow. She was married to Yisrael and was a housewife. Deported from Rymanow during 1942 to Belzec.

TEITELBAUM, Miriam. Born in 1910, in Vienna, Austria. She was single. Deported from Rymanow to Belzec during 1942.

TENCER, Icchak. Born in 1883, in Strzyzow. He was married and was a merchant by profession.

TENCER, Szmuel. Born in 1898, in Strzyzow. He was married and was a merchant by profession.

TENENBAUM, Hene. Born in Dzialoszyce, née Platkeiwicz. She was a housewife. Deported to Belzec during 1942.

TENENBAUM, Klara. Born in 1915, in Zloczow. She was married and was housewife. Deported to Belzec during 1942.

TIRGFELD, Rejzel. Born in 1884, in Zborow. She was married to Yaakov and was a housewife. Deported from Slawna to Belzec during August 1942.

TIRKILTOUB, Wolf. Born in 1905, in Chrobjeszow. He was married and was a carriage owner by profession. Deported from Ludma to Belzec.

TOBIAS, Berta. Born in 1911, née Shvartz, in Oswiecim. She was married to Herman and was a housewife. Deported during 1942 from Krakow to Belzec.

TROHM, Israel. Born in 1890, in Frysztak. He was married to Ida and was a merchant by profession. Deported from Rzeszow to Belzec during 1942.

TURM, Malka. Born in 1872, née Likhtenshtein, in Komarow. She was married to Yisrael and was a housewife. Deported from Komarow to Belzec during 1942.

VEINBERG, Shalom. Born in Turobin. Married to Matil. Deported from Bychawa to Belzec.

WACHMAN, Dr. A lawyer from Lvov. Deported from the Lvov ghetto to Belzec in March 1942.

WAJNSZTOK, Fajga. Born in 1884. Deported from Szcebrzeszyn to Belzec during 1942.

WAJSBROT. He was a Hassidic rabbi from Turobin. During the war he was in the Krasnik ghetto together with his son and his family. In October 1942, during the "Second Action" in the Krasnik ghetto, they were deported to Zaklikow, which was the main collecting point for the Jews in Krasnik county. From there, he and his family members were deported to Belzec.

WAJSELFISZ, Josef. Born on August 1, 1898. He was an activist of the Zionist Organization in Lublin, and a member of the Jewish Community Council, who worked with Hebrew schools in Lublin. During the Nazi occupation, he was a member of the *Judenrat*. Deported to Belzec together with his whole family on March 31, 1942.

WEB, David. Born in 1893, in Rawa Mazowiecka. He was married to Masha and was a rabbi. Deported from Rawa Mazowiecka to Belzec.

WEINBAUM, Jehuda. Born in 1887, in Stojanow. He was married and an engineer by profession. Deported from Sambor to Belzec.

WEINBERG, Riwka. Born in 1882, née Katz. She was married to Yisrael and was a housewife. Deported from Sokal to Belzec.

WEINBERG, Shmuel. Born in 1892, in Rowne. He was married to Mala and was a merchant by profession. Perished in Belzec during 1942.

WEINSTOCK, Berthold (Olek). Born in 1897. He was an electrical engineer by profession. Deported from the Przemysl ghetto to Belzec during the "First Action" on July 27, 1942.

WEINSTOCK, Irena. Born in 1903, née Reisner. She was a school teacher by profession. Deported from the Przemysl ghetto to Belzec during the "First Action" on July 27, 1942.

WEINSTOCK, Izydor (Chaskel). Born in 1865. He was a jeweler by profession. Deported from the Przemysl ghetto to Belzec during the "First Action" on July 27, 1942.

WEINSTOCK, Ludwiczek. Born in 1934. Deported from the Przemysl ghetto to Belzec during the "First Action" on July 27, 1942.

WEJNRATH, Szejndel. Born in 1902, in Lubaczow. She was married. Perished in Belzec during 1942.

WEJNSZTOK, Gustav. Born in 1914, in Lvov. He was married and a school teacher by profession.

WELC, Cwy. Born in 1918, in Tarnogrod. He was single. Deported from Tarnogrod to Belzec.

WELICZKER, Abraham. Born in 1894, in Stojanov. He was a timber merchant and was associated with a company that exported eggs, and was a partner in a cement-pipe company in Stojanov. When the famly moved to Lvov, he designed houses. Deported from Lvov on November 19, 1942 to Belzec.

WERDINGER, Ana. Born in 1908, née Roka, in Boryslaw. She was a clerk by profession. Perished in Belzec during 1942.

WERTMAN, Ichak. Born in 1896, in Izbica. He was married to Mendel and was a merchant by profession.

WERTMAN, Pinie. Born in 1910, in Tomaszow Lubelski. He was married and was a merchant by profession.

WICKLER, Rachel. Born in 1876. Deported from Probuzna to Belzec during 1942.

WIENER, Stefa. Born in 1900, in Krakow. She was married to Yulius and was a housewife. Deported from Krakow to Belzec during 1942.

WIKLER, Abraham. Born in Probuzna.

WILF, Isser. Born in 1905, in Boryslaw. He was married and an engineer by profession. Perished in Belzec during 1942.

WITLIN, Abraham. Born in 1910, in Zolkiew. He was a grocer by profession and single.

WITMAN, Ysak. Born in 1888, in Sobibor. Married to Sara. Perished in Belzec during 1942.

WOLBROMSKI, Sara. Born in 1918, in Ksiaz Wielki. Perished in Belzec during 1942.

WOLBROMSKI, Tzirel. Born in 1886, in Wodzislaw. She was married to Aahron and lived in Ksiaz Wielki. Perished in Belzec during 1942.

WOLF, Sara. Born in 1910, in Zwadka. She was married to Yosef and was a housewife. Deported from the Lvov ghetto to Belzec during 1942.

WOLKENFELD, Juda. Born in 1895. He was married to Tziporan and lived in Biecz. Perished in Belzec on November 11, 1942.

WOLMAN, Szmul. Born on November 4, 1889, in Lublin. He was the owner of large hardware stores in Lublin. Deported in March 1942 to Belzec.

WOLSZTAJN, Lejb. Born in 1927, in Wloclawek. He was resettled to Zamosc in 1940. He was sent to Belzec during the "First Action" on April 11, 1942, together with his mother and sister.

Lejb managed to escape and he returned to the Zamosc Ghetto. He told the *Judenrat* in Zamosc about the death camp and the fate of the Jews transported there. In August 1942, he was again deported to Belzec, together with his father Szmul. Both of them perished in Belzec.

WOLSZTAJN, Rojza. Born in 1921. Daughter of Szmul and Zera.

WOLSZTAJN, Szmul. Born in 1890. Father of Lejb and Rojza. He was resettled to Zamosc in 1940 together with his family. He was a member of the Jewish Social Self-Help (*Judische Soziale Selbshilfe*) in the Zamosc ghetto. Deported to Belzec along with his son Lejb, in August 1942. They both perished in Belzec.

WOLSZTAJN, Zera. Born in 1892. She was the mother of Lejb and Rojza, and wife to Szmul. Perished in Belzec during August 1942.

ZAJDENFODEM, Szymon. Born in 1920, in Chelm. He was married to Pesa and was a metalworker by profession. Deported from Chelm to Belzec during 1942.

ZALCBERG, Sara. Born in 1900, née Tzukerman, in Miechow. She was a housewife. Perished in Belzec during 1942.

ZAUER, Sara. Born in 1918, in Limanowa. Deported from Chelmiec during 1942 to Belzec.

ZEIDENWEG, Fawel. He was single and lived in Zakilow. Deported from there to Belzec.

ZEMLER, Fawl. Born in 1887, in Nemirow. He was married to Roshi and was a merchant by profession. Deported during 1942 from Rawa Ruska to Belzec.

ZIEGEL, Berl. Born in 1913, in Laski. He was single and was a merchant by profession. Perished in Belzec during 1942.

ZIEGEL, Josef. Born in 1900, in Cieszanow. He was married to Pesel and was a merchant by profession. Deported from the Lvov ghetto in 1942 to Belzec.

ZIGEL, Amalia. Born in 1890, in Uhnow. Married to Moshe. Deported to Belzec during 1942.

ZILBERGER, Amalia. Born in 1892, née Brandsdorfer, in Brzesko. Married to Shimon. Deported during 1942 to Belzec.

ZILBERNADEL, Ester. Born in 1908, in Belzec.

ZILBERSZTEIN, Fejga. Born in 1895. She was married to Yosef and was a housewife in Tomaszow Lubelski. Deported from Tomaszow Lubelski to Belzec.

ZINGER, Mirjam. Born in 1884, in Tomaszow Lubelski. Married to Iasha. Deported to Belzec during 1942.

ZIS, Faivel. Born in 1874, in Zamosc. Married to Ester.

ZISKIND, Rosalia. Born in 1921, in Gorlice. She was single. Deported to Belzec during 1942.

ZLOCZOWER, Chana. Born in 1920, in Lvov. Daughter of Rachel and Shlomo Zloczower. Perished in Belzec together with her parents and sister Rena during 1942.

ZLOCZOWER, Israel. Born in 1900, in Lvov. He was a tailor by profession. Perished in Belzec during 1942.

ZLOCZOWER, Rachel. Married to Shlomo. Deported from the Lvov ghetto to Belzec during 1942, where she perished with other members of her family.

ZLOCZOWER, Rena. Born in 1924, in Lvov. Daughter of Rachel and Shlomo Zloczower. Perished in Belzec together with her parents and sister Chana during 1942.

ZLOCZOWER, Shlomo. Born in 1890, in Lvov. He was married to Rachel, with whome he had two daughters—Chana and Rena—and he was a tailor by profession. Perished in Belzec during 1942, along with the rest of his family.

ZMISZLONO, Jakob. Born in 1910, in Dzaloszice. He was married to Sara and was a merchant by profession. Deported from Dzaloszice to Belzec during 1942.

ZOMMER, Brajndel. Born in 1920, in Debica. She was a pupil and single. Deported from Debica to Belzec during 1942.

ZYLBER, Szlomo. Born in 1888, in Zamosc. He was married to Reizl and was a worker by profession. Deported in 1942 from Zamosc to Belzec.

ZYLBERBERG, David. Born in 1902, in Tomaszow Lubelski. He was married to Miril and was a driver by profession.

ZYLBERBERG, Miril. Born in 1902, in Tomaszow Lubelski. She was married to David and was a housewife. Perished in Belzec during 1942.

ZYSKIND, Michael. Born in 1875, in Rozyszcze. He was married to Khala and was an agent by profession. Perished in Belzec during 1942.

ZYSKIND, Sheindl. Born in 1910, in Kowel. She was single. Perished in Belzec during 1942.

Chapter XIV
The Perpetrators

The following chapter is based on information disclosed at the trials of those men who served at the *Aktion Reinhardt* camps, or from survivor accounts and accounts by their fellow officers.

Almost all of them came from the lower middle class—their fathers were factory workers, craftsmen, salesmen, or shop workers. Most of the men who served in the death camps had finished extended elementary school, some lower high school, and a few had attended secondary school. Some had attended commercial schools, or had received vocational training. Those who were former euthanasia program employees were mostly former nurses, craftsmen, farm workers, or salesmen.

Almost all of the accused were members of either the Nationalsozialistische Deutsche Arbeitspartei (NSDAP)—the Nazi Party—the police, the *Schutzstaffel* (SS) or the *Sturmabteilung* (SA). Some had joined these organisations before Hitler came to power, others joined the Party later. Their average age was between thirty and forty at the time they served in the death camps.

The personnel who ran the camps and supervised the extermination activities were absolutely ordinary people. They were not assigned to these roles because of any exceptional qualities or characteristics. The anti-Semitism that festered within them was no doubt part of their milieu and was an accepted phenomenon among large segments of German society. Many of them were married, and most had no criminal record. They had either volunteered to serve in the SS or had been drafted into its ranks. So it was not unusual that a man wore an SS uniform but received his salary from his real employer, the German police, or *Aktion T4,* the Nazi euthanasia program.

These men carried out the murder of hundreds of thousands of men, women, and children—always loyally and without question.

What is more, they constantly displayed initiative in trying to improve the extermination process. An integral aspect of their duties was that they were also to exhibit cruelty towards their victims, and many of them contributed their own ideas and innovations for various forms of torture that served to entertain them all. Under the Nazi regime, these perfectly ordinary people were turned into something extraordinarily inhuman.

Source and pertinent material on the daily lives of these men in Belzec, on their personal feelings about the tasks that they carried out, and their relationship to their innocent victims is almost non-existent—men more than anxious to cover up their past were not about to sit down and record their memoirs. Even at their trials, when some of them were forced to attest to their deeds, very little was brought out about their personal feelings and experiences. The primary sources on the behavior of these perpetrators and their actual relationship to their victims are the testimonies of those who survived the camps, as well as some material and evidence that was submitted during the trials. Prisoners used to give nicknames to the various men in SS uniform, and these were indicative of their reputations and activities in the camp. These nicknames were also a type of code to be used as a warning when a particular SS-man appeared in a certain area of the camp.

Taking the above restrictions on information into account, it is nevertheless possible to compile a reasonably comprehensive staff list of Belzec perpetrators. The list is assembled based on known evidence and information from various sources, however scant, about the perpetrators. The SS garrison only comprised of about twenty to thirty men stationed in the camp at any given time, and this list contains the names of mainly SS-men who were assigned duties at Belzec during the time of its existence.

Members of the SS held key positions in the camp, and many of the staff belonged to a police detachment of unknown origin—a few were civilians. SS-men were sometimes transferred between the three *Aktion Reinhardt* camps, and may have served in Belzec only briefly. It cannot be ascertained if this list contains all of the staff that served at the camp, as not all of the names of the camp staff or their specific functions could be gleaned from eyewitness reports. Most of the SS camp personnel first worked in the euthanasia program (*Aktion T4*), although not all functions were known, but where this is known it has been included.

After the three *Aktion Reinhardt* camps were demolished, most of the personnel were posted to northern Italy, assisting with the suppression of partisan activities, rounding-up Jews, and confiscating Jewish property and valuables. As the war drew to a close, the Nazi command realized that the staff and commanders could incriminate their superiors, and they were consequently sent to dangerous areas where some of them, such as Christian Wirth and Franz Reichleitner, were killed by partisans. As Franz Stangl said afterwards, "We were an embarrassment to the brass. They wanted to find ways to incinerate us."

*

Richard THOMALLA
Belzec Death Camp—Construction Supervisor (Latter Stages)

Born on October 23, 1903, in Sabine-bei-Annahof (today, Sowin, in Polish Silesia), in the Falkenberg district of Upper Silesia. A builder by profession, he was bi-lingual in German and Polish, and joined the SS on July 1, 1932, and the Nazi Party a month later. On October 5, 1935, Thomalla married Margarete Bruckner. He saw military service in Falkenberg and Oppeln, and service in the SS in Wohlau and Breslau (Wroclaw) in the present-day southeastern part of Polish Lower Silesia.

On September 6, 1940, Thomalla was transferred from Breslau to the *Generalgouvernment*, where he was a member of the *SS-Hilfspolizei* (auxiliary police), in the cities of Czestochowa and Radom. On August 22, 1940, he was transferred by Friedrich-Wilhelm Krüger, the *Höhere SS- und Polizeiführer Ost* (*HSSPF*), based in Krakow, to serve under Odilo Globocnik, *SS- und Polizeiführer* (SSPF) Lublin. From August to October 1940, he was section leader of the SS Border Defence Construction Service (*SS-Grenzschutz Baudienst*) in Belzec, on the demarcation line between the *Generalgouvernement* and Soviet-occupied Galicia (western Ukraine). His first task was the establishment of a construction depot of the *Waffen-SS* and police in Zamosc, about 40 kilometers north of Belzec.

After the invasion of Russia, Thomalla was also in charge of constructing SS Strongpoints in the Ukraine, with branch offices in Zwiahel and Kiev. He was recalled by Globocnik to Lublin at the beginning of 1942 to take over supervision of constructon of the first *Aktion Reinhardt* death camp at Belzec. Thereafter, he also oversaw construction of the other *Aktion Reinhardt* camps at Sobibor and Treblinka; as such, he was the senior SS officer at each site until the camps became operational.

In 1943, he headed *Waffen-SS* construction offices in Riga, the capital of Nazi-occupied Latvia, and Mogilev in Belorussia. Later, during 1943–44, Thomalla also played a role in the "pacification" operations of the SS and the police in Zamosc district.

He was last seen in Zamosc in June 1944, a few weeks before the entry of the Red Army into the town the following month. He was arrested by the Russians near Jicin, on the Czechoslovakian side of the Czech-Polish border. He was held nearby, in a special prison for members of the SS and Nazi Party officials at Karthaus-Walditz. On May 12, 1945, Thomalla was "ordered out of his cell, with all his belongings." This was a typical order by the Soviet NKVD immediately before the prisoner was executed.

Christian WIRTH
Belzec Death Camp Commandant & Inspector of *SS-Sonderkommandos Aktion Reinhard*

Born on November 24, 1885, in Oberbalzheim, a small village in the Upper Swabian part of Württemberg in southwest Germany. After completing elementary education at the age of 14, he was employed as an apprentice carpenter with the Bühler brothers' timber firm in Oberbalzheim. From 1905 to 1907, he served his two-year draft with Grenadier Regiment 123 in Ulm, and, after a short break, re-enlisted for another two years as an army instructor.

After honorable discharge from the army in 1910, Wirth joined the Württemberg state police as a uniformed constable in Heilbronn, and in the same year married Maria Bantel, with whom he had two sons. In 1913, Wirth transferred to the *Kriminalpolizei* (*Kripo*)—the plainclothes detective squads—at their headquarters on Büchsenstraße near the city center in Stuttgart.

In October 1941, two months after the outbreak of World War I, he volunteered to serve in the army of Kaiser Wilhelm II and saw action on the Western Front in Flanders and northern France in the ranks of Reserve Infantry Regiment 246. He received a field promotion to *Offiziersstellvertreter* (acting officer) and was awarded several medals and decorations for bravery, including the Iron Cross I and II Class, and the Gold Württemberg Military Service Medal. At the end of 1917, Wirth was transferred back to Stuttgart as an officer in the military police, guarding a supply depot for Reserve Infantry Regiment 119. During this duty, he won high praise for defending the depot against the *Spartakists*, the forerunners of the German Communist Party, who attempted to raid the depot for weapons and ammunition.

Wirth rejoined the *Kripo* in 1919 and by 1923 was the head of Precinct II (*Dienststelle II)* on Büchsenstrasse in Stuttgart. He earned a reputation for solving difficult crimes that had defeated other officers, often through brutal interrogation. His "dedication and zealous methods" finally led to questions being asked about him in the Württemberg Regional Parliament (*Landtag*).

In 1937, Wirth was the deputy head of all police and party organizations, not only in Stuttgart, but the whole of Württemberg, which resulted in his recruitment by Reinhard Heydrich's Security Service (*Sicherheitsdienst-SD*) as a "*V-Mann*" (*Vertrauensmann*)—a confidential agent spying and informing on his party and police comrades.

By 1939, Wirth had reached the rank of *Kriminalinspektor*, in charge of *Kommissariat* 5, a special detective squad for investigating serious crimes, including murder. Wirth then carried out special police duties in Vienna, Austria, and in Olmütz, Czechoslovakia. In the spring of 1939, a special remark was inserted into his personal file: "At the disposal of the *Führer* ('z.V. *Führer*')." He had been earmarked for future "special tasks."

In the autumn of 1939, Wirth began the first "special task" as a founding member of the euthanasia planning team in Hitler's private Chancellery. His well-known reputation for "meticulous administration and organization" was put to use in setting up the bureaucracy. In mid-January 1940, he was among a group of high-ranking Nazi officials who witnessed the first test gassing of psychiatric patients in the abandoned prison in Brandenburg-an-der-Havel. Among this group were *Reichsleiter* Philipp Bouhler, head of the Chancellery, Dr. Karl Brandt, Hitler's escorting physician, Dr. Leonardo Conti, secretary of state for health and *SS-Standartenführer* Viktor Brack, chief of Head Office II. Brack was soon to be in charge of the daily running of the euthanasia operation under the code designation T4, named after its headquarters in a villa at Tiergartenstraße 4 in Berlin-Charlottenburg.

At the beginning of February 1940, Wirth arrived at the first T4 euthanasia institute established in Grafeneck castle in the Swabian mountains, 60 kilometers south of Stuttgart, in charge of administration and security. In May 1940, he was appointed "roving inspector" of the euthanasia institutions to tighten-up discipline among the staff, which had deteriorated alarmingly, improve security, and streamline the killing process and ensuing paperwork. He spent much of his time in the euthanasia instituton in Hartheim castle, near Linz in Upper Austria. It was here that he encountered the police officer Franz Stangl, the future commandant of the *Aktion Reinhardt* death camps at Sobibor and Treblinka. At Hartheim castle, Stangl was in charge of administration and security, and his first meeting with Wirth made a profound impression on him:

> Wirth was a gross and florid man. My heart sank when I met him. He stayed at Hartheim for several days that time and often came back. Whenever he was there he addressed us daily at lunch. And here it was again this awful verbal crudity: when he spoke about the necessity for this euthanasia operation, he was not speaking in humane or scientific terms ... he laughed. He spoke of 'doing away with useless mouth's, and that sentimental slobber about such people made him puke'.[142]

Just before Christmas 1941, Wirth arrived in Bełżec where the first *Aktion Reinhardt* death camp was under construction, and in the new year returned to the T4 euthanasia institution at Bernburg to select the first group of 15 men to staff the camp.

Between mid-January and the beginning of March 1942, he experimented with different methods of gassing, including, in the early days, using the exhaust fumes from a Post Office parcel delivery van converted into a mobile gas chamber. He also tried pumping the exhaust fumes from army trucks into three primitive gas chambers, before trying *Zyklon B*, a pesticide issued to all German military units in the field, and bottled carbon monoxide (CO) gas. This was the method used in the T4 euthanasia institutes.

He finally decided that CO gas produced from engines was the most efficient and had a Russian tank engine brought from a depot of captured Russian vehicles in *Lemberg* (today Lvov in the Ukraine). This method was then applied in the other two *Aktion Reinhardt* death camps Sobibor and Treblinka.

In time, Wirth also perfected the "conveyor-belt" method of mass murder, in which the Jews themselves carried out most of the tasks in the extermination process, working permanently at specific points to ensure its smooth continuity. This method, too, was also adopted at Sobibor and Treblinka. Wirth ran the Belzec

---

142 Sereny, *Into That Darkness*, op. cit., p. 54.

death camp with an iron fist, feared not only by Jews, but also by his own staff—Germans and Ukrainians alike.

After ensuring that Belzec was operating efficiently, on August 1, 1942, *SS-Brigadeführer* Globocnik appointed Wirth to the post of inspector of the three *SS-Sonderkommandos* operating at Belzec, Sobibor, and Treblinka *"Abteilung Reinhard—Inspekteur der SS-Sonderkommandos Aktion Reinhard"* with his office at first in the Julius Schreck Barracks, the headquarters of *Aktion Reinhardt* in Lublin. At the end of the year, Wirth's inspectorate was moved to a building on the Old Airfield just outside Lublin, close to Lublin concentration camp (Majdanek).

From mid-August 1942, Wirth played a leading role in the re-organization of Treblinka, including the construction of the new gas chambers, and thereafter visited the camp frequently. Wirth was also present when *Reichsführer-SS* (RFSS) Heinrich Himmler visited Sobibor death camp on February 12, 1943.

On September 20, 1943, Globocnik, Wirth, Stangl, and several Ukrainian guards from the *Aktion Reinhardt* death camps were transferred to Trieste in northern Italy, where Globocnik had been appointed the Higher SS and Police Leader for the Adriatic coastal region. Wirth was given command of three special units formed from former *Aktion Reinhardt* personnel, including many of the Ukrainian guards, most of whom had arrived in Trieste by the end of the year.

Based in the buildings of an old rice-husking factory in the San Sabba suburb of Trieste, their task was rounding-up and deporting the remaining Italian Jews to Auschwitz-Birkenau and confiscating their property. Under the code designation *Einsatz R* (Operation "R") these tasks were merely an extension of *Aktion Reinhardt*, albeit on a far smaller scale.

Wirth, however, turned the San Sabba factory into an interrogation center and mini-death camp for Jews and captured Italian and Yugoslav partisans. Executions were carried out by shooting, hanging, or beating to death with a mallet. For a time, a gas van was also used. Erwin Lambert, who had constructed the gas chambers at the T4 euthanasia institutions and supervised construction of the new and bigger gas chambers at Treblinka and Sobibor, converted a basement heating furnace into a crematorium to dispose of the bodies of the victims. The charred and burnt human bones and ashes were dumped into the Adriatic from a boat or a jetty in the harbor.

Christian Wirth returned to Lublin and, on behalf of Globocnik, played a leading role in the mass murder of the Jewish workers employed in a number of labor camps within the Lublin district, in Lublin itself, and at Poniatowa and Trawniki. The mass murder of 18,000 Jews alone at Lublin, 15,000 at Poniatowa, and 10,000 at Trawniki, was the last mass killing of the Jews within the *Generalgouvernement.* Wirth's involvement in these mass killings was revealed during postwar interrogations with Jakob Sporrenberg, SSPF Lublin, who had taken over this post from Globocnik.

By the spring of 1944, Globocnik was aware that the tide of the war was turning against Germany and became concerned about the mass murders in Poland and Italy, for which he was ultimately responsible. He therefore forbade Wirth to carry out any more killing of prisoners in San Sabba. Wirth's special units were switched instead to anti-partisan duty on the Istrian peninsula, where they committed atrocities against the Yugoslav and Italian population under the guise of "pacification operations."

Christian Wirth was ambushed and killed by Yugoslav partisans of the First Battalion of the *Istrska* (Istrian) Division on May 26, 1944, near Kozina, just outside Trieste. He was on his way by car to inspect one of his SS units in Fiume (today Rijeka, in Croatia) on the other side of the peninsula.

Wirth was buried with full military honors in the German military cemetery in the small village of Opicina, up on the Karst above Trieste. During the late 1950s and early 1960s, the remains of all German war dead in Italy were exhumed from their widely-scattered graves and reinterred in a new and big German military cemetery at Costermano, on the southeastern shore of Lake Garda, near Verona in northern Italy. For many years, the presence of Wirth's grave at Costermano has been a matter of bitter dispute, although his SS rank has been erased from his gravestone and his name removed from the Roll of Honor in the Propyleum.

Gottlieb Jakub HERING
Second Commandant Belzec
August 1942-May 1943
Temporary Commandant Sobibor

Born on June 2, 1887, in Warmbronn, near Leonberg, Württemberg. After leaving school, he worked as an agricultural laborer on estates in the Leonberg area. In 1915, he was conscripted into a machine gun company of Grenadier Regiment 123. He fought on the Western Front in northern France and was awarded the Iron Cross I Class among other medals. Discharged from the army in 1918, he joined the police at the end of December and served in the *Kripo* office at Goppingen, Württemberg. He later worked for the Stuttgart CID, where he became acquainted with Christian Wirth.

From December 1939 until December 1940, he served in a team of *Kripo* officers in Gotenhafen (Gdynia), dealing with the resettlement of ethnic Germans on the Baltic coast. In 1941, Hering was drafted into T4 and served in Bernburg, then later at Hadamar, Pirna-Sonnenstein, before arriving in Belzec in July 1942. One month later, in August 1942, he was appointed commandant of Belzec, when Wirth became the inspector of *SS-Sonderkommandos Aktion Reinhard.*

After the liquidation of Belzec in May 1943, he became the commandant of the Jewish labor camp at Poniatowa, until its liquidation on November 4, 1943, as part of *Aktion Erntefest* (Harvest Festival). Hering was temporary commandant of the Sobibor death camp, during its dismantling and closure in November 1943. In 1944, he was ordered to Italy, where he again replaced Christian Wirth as chief of *Kommando R1* in Trieste, after

Wirth was killed by partisans. On October 9, 1945, Hering died under unknown circumstances in the patient's waiting room of the Katherinen Hospital in Stetten-in-Remstal, Württemberg, while under investigation by the French military authorities.

Belzec Death Camp Garrison
Listed in Alphabetical Order

BAER, Rudolf. Born on March 28, 1906 in Leipzig. He was a carpenter from Halle-an-der-Saale in Saxony-Anhalt. He worked for T4 institution as a cook at Bernburg. Served at Belzec and Treblinka death camps in the administration office. He served at the Old Airfield camp in Lublin, and later in Trieste In May 1945, he was interned in a POW camp near Kircbach, Austria. He escaped and has never been traced.

BARBL, Heinrich. Born on March 3, 1900, in Sarleinsbach, Austria. He worked at the T4 institution at Hartheim before being sent to the Belzec death camp in Poland, where he helped install the gas pipes. He referred to himself as the *Hausklemper (*plumber) and worked with Erich Fuchs on the installation of pipes in the gas chambers in Sobibor.

BLAUROCK, Emil. Born on January 25, 1897. He was a male nurse at Pirna-Sonnenstein. Served in Sobibor death camp. He was detained by the US Army in Bad Aiblingen, Bavaria. He was discharged from internment on April 19, 1946.

BOROWSKI, Werner. Born on October 23, 1913, in Sprottau in the Prussian province of Lower Silesia. Served at the Bernburg T4 institution as head of the economics office. Posted to the Belzec death camp in early 1942, and then to Treblinka death camp. Because he fell victim to the typhus epidemic in the camp, he was sent back to Bernburg after recovering. He joined the *Luftwaffe* and was reported "missing in action, presumed killed."

BREE, Max. Born during 1914 in Lübben im Spreewald. Following service in T4 he served in Belzec from June / July 1942 until September 1942, when he was transferred to Treblinka. In the spring of 1943, he was transferred to Sobibor. He was killed during the prisoner revolt on October 14, 1943.

DACHSEL, Arthur. Born during 1890, in Böhlen, Sachsen. Arthur Dachsel worked at the T4 institution at Pirna-Sonnenstein, where he incinerated bodies. Served at the Belzec death camp in Poland and in July 1942 was transferred to the Sobibor death camp, where he supervised the *Waldkommando*. Promoted to the rank of *Oberwachtmeister* in March 1943. He was remembered by Thomas (Toivi) Blatt as one of the least brutal SS-men.

DUBOIS, Werner. Born on February 26, 1913, in Wuppertal-Langenfeld. He was brought up by his grandmother. After school he worked as a joiner, brushmaker, printer and on a farm. Joined the SS in January 1937 and worked as a driver for the *Gruppenkommando Oranienburg*. Also served as a driver and a guard at the Sachsenhausen concentration camp.

In August 1939, he was transferred to the T4 organization where he drove buses and worked as a burner in a number of T4 institutions in Bernburg, Brandenburg, Grafeneck, and Hadamar. Following a brief spell in Russia working for the *Organisation Todt*, he was transferred to the Belzec death camp in April 1942, where he admitted shooting Jewish prisoners. In the summer of 1943, he was transferred to the Sobibor death camp, after Belzec was closed.

At Sobibor, he was in charge of the *Waldkommando* and was attacked in the armory on the day of the prisoner revolt on October 14, 1943, and suffered serious wounds. Dubois was acquitted at the Belzec trial in August 1963. However, he was sentenced to three years imprisonment at the Sobibor trial in Hagen in 1966.

FEIX, Reinhold. Born on July 3, 1909, in Neundorf / Oberschwarzbrunn, Sudetenland, and settled in Gablonz on the Neisse River. Following his time in the SS training camp at Trawniki, he served in the Belzec death camp. At Belzec, he was one of the most brutal and feared SS-men on the camp's staff.

He accompanied the last Jewish workers to the Sobibor death camp in May 1943. He was then appointed commandant of the Jewish labor camp in Budzyn. He left Budzyn, during August 1943, and disappeared. He survived the war and died at his home in Amberg, Bavaria on May 30, 1969.

FICHTNER, Erwin. Born on January 12, 1912, in Trachenberg. Served as a cook at the T4 institution at Bernburg. At Belzec, he was the camp quartermaster. Killed by Polish partisans on March 29, 1943, near Tarnawatka, 17 kilometers north of Belzec, on the road to Zamosc. He was buried in the German military cemetery in Tomaszow Lubelski, and his remains were exhumed in 1996 and re-buried in the German military cemetery in Przemysl.

FLOSS, Erich Herbert. Born on August 25, 1912, in Reinholdsheim. Attended elementary school. After graduating, he trained in textile dyeing but could not secure a position in this line of work and consequently worked in several other jobs.

From April 1, 1935, he served in the 2 *Totenkopfsturmban Elbe* (Death Head Unit Elbe), saw service in the Buchenwald concentration camp, and also served at the T4 institution at Bernburg.

Floss was to make a name for himself as the *Aktion Reinhardt* cremation expert, which he put to good effect at Belzec, Sobibor, and Treblinka death camps during 1943. Floss was nicknamed *Tadellos* ("Perfect") by the Jews at Treblinka—this was his favorite expression. Floss served mainly at Sobibor. He was one of the SS-men who took the victims' last possessions before they entered the "tube" leading from *Lager II* (Camp II) to the gas chambers.

One week after the prisoners revolted at Sobibor on October 22, 1943, Floss was escorting a group of Ukrainian guards to the Trawniki training camp when he was killed by shots from his own machine gun by *Trawnikimänner* Wasil Hetmaniec, between Chelm and the village of Zawadowka.

FRANZ, Kurt Hubert. Born on January 17, 1914, in Dusseldorf. He attended elementary school from 1920 until 1928 in his home town. From 1929, he trained as a cook, firstly at the *Hirschquelle* restaurant, then in *Hotel Wittelsbacher Hof* in Dusseldorf, without taking his final examination.

Franz then served as a soldier between 1935 and 1937, and in October 1937 joined the *Waffen-SS* as part of the *SS-Totenkopfstandarte Thüringen.* As a member of the 6th battalion he served at the Buchenwald concentration camp, as part of the guard unit. At the end of 1939, Franz was summoned to the Führer's Chancellery in Berlin and detailed for service as a kitchen chief in the T4 institutions at Grafeneck, Hartheim, Sonnenstein and Brandenburg.

During March 1942, he was ordered to the *Generalgouvernment* and reported to Odilo Globocnik, SSPF in Lublin, and was then posted to the Belzec death camp. In Belzec, Kurt Franz was responsible for supervising the Ukrainian guards and military training, and he was promoted to the rank of *SS-Oberscharführer* on April 20, 1942.

In August 1942, he was ordered to the Treblinka death camp as deputy camp commandant and took over control of the Ukrainian guard unit. After the revolt in August 1943, he was appointed as the last commandant of the camp, responsible for the liquidation of the death camp, from August 27, 1943, until November 1943.

Franz was one of the most brutal and murderous members of staff when it came to the day-to-day running of the camp. To the prisoners, Franz was the cruelest and most feared among the SS personnel. His physical appearance was extremely deceiving—he was handsome and had a round, almost babyish face, and was nicknamed *Lalka* ("Doll") by the prisoners. He was accompanied on his rounds of the camp by Barry, a Saint Bernard cross, who attacked and maimed prisoners on Franz's command. Franz is mentioned frequently in survivor accounts, and all paint the same evil picture.

When Treblinka closed down, he briefly relocatd to Sobibor, and then to Trieste and Goriza in Italy, where he was head of the *Landeschutz* school.

In May 1945, he was arrested by the Americans but escaped back to Germany, where he was re-arrested again but later released. He then lived undisturbed in Düsseldorf until his arrerst in 1959. He was tried as a war criminal in the Treblinka trial in Düsseldorf and sentenced to life imprisonment by the German *Landesgericht* on September 3, 1965. Kurt Franz died in an old people's home in Wuppertal on July 4, 1998.

FUCHS, Erich. Born on April 9, 1902, in Berlin. After his education in an elementary school he trained to become a skilled motor mechanic and automative foreman. Before the Second World War, he was a driver in Berlin and joined the Nazi Party in the early 1930's, becaming a member of the SA and later the SS.

He was drafted to T4 he worked as Dr. Eberl's driver in the T4 institutions at Brandenburg and Bernburg, and was, as he expressed himself, "an interested spectator" at the gassing of 50 mental patients.

In the winter of 1941, Fuchs was selected at Bernburg by Christian Wirth and posted to the Belzec death camp. At Belzec, he installed "showers"—the disguised gassing facilties—and worked as a truck driver in the motor pool, transporting material to the death camp site. In April 1942, he collected a Russian water-cooled petrol engine from Lvov, which was to produce the lethal gas for exterminating the Jews at Sobibor. He installed the engine with Erich Bauer and ensured it worked with a trial gassing.

Erich Fuchs was then posted to Treblinka to assist with the installation of an engine in the gas chamber: "Subsequently I went to Treblinka. In this extermination camp I installed a generator which supplied electric light for the barracks. The work in Treblinka took me about three to four busy months. During my stay there transports of Jews who were gassed were coming in daily."

In December 1942, Fuchs managed to arrange his release from T4, and from early 1943 worked for the German oil company *Ostland-Öl-Vertriebsgesellschaft* in Riga. In February 1945, he became a soldier and member of the *Waffen-SS*, where he served in a tank transport unit. In March 1945, he was wounded during a bombing raid. Fuchs was taken prisoner by the Russians, and then subsequently held as a prisoner of war by the Americans in western Germany. He was employed by the British Army as a driver / mechanic in Bergen Belsen, until his release in 1946.

Fuchs worked at a number of jobs as an assistant worker, locksmith, and truck inspector at the Technical Inspection Agency (*Technischer Überwachungsverein*, TUV) in Koblenz until 1962; he was arrested and held in custody from April 8, 1963. The *Schwurgericht am Landgericht* Hagen sentenced him to four years imprisonment on December 20, 1966, for being an accessory to the murder of at least 79,000 people. He died in Koblenz on July 25, 1980.

GIRTZIG, Hans. Born on April 23, 1905, in Berlin. Served in the canteen in the T4 Institutions of Grafeneck, Hadamar, and Hartheim. Transferred to Belzec in the middle of 1942. When Belzec was closed down, he served at the Poniatowa Jewish labor camp. After the war he returned to Berlin. Arrested to stand trial during the 1960's, he was released due to ill health (multiple sclerosis).

GLEY, Heinrich. Born on February 16, 1901, in Rödlin, Mecklenburg. After completing elementary school education, he worked on a farm until 1919. From 1929 he worked as a male nurse. He joined the NSDAP in 1932 and entered the SS in 1934. He joined the T4 organization on January 4, 1940. He served at the T4 institutions at Grafeneck and Pirna-Sonnenstein. During the winter of 1941–42, he served in an *Organisation Todt* transportation unit for wounded soldiers.

In mid-August 1942 he was transferred to Belzec, where he worked in the Ramp and the Undressing barracks. When Belzec was closed down, he was transferred to Poniatowa Jewish Labor camp. He served in Italy, but was sent to Berlin in late 1944 due to ill health. He was discharged from prisoner of war status on December 29, 1947, and worked as a bricklayer in Munster. He was acquitted at the Belzec trial .

GRAETSCHUS, Siegfried. Born on June 9, 1916, in Tilsit, east Prussia. After extended elementary education, he became a farmer and a member of the NSDAP from 1936. He served at the Sachsenhausen concentration camp, as confirmed by the War Crimes Group in 1947.

Graetschus was posted to Belzec and was involved in the early gassing experiments, including the conversion of a Post Office parcel van into a gas wagon. Graetschus was transferred to Treblinka in May 1942, until September 1942, when he was posted to Sobibor where he commanded the Ukrainian guards, replacing Erich Lachmann as their chief. He was killed during the prisoner revolt on October 14, 1943, by Jehuda Lerner.

GRINGERS, Karl. Born during 1898. Served at the T4 Institutions of Bernburg, Hadamar, and Hartheim. Served in Belzec. He was killed in active service in Italy during 1944. He was buried at the German military cemetery in Costermano, Italy.

GROTH, Paul Johannes. Born on February 9, 1922, in Holthausen, Schwein. Served at the T4 institute at Hartheim near Linz, Austria. Groth was posted to the Belzec death camp in January 1942. Christian Wirth transferred Groth to Sobibor in April 1942, where he supervised the sorting activities in *Lager II.* He was regarded by the prisoners as one of the worst sadists among the staff. However, Groth fell in love with a Jewish girl called Ruth, who was shot in *Lager III.* Groth was transferred back to Belzec death camp in December 1942. He was in charge of the transport that brought the last Jewish work-brigade from Belzec to Sobibor in May 1943 . In 1951 his wife declared that Groth had died, in order to claim her widow's pension.

HACKENHOLT, Lorenz Maria. Born on June 25, 1914, in the coal mining area of Gelsenkirchen, Northrhine-Westphalia, in the northern part of the Ruhr. After attending the local elementary school until the age of 14, he became an apprentice bricklayer and, on passing the trade examinations, worked on various building sites.

In 1934, he joined the 2 *Totenkopfstandarte* (Death's Head Regiment) Brandenburg, stationed at Oranienburg, north of Berlin. In March 1938, he was transferred to the nearby Sachsenhausen concentration camp, where he was employed in the motor pool and as a driver for the camp *Kommandantur* and personnel.

In November 1939, he was one of a group of 10 SS NCOs summoned to the Führer's Chancellery on Vosstraße in Berlin. During a meeting with *SS-Standartenführer* Viktor Brack, the head of Main Office II of the Chancellery, they were informed of the euthanasia program and their roles within it, mainly as bus-drivers conveying the patients, and as corpse incinerators. This duty was to be performed in civilian clothes. After the SS NCOs were sworn to secrecy, civilian clothes were brought for them, and Hackenholt drove them in a bus to Grafeneck Castle in the Swabian mountains south of Stuttgart. From the beginning of 1940, when Grafeneck became operational, until the summer of 1941, when the gassings were temporarily halted on Hitler's orders, Lorenz Hackenholt served in all six T4 euthanasia institutions, both as a bus driver and as a so-called "disinfector / burner," unloading the corpses from the gas chambers and incinerating them.

After the temporary halt in the T4 gassings, Hackenholt, together with a small group of SS NCOs from T4, was transferred in the autumn of 1941 to serve under *SS-Brigadeführer* Odilo Globocnik, the SS and Police Leader of the Lublin district in the *Generalgouvernement*. Hackenholt was assigned to Belzec, a remote village in the far southeastern corner of the Lublin district, on the main road and railroad between Lublin and Lvov.

Here, on the outskirts of the village, the first *Aktion Reinhardt* death camp was under construction. When the camp became operational on March 17, 1942, Hackenholt became the supervising mechanic who started the Russian tank engine that pumped its lethal exhaust fumes into three primitive gas chambers in a wooden shed. He rapidly became the gassing expert of *Aktion Reinhardt*, and a few months later designed and supervised the construction of a new and bigger gassing building with six chambers. It was named the Hackenholt Foundation (*Stiftung Hackenholt*) in his honor.

In August 1942, Hackenholt was ordered to Treblinka by Christian Wirth, by then the inspector of the three *Aktion Reinhardt SS-Sonderkommandos* operating at Belzec, Sobibor and Treblinka, to replace the original three gas chambers with a new and bigger building containing 10 chambers. He was assisted in this task by Erwin Lambert, the T4 construction expert. On completion of this task both men were sent by

Wirth to Sobibor to construct new and bigger gassing facilities there.

Hackenholt then returned to Belzec, where, in the late autumn of 1942, he became involved in the exhumation and cremation of the hundreds of thousands of corpses buried in the mass graves. In the spring of 1943, Hackenholt returned to Treblinka on orders from Wirth to assist with the exhumation and cremation operations as one of the excavator drivers. Follwing the liquidation of Belzec duing May 1943, Hackenholt was transferred to the Old Airfield camp just outside Lublin, which was the main sorting, cleaning and storage depot for the vast amounts of belongings and valuables seized from the Jews murdered in the *Aktion Reinhardt* death camps.

Valuable furs were disinfected with *Zyklon B* in four specially constructed chambers. After Hackenholt arrived at the airfield, he used the chambers for killing prisoners who were unfit for work, instead of sending them to the gas chambers in the nearby Lublin concentration camp (Majdanek).

In the autumn of 1943, Hackenholt was transferred to Trieste in northern Italy, where he served in the *R-I Sonderkommando* of *Einsatz R* at San Sabba. In 1944, he was awarded the Iron Cross II Class for his dedicated service to *Aktion Reinhardt*. Shortly after Easter 1945, he was arrested and interned in San Sabba, awaiting execution for selling arms to partisans. However, Dieter Allers, the head of *Aktion T4* and *Einsatz R*, who had replaced Christian Wirth after his assassination, realized that the war was all but over and released Hackenholt, who promptly disappeared. He was next seen driving a bus for a Trieste motor company.

Hackenholt was next seen during the retreat of the *Einsatz R* troops ino Austria. A convoy passed him on the road to Kirbach, driving a horse-drawn milk float. In the summer of 1945, his wife Ilse received news of him in Berlin from Rudolf Kamm, a former SS comrade from Belzec. He wanted to collect

Hackenholt's civilian clothing. In 1946, two former SS comrades from Sobibor, Erich Bauer and Wenzel Rehwald, claim to have met him near Ingolstadt in Bavaria, where he was living under an assumed name and employed in a motor accessories shop.

A year later, Hackenholt's brother, Theo, believed he passed him driving a delivery van near their hometown of Gelsenkirchen in the Ruhr. After that nothing more was heard of Lorenz Hackenholt. However, after a fruitless four-year hunt by the West German police, and intensive, and repeated interrogations of his wife Ilse and other family members, it seemed likely that Hackenholt could have been living under a false name in the area of Memmingen, in the Allgau region of southern Germany. His wife Ilse lived in the same area. The Allgau region was close to the border with Austria, a country that had no extradition treaty with West Germany. Lorenz Hackenholt, wanted for participation in the mass murder of at least 1.5 million people, has never been found.

HIRCHE, Fritz. Born on June 10, 1893, in Penzig, Oberlausitz. He was employed as a manual laborer, before becoming Assistant Detective (*Kriminalobersekretär)*. He was a member of the NSDAP since 1933 and joined the T4 in 1939.

He was chief of the office and captain of the *Schutzpolizei* at Bernburg and then at Hartheim. He was transferred to Belzec. Committed suicide.

JIRMANN, Fritz. Born on January 11, 1914, in Barzdorf, Braunau. He served at the Buchenwald concentration camp before being recruited along with Kurt Franz and Erich Floss into the T4 organization. He was posted to the T4 euthanasia institute at Grafeneck. Later posted to Belzec, where he was feared as a brutal member of the camp staff, as recalled by Rudolf Reder. He was killed by Heinrich Gley, in an accidental shooting on March 1, 1943, involving two Ukrainian guards in the dark at the punishment bunker, near the *Kommandantur*. He was buried at the German military cemetery at Tomaszow Lubelski. In 1995 his remains were moved to the German military cemetery in Przemysl.

JUHRS, Robert Emil. Born on October 17, 1911, in Frankfurt am Main. Painter by profession, but he also worked as a laborer, caretaker, and usher at the Frankfurt Opera House, and as an office clerk. He served at the T4 institute at Hadamar, working as a male nurse, painter, and clerk until late 1941.

He was posted to Belzec in June 1942, where he served at the Ramp and at the *Lazarett* (field hospital), shooting the sick and disabled. In March 1943, he was posted to the Jewish labor camp at Dorohucza, where peat was dug, and he remained until early November 1943.

Juhrs escorted the working prisoners (*Arbeitshaftlinge)* from Dorohucza to Trawnki, where all of them were shot during *Aktion Erntefest* (Harvest Festival). Following the revolt in Sobibor in October 1943, Juhrs was sent to help with the dismantling of the camp and formed a guard cordon of the last prisoners to be killed at Sobibor, once they had finished with the clean-up of the death camp.

Juhrs was ordered to Italy in December 1943. He was acquitted at the Belzec trial at the *Landgericht* Munich in 1963, and he was also acquited at the Sobibor trial in Hagen on December 20, 1966, on charges arising from his involvement in the demolition of the camp.

KAMM, Rudolf. Born in 1905, in Sedenz, a village near Teplitz Schonau in the *Sudetenland*. He served at the T4 institute at Pirna-Sonnenstein as a "burner."

He was posted to the death camp at Belzec in 1942, and records from the nearby hospital at Tomaszow Lubelski show that he was hospitalized on June 17, 1942, until June 25, 1942, and again on the December 30, 1942, until January 31, 1943, with typhus.[143]

He was transferred to Sobibor in 1943, where he supervised the sorting barracks. He was then posted to Italy. Franz Suchomel testified that he saw him for the last time after the end of the war, in a *Gasthaus* between Mauthern and Hermagor, Carinthia (Austria), the last lodgings of the former unit (R-1 in Trieste).

KLEMINSKY, Otto. Born during 1906, possibly in Berlin. After service in T4, he was posted to Belze, from July 1942 until the spring of 1943. He was then transferred to Udine in Italy. Post war fate unknown.

KLOS, Walter. Served as a T4 driver at the Bernburg and Pirna-Sonnenstein institutions. Also served at the Belzec and Sobibor death camps. He was transferred to the Lublin concentration camp, where he died in unknown circumstances.

KRASCHEWSKI, Friedrich. Served at Belzec until September 1942. Wirth transferred him. Later served in Trieste.

NIEMANN, Johann. Born on August 4, 1913, in Wollern Ostfriesland. Served at a number of concentration camps such as Oranienburg, Esterwegen, and Sachsenhausen between the years 1934–1941. He was a member of T4 and was employed as a "burner" at the Bernburg institute.

Niemann was posted to service in the east at the Belzec death camp, before being posted to Sobibor in January 1943. He was promoted to the rank of *SS-Untersturmführer* following Himmler's visit to the camp on February 12, 1943, He was acting camp commandant when the prisoner revolt took place on October 14, 1943, and he was killed in the tailors' barracks by a blow from an axe wielded by Alexander (Kalimali) Shubayev.

---

143 A number of the SS garrison were also hospitalised at Tomaszow Lubelski, including Gottfried Schwarz and Heinrich Unverhau as well as Kamm, and a number of *Trawnikimänner*.

OBERHAUSER, Josef. Born on September 20, 1915, in Munich. Worked on farms after leaving school. In 1935 he joined the SS and the NSDAP. At the outbreak of the war he served with the *Liebstandarte* Adolf Hitler. From 1940, worked in the T4 institutes at Bernburg, Brandenburg, and Grafeneck, burning corpses.

In November 1941, he was assigned to the SS- and Police Leader Lublin and was responsible for the construction of the Belzec camp that commenced in November 1941. Served at Belzec until August 1942, when he became Christian Wirth's adjutant, as Wirth became inspector of the *SS-Sonderkommandos Aktion Reinhard*. Oberhauser was promoted to the rank of *SS-Untersturmführer* because of his service in *Aktion Reinhardt*.

In the autumn of 1943 he was ordered to Italy, where he became commandant of the camp at San Sabba, Trieste. Captured by British troops in Bad Gastein, Austria, in May 1945. In 1948, he was sentenced to fifteen years' imprisonment by the Magdeburg *Landesgericht* for participation in euthanasia crimes. He was released in April 1956, and he was employed as a casual worker and a barman in Munich.

In 1965, he was tried by jury in *Landesgericht I* in Munich at the Belzec trial and was sentenced to a total of four years and six months imprisonment for the crime of acting as an accessory in the common murder of 300,000 people, and for his role in the common murder of 150 people. Oberhauser was interviewed by Claude Lanzmann in the film *Shoah*, in the *Franziskaner Poststubl* about Christian Wirth and the number of Jews murdered at Belzec.

ORLIEWSKI, Eduard. Born during 1905 in Berlin. Served at the T4 institution at Pirna-Sonnenstein as a "burner." Served at Belzec. Fate unknown.

SCHEMMEL, Ernst. Born on September 11, 1883, in Kirchhain, north Saxony. A career police officer, he was a member of the

Kriminalpolizei (*Kripo*), the plainclothes detective squads. Commandeered to T4, he was employed as head of administration at the Pirna-Sonnenstein and Hartheim institutions. Transferred in early 1942 to the Belzec administative office, and then, for a short time—late September to early October 1942—as acting commandant at Treblinka. He died in Dresden on December 10, 1943, whilst home on leave, aged 60.

SCHLUCH, Karl Alfred. Born on October 25, 1905, in Lauenburg, Pommern. He spent his childhood with his grandparents. After attending elementary school he became an agricultural worker. From April 1930 he was employed as an attendant at the sanatorium run by Dr. Wiener in Bernau, near Berlin. He passed his public nursing examinaion in 1932.

He joined the NSDAP in 1936 and the T4 organization on June 13, 1940, where he served at Grafeneck and Hadamar institutions. During the winter of 1941–42 he served in an *Organisation Todt* transportation unit for wounded soldiers on the Eastern Front.

Schluch was transferred to Belzec during June 1942, where he served on the Ramp and accompanied the naked Jews through "*der Schlauch*" to the gas chambers. After Belzec was closed down, he served in the Poniatowa Jewish labor camp. In the autumn of 1943 he was sent to Italy to fight the partisans. At the end of the war, he was arrested by US forces, but released on July 6, 1945.

After the war, he returned to being an agricultural and then construction worker, before returning to the nursing profession at a hospital in Bedburg-Hau.

SCHMIDT, Fritz. Born on November 29, 1906 in Eibau, Görlitz district in eastern Saxony. A motor mechanic by trade, he was employed in the T4 euthanasia institute at Pirna-Sonnenstein in 1940 as a guard and driver and in 1941 he was transferred to

Bernburg euthanasia institute. He served in Belzec from June / July 1942 until September 1942, when he was transferred to Treblinka to supervise the maintenance and running of the gassing engines in the Upper Camp. He was also in charge of the SS-garage and supervised the metal-work shop. He was transferred to Sobibor during September 1943 and he stayed there until the camp was liquidated in November 1943. After Treblinka he served with Einsatz R in Trieste, northern Italy. Captured by the Americans at the end of the war, he was released and he returned to Germany. He was arrested by the Soviet millitary authorities, placed on trial, and on December 14, 1949, was sentenced to nine years imprisoment. He escaped and fled to West Germany, where he died on February 4, 1982, aged 76.

SCHNIEDER, Friedrich. A *Volksdeutscher* who was in charge of the *Trawnikimänner* at Belzec.

SCHWARZ, Gottfried. Born in 1913, in Furth. He served at Brandenburg, Grafeneck, and Bernburg T4 institutes as a "burner." Schwarz was deputy commandant of Belzec and assisted in the construction of the death camp. According to Erich Fuchs, Schwarz also served at Sobibor, taking part in trial gassings.

Schwarz was regarded by Rudolf Reder as one of the most cruel SS guards. When Belzec was liquidated, he was appointed commandant of the Dorohucza labor camp. Schwarz was ordered to Trieste and was killed by Italian communist partisans in San Pietro, near Civdale, on June 19, 1944. He was buried at the German millitary cemetery at Costermano, Italy.

TAUSCHER, Fritz. Born on May 20, 1903, in Planitz, near Zwickau. Worked as a supervisor at the registry office in Pirna-Sonnenstein. Also served at Brandenburg and Hartheim T4 institutes.

Transferred to Belzec in October 1942, he served there until March 1943 and was in charge of the cremation of the exhumed bodies. Tauscher, according to SS NCO's Juhrs and Zierke, was the last commandant of Dorohucza—the Jewish labor camp—after also having served at Budzyn Jewish labor camp. He was then posted to Trieste. Committed suicide whilst on a remand prison in Hamburg.

UNVERHAU, Heinrich. Born on November 26, 1911, in Vienenburg, Goslar. In April 1925 he became a plumber's apprentice, but, as a result of an accident at work, he lost the sight in his right eye and was forced to end his apprenticeship. He became a muscian, and from 1934 worked as a nurse.

In January 1940 he was ordered to join T4, and he was employed at Gafeneck and Hadamar institutes as a nurse. In the winter of 1941–42 he was drafted to the Eastern Front for service in the *Organisation Todt*, looking after the wounded in Raume Wjasma.

In June 1942 he was posted to the Belzec death camp, and, in November 1942, he was hospitalized at Tomaszow Lubelski with spotted typhus that caused him to lose his right eye completely. At the death camp he was responsible for sorting the possessions in the railway sheds located just outside the camp, opposite Belzec railway station.

In the summer of 1943 he was posted to Sobibor, where he supervised the cleaning up the undressing area in *Lager II* and one of the sorting barracks. Unverhau was ordered back to the former death camp site at Belzec to help with the planting of trees to cover the traces of the crimes committed there. He repeated this role at Treblinka in September 1943, returning to Sobibor in November 1943, just in time to help with the re-planting there.

Unverhau was cleared at the Belzec trial in 1963, and was also acquitted at the Sobibor trial in Hagen in 1966.

VALLASTER, Josef. Born on February 5, 1910, in Silbertal, Austria. Served in the T4 institutes of Hadamar and Hartheim. Posted to Belzec, he served there between January and April 1942, and from there went to Sobibor, the same month. He worked in *Lager III,* supervising the gassing and burial—and later burning—of the victims. He often drove the narrow-gauge railway engine that pulled the trucks filled with the elderly and disabled from the ramp to *Lager III*. One of the most brutal SS NCOs in Sobibor, he was killed in the prisoner revolt on October 14, 1943, in the shoemakers workshop.

ZANKER, Hans. Born on September 8, 1905 in Sachsen. He served in the T4 institutes of Pirna-Sonnenstein as a cook. Served at the death camps in Poland including, Belzec, from September 1942 until May 1943, when the camp closed. Also served at Sobibor, and Treblinka. He was posted to Trieste, Italy. No more details known.

ZIERKE, Ernst Theodor Franz. Born on May 6, 1905, in Krampe. Son of a railroad worker. After graduating from elementary school he worked as a forester, and in 1921 was apprenticed to be a blacksmith. After passing the blacksmith apprenticeship exams he was employed in agriculture from 1925.

In 1934, he changed careers and became a nurse at a clinic at Neuruppin near Brandenburg, and was summoned to the T4 Main Office in Berlin in December 1939. Served at the T4 institutes at Grafeneck and Hadamar.

In the winter of 1941–42, he was drafted into the *Organisation Todt* to care for the wounded in Russia. He returned to Germany and worked at a T4 institute at Eichberg, near Rudesheim. Posted to Belzec in June 1942, where he served until March 1943. At Belzec he served on the Ramp.

In March 1943, he was transferred along with Robert Juhrs to the Jewish labor camp at Dorohucza, where peat was dug, until November 1943. Zierke was amongst the SS who escorted the

Jewish *Arbeitshaftlinge* from Dorohucza to the neaby Jewish labor camp at Trawniki, where all of them were shot as part of *Aktion Erntefest*

Zierke was sent to Sobibor to help with the closure of the camp, and he formed part of the cordon that watched over the final liquidation of the Jewish workers from Treblinka. He was then posted to Italy. Zierke was acquitted at the Belzec trial in Munich in 1964, and was released from custody during the Sobibor trial in Hagen on health grounds. Zierke died on May 23, 1972.

SUPPORT STAFF

GOCKEL, Rudolf. Worked for the *Reichsbahn*, was responsible for the Belzec railway station, and drove the trains packed with deportees into the death camp. He was imprisoned in Zamosc for three years, but never charged. He died in 1965 in Lauffen am Neckar, near Stuttgart.

Chapter XV
Wartime Reports About the Death Camp

The Polish Underground passed on information about Belzec to the Polish government-in-exile in London, and some of these reports were published by the Polish Ministry of Information. The Home Army (*Armia Krajowa*), or the *Delegatura*, passed on information via monthly reports using a network of Underground messengers, who travelled through occupied Europe via neutral countries such as Spain or Sweden to reach the government-in-exile.

The *Delegatura* report for April 1942 included a comprehensive account of the Belzec extermination camp:

> The camp was fully completed a few days before March 17, 1942. From that day transports with Jews began to arrive from the direction of Lvov and Warsaw. On the first day five transports arrived, afterward, one transport arrived daily from each direction. The transport enters the railway spur of Belzec camp after disembarkation, lasting half an hour, the train returns empty. The observations of the local people (the camp is within sight and hearing distance of the inhabitants near the railway station) led all of them to one conclusion: that there is a mass murder of the Jews inside the camp. The following facts testify to this:

1. Between March 17 and April 13, about fifty-two transports (each of eighteen to thirty-five freight cars with an average of 1,500 people) arrived in the camp.
2. No Jews left the camp, neither during the day nor the night.
3. No food was supplied to the camp (whereas bread and other food articles had been dispatched to the Jews who had worked earlier on the construction of the camp).
4. Lime was brought to the camp.
5. The transports arrived at a fixed time. Before the arrival of a transport, no Jews were seen in the camp.

6. After each transport, about two freight cars with clothing are removed from the camp to the railway stores. (The guards steal clothes.)
7. Jews in underwear were seen in the area of the camp.
8. In the area of the camp there are three barracks; they cannot accommodate even one-tenth of the Jews.
9. In the area of the camp, a strong odor can be smelled on warmer days.
10. The guards pay for vodka, which they drink in large quantities, with any requested sum, and frequently with watches and valuables.
11. Jews arrived in Belzec (the township) looking for a witness who would testify that Jews are being killed there. They were ready to pay 120,000 zloty..... They did not find a volunteer. It is unknown by which means the Jews are liquidated in the camp. There are three assumptions: (1) electricity; (2) gas; (3) by pumping out the air. With regard to (1) : there is no visible source of electricity; with regard to (2): no supply of gas and no residue of the remaining gas after the ventilation of the gas chamber were observed; with regard to (3): there are no factors that deny this possibility. It was even verified that during the building of one of the barracks, the walls and floor were covered with metal sheets (for some purpose). In the area of the camp huge pits were dug in the autumn. At that time it was assumed that there would be underground stores. Now the purpose of this work is clear. From the particular barrack where the Jews are taken for so-called disinfection, a narrow railway leads to these pits. It was observed that the 'disinfected' Jews were transported to a common grave by this trolley.In Belzec the term '*Totenlager*' (death camp) was heard in connection with the Jewish camp. The leadership of the camp is in the hands of twelve SS-men (the commander is *Hauptmann* Wirth) who have forty guards for help.[144]

Dr. Ignacy Schwarzbart, a member of the Polish National Council, stated in London on November 15, 1942:

> The methods applied in this mass extermination are, apart from executions, firing squads, electrocution and lethal gas-chambers. An electrocution station is installed at Belzec camp. Transport of settlers arrive at a siding, on the spot, where the execution is to take place. The camp is policed by Ukrainians. The victims are

---

[144] Delegatura Report, April 1942 YVA o-25/140-8.

ordered to strip naked, ostensibly to have a bath, and are then led to a barracks with a metal plate for a floor. The door is then locked, electric current passes through the victims, and their death is almost instantaneous. The bodies are loaded on the wagons and taken to a mass grave, some distance from the camp.[145]

In the *Polish Fortnightly Review* dated Tuesday, December 1, 1942, published in London by the Polish Ministry of Information, the main feature was a report on the extermination of Jews in the Warsaw ghetto. It also briefly mentioned Belzec, and, in an annexe to the main report, a fuller account regarding the extermination camp at Belzec was also covered:

Main Report

A camp was organised at Belzec for the special purpose of execution by electrocution and here in the course of about a month, in March and April 1942, 80,000 Jews from the Lublin, Lwow, and part of the Kielce provinces were executed. Out of Lublin's 30,000 Jews only 2,500 were left, 70 of them being women.[146]

Extraordinary Report from the Jew-extermination Camp at Belzec-Annex, July 10th 1942

According to information from a German employed at the extermination camp, it is situated in Belzec, by the station, and is barred off by barriers of barbed wire. Inside the wire, and all round the outside, Ukrainians are on guard. The executions are carried out in the following fashion: When a trainload of Jews arrives at the station in Belzec, it is shunted by a side-track up to the wire surrounding the place of execution, at which point there is a change in the engine crew and train guards.

From the wire onward the train is serviced by German drivers who take it to the unloading point, where the track ends. After unloading, the men go to a barracks on the right, the women to a barracks situated on the left, where they strip, ostensibly in readiness for a bath.After they have undressed both groups go to a third barracks where there is an electrified plate, where the

145 The Black Book of Polish Jewry.
146 National Archives Kew FO 371/ 31097, p. 2.

> executions are carried out. Then the bodies are taken by train to a trench situated outside the wire, and some thirty metres deep. This trench was dug by Jews, who were all executed afterwards. The Ukrainians on guard are also to be executed when the job is finished. The Ukrainians acting as guards are loaded with money and stolen valuables; they pay 400 zlotys for a litre of vodka, 2,000 zlotys and jewellery for relations with a woman.[147]

The Polish Underground reported on a spontaneous act of resistance took place in Belzec on June 13, 1942:

> The revolt in the camp, probably the first one, took place on June 13th, when Jews were summoned to remove the corpses of murdered women and children: at the horrible sight (they were standing in the gas chamber holding each others' waists and necks, presumably in the prenatal reflexes), they attacked the *'Wachmannschaft'* (the guards), which resulted in a struggle in which 4–6 Germans and nearly all the Jews died; several Jews managed to escape.[148]

Dr. Schwarzbart sent a telegram to the Jewish Congress in New York on December 5, 1942, regarding the extermination of the Jews in Poland, including the mass gassing of Jews in Belzec. The extract read as follows: "Special official envoy Gentile escaped and arrived here left capital this October Saw Warsaw Ghetto on last August and September. Witnessed mass murder of one transport six thousand Jews at Belzec. Spoke to him yesterday 3 hours confirm all most horrible mass atrocities......"[149] This telegram can be seen in the chapter marked "Illustrations."

A British Intelligence report dated March 16, 1945, mentions a transport of Polish people to the Belzec death camp:

---

147 National Archives Kew FO 371/ 31097, p. 4.

148 Arad, *Belzec, Sobibor, Treblinka*, p. 257.

149 National Archives Kew FO 371/ 30924

It might be interesting to learn that during an 'Action' directed spefically against Aryan Poles, the latter were kidnapped in the streets, from streetcars, in stores, and public places. A transport consisting entirely of Aryan Poles was sent to Belzec, where they shared the fate of their Jewish compatriots. This however, only happened once.[150]

150 National Archives Kew FO 371/50971, p. 4.

Chapter XVI
The Long Road to Justice

Given that nearly half a million innocent Jewish men, women, and children were murdered in Belzec, the long road to justice is poorly traveled, with only Josef Oberhauser brought to stand trial in the 1960s for crimes committed at the Belzec extermination camp.

One of the Belzec SS NCO's, Heinrich Unverhau, was arrested and charged in 1948, accused of killing patients at the Grafeneck T4 institution. At Belzec, Unverhau had been in charge of the sorting depot, housed in the locomotive sheds, opposite the Belzec railway station. It was during the course of this trial that details began to emerge about the Belzec death camp and other *Aktion Reinhardt* camps. His testimony about Belzec and Sobibor death camps were discounted by the court as being irrelevant to the Grafeneck proceedings. After a lengthy hearing, Heinrich Unverhau was acquitted of all charges, as it was proven he had not participated in the killings.[151]

Between the years 1959 and 1963, former SS NCO's who had served at Belzec and other death camps that were part of *Aktion Reinhardt*, were arrested and subjected to pre-trial interrogations and pre-trial court hearings. These included Werner Dubois, Erich Fuchs, Heinrich Gley, Hans Girtzig, Robert Juhrs, Josef Oberhauser, Karl Schluch, Heinrich Unverhau, and Ernst Zierke. One of them, Hans Girtzig, was released due to ill-health, as he suffered from multiple sclerosis.[152]

Robert Lorent, a member of the T4 organisation, made a statement regarding his visits to Belzec and a number of the camp personnel who were under investigation, on May 4, 1961, in the German city of Cologne:

---

151 O'Neil, *Belzec*, p. 206.

152 Ernst Klee, *Das Kulturlexikon Zum Dritten Reich*, S. Fischer Verlag GmbH, Frankurt am Main, 2007, p. 184.

In February 1942 I reported to the Community Charity Foundation in Berlin, which was then in the process of dissolution. The personnel were largely passed to the office of Globocnik. I need to amend this statement and say that about 20% of the personnel were thus transferred and of these a large part continued to be paid by the foundation. These payments were made by a Loans Office, of which I was in charge. My knowledge of the camp Belzec and its staff stem from this arrangement.

I went to Belzec twice. I no longer remember the exact dates.There was an interval of about six weeks to two months between these visits. The second visit in 1942 must have taken place before the weather turned cold, as I clearly recall that I spent the night in a PKW, near the railway station Rawa Ruska, there was a guarded market-place—which I could not have done had it been really cold.

The purpose of my visit was to deliver supplies to the camps in the Lublin region. I seem to remember that the goods train was shunted into sidings at the camp (Belzec) and that I spent the night in a sturdily constructed brick building, on a road about 500 metres distant from the camp.

Close to this was the billet of Wirth. The staff which accompanied the goods train became the responsibility of the admin staff member Fichtner. I already knew him from a previous meeting. I am of the opinion he must also have been employed in another Foundation and that I must have got to know him, when this was dissolved.

From my two visits I clearly remember only Wirth and Fichtner. In the course of the dissolution of these organizations, mainly at evening get-togethers, I learned the names of other people, and likewise because I was in charge of these organizations, but this did not mean I could recall individuals.

On one occasion—I no longer remember whether it was my first or second visit—a trainload of Jews arrived while I was there. Accompanied by a SS-man I was able to watch the unloading of the Jews. Who this SS-man was I cannot now say. I also do not know what rank he had. There would be no point in showing me photos of possible people for me to identify, nor any purpose in naming them. One has to take account that 20 years have since passed.

The question as to who were materially involved in driving the Jews out of their carriages, is not one I can give a straight answer. The train consisted of ordinary passenger carriages. The disembarkation of the Jews took place with relatively little trouble, and I gained the impression that after a long journey the Jews were glad to be able to breathe some fresh air.

Where there was a certain melee, order was restored with the help of a Jewish working party and other volunteers. After a short while the Jews were addressed, possibly by Wirth, but I cannot be certain about this, as I was not interested in these details. The way I have put this, does not do justice to my attitude. I should like to reply to the question in a useful manner, but I found this experience too upsetting for me to be able to remember these things.

After the address, the Jews, though clearly disturbed went surprisingly peacefully along the way pointed out to them, which led to the huts. I do not believe that the Jews knew what was in store for them. I did see, for example, how an SS-man supervised the hut where the Jews had to undress and another SS-man then pointed them in the direction they had to follow, but I cannot say who these SS-men were. I mean that I am not in a position to say it was this, or other SS-men who carried out this given function.

I am unable to answer the question regarding the organization of the SS staff or which rank was responsible for which function. I never knew who was camp commandant or his deputy, or who was chief NCO, or section leader. In my opinion the camp commandant was Wirth. I cannot say whether Wirth had an adjutant, or who he might have been.

According to my information after the closure of the camps in the Lublin area, four men belonging to the volunteer group went to Italy. I do not know their names. A number of names were mentioned to me, regarding which I can say the following:

Barbel—He probably came from Linz and was Austrian.[153]

Girtzig—I know his name, but I have nothing further to say.

---

153 Correct name Barbl. Served in Belzec and Sobibor death camps.

Groot—Came from Hamburg, was rather young, as I remember came from Hartheim Institution. I noted that he was unable or unwilling to reply to me in a low-German dialect.[154]

Häusler—Was originally in the administration of T4 and later on the Lublin administrative staff.[155]

Hodl—Was possibly a driver in Hartheim. I do not know if he was posted to the East.[156]

Kriegas—Or Kriegad—was possibly correct name **Gringers.** I know nothing more.[157]

Münzberger—Was possibly Austrian and to my knowledge was not posted to the East, as he was probably too old. He must now be in his early sixties.[158]

Oberhauser—I do know but can no longer describe him. He was possibly a section leader

Zierke—I have heard this name, but I cannot say if he belonged to the T4 office staff or was transferred to the East.[159]

I am unable to answer the question which actual duties were performed in Belzec by Oberhauser, Girtzig, Unverhau or Gley, as I do not know. I am unable to provide further information regarding the events and conditions in camp Belzec or about people on the camp staff.

Signed: R.Lorent [160]

*

In August 1963 the eight former SS NCOs were brought before examining magistrates to answer for their alleged war crimes committed at Belzec. During these pre-trial hearings, Rudolf

---

154 Correct name Paul Groth. Served in Belzec and Sobibor death camps.

155 Willi Hausler served with Christian Wirth as part of the Inspector of SS Sonderkommandos Abteilung Reinhard in Lublin.

156 Franz Hodl served in the Sobibor death camp.

157 Correct name was Karl Gringers.

158 Gustav Munzberger served at the Treblinka death camp.

159 Ernst Zierke served at the Belzec and Sobibor death camps.

160 Robert Lorent Interrogation, May 4, 1961. Zentralle Stelle Ludwigsburg 208 AR-Z 252/59 .

Reder, now known as Roman Robak, traveled from Toronto in Canada, but was unable to positively identify any of the accused.

Although those charged tried to minimize the roles they played in the extermination of the Jews in Belzec, they admitted their guilt, but pleaded mitigating circumstances. They claimed they had carried out their duties in Belzec, in fear of their lives—so brutal were commandants Wirth and Hering. As a consequence of this, the examining magistrates decided not to proceed with a public trial for seven out of the eight men accused. They ruled that Josef Oberhauser would stand trial because of his close relationship with Christian Wirth, and his wider involvement with *Aktion Reinhardt*. The rest were acquitted.

Werner Dubois, Erich Fuchs, Robert Juhrs, Heinrich Unverhau, and Ernst Zierke did not enjoy their freedom, as immediately after leaving the courtroom, they were once again arrested and taken into custody to face similar war crimes charges, in connection with their service at the Sobibor death camp.

Josef Oberhauser faced justice at the Munich Assize Court on January 18, 1965, in a trial that only lasted four days. One of his former collegues in the SS, Karl Schluch, was particularly scathing about Oberhauser:

> If Oberhauser maintained that he did not partipate in the extermination of the Jews in Belzec, or that he did not see the whole operation from beginning to end—from the unloading to the removal of the bodies—then I say, try another one. Oberhauser not only knew the entire running of the extermination operation well, but also took part in it. In my opinion, there is no doubt that Oberhauser was an authoratiative person in the killing of the Jews in Belzec camp. The Belzec camp operated for only one reason and for what Oberhauser did he was well promoted.[161]

Oberhauser claimed at the start of his trial that he had already been tried in a Magdeburg court, for crimes committed at Belzec, and had been found guilty and sentenced to 15 years in prison, but the court investigated this claim and established that Oberhauser

---

161 O'Neil, *Belzec*, p. 208.

had been tried and sentenced for crimes relating to euthanasia, and thus the trial proceeded.

Despite Oberhauser's defence of only being on the periphery of the mass extermination of the Jews in Belzec, he was found guilty of war crimes and sentenced to four-and-a-half years imprisonment, the only defendant to answer for the death of nearly half a million innocent men, women, and children. He only served half the sentence and returned to his old job as a barman in the *Franziskaner Postubel* in Munich. It was at this bar that Oberhauser was confronted by Claude Lanzmann, who, in the film *Shoah*, released in 1985, held up a photograph of Christian Wirth. "Do you recognise this man? No? Christian Wirth? Mr. Oberhauser! Do you remember Belzec? No memories of Belzec? Of the overflowing graves? You don't remember?"

Josef Oberhauser passed away in Munich during 1979. He was 64 years old.

A number of the *Trawnikimänner* who had served at Belzec death camp were brought to trial by the Soviets. B. Bielakow, M. Matwijenko, I. Nikoforow, W. Podienko, F. Tichonowski, F. Schultz, J. Zajczew, and several others were tried, found guilty of war crimes, and executed. Two further trials were held in Kiev, and 13 former Ukrainian SS guards shared the same fate.

Samuel Kunz, was an ethnic German born in August 1921, in a small village on the River Volga, who joined the Red Army and fought against the invading Germans. He was captured and, whilst a prisoner of war, volunteered to join the SS, and was trained at the SS training camp at Trawniki, near Lublin. Kunz was then posted to the Belzec death camp, where he served from January 1942 to May 1943, as a *Volksdeutsch* member of the camp staff.

After the war he settled near Bonn—then West Germany—where he worked as a technician for the Buildings Ministry. Kunz was questioned on numerous occasions, in 1969, 1975, and 1980, but he evaded justice due to his lowly rank. He was finally charged in July 2010 with assisting in the murder of 430,000 Jews. It was also alleged that he murdered ten Jews by shooting them in two separate incidents.

On November 22, 2010, a Bonn court spokesman Joachim Klages confirmed that Samuel Kunz had died, aged 89, in his hometown near Bonn, although the causes of death were unknown.[162]

So Samuel Kunz had at least been charged—though somewhat belatedly—for his alleged crimes, but had evaded justice. It is highly unlikely that anyone else will stand trial for war crimes committed at the Belzec death camp. The long road to justice has finally come to an end.

---

162 Topping—*Suspected Nazi Death Camp Guard Samuel Kunz dies before trial*—www.guardian.co.uk, 22 November, 2010.

Chapter XVII The Paintings of Waclaw Kolodziejcyk

During the 1960s, Waclaw Kolodziejczyk, a former railway employee at Belzec station, created six paintings showing the Belzec death camp and the village during the German occupation. He and his family were eye-witnesses to the brutal conditions of the transports, as they passed through the station on the way to the death camp.

Shortly before his death, Waclaw Kolodziejczyk donated the paintings to the local parish church in the Belzec village, four of which are reproduced in this book. It must be stressed that Kolodziejczyk never set foot in the death camp, and the two paintings of the camp were from a combination of second-hand knowledge, along with a degree of artistic licence, and therefore cannot be treated as definitive illustrations. For example, the heavy wooden entrance gate has been replaced by a see-through iron gate:

Belzec Death Camp—Arrival of a Jewish Transport

Belzec Death Camp—Burning of Corpses

The Punishment of Bartlomiej Panasowiec

This painting shows the punishment of Bartlomiej Panasowiec, a resident of Belzec village who was caught by the Germans spying on the camp. Christian Wirth and Gottlieb Hering on horse-back chased him through the village, setting their dogs on him and beating him with whips. Panasowiec was seriously injured but he survived the ordeal, and, as a Ukrainian, he and some of his family were resettled to the Ukraine. It is worth pointing out that the two SS-men were pictured wearing German Army uniforms, which is incorrect.

Belzec Railway Station

This is a fine painting of the old railway station before it was destroyed. On July 5, 1944, a German ammunition train was standing at the Belzec station when it was bombed in an attack by a lone Soviet fighter plane. In the ensuing explosion the station and a number of adjacent buildings were destroyed completely.

All the color reprints are courtesy of the Holocaust Historical Society.

Chapter XVIII
The Number of Victims

As a result of recent research, most notably by Steven Tyas, which considerably helped my own work at the National Archives in Kew, a German police message sent by Herman Höfle was intercepted and decoded by the British Intelligence staff at Bletchley Park. It is thanks to the sterling research of Tyas that this decode became known.

The message sent by Herman Höfle to *SS-Obersturmbannführer* Franz Heim, Commander-in-Chief (*Befehlshaber der Sicherheitspolizei*, BdS) office in Krakow, was a 14-day report for *Aktion Reinhardt* and a year-end report up to December 31, 1942. This was the second of two messages intercepted by the British—the first one Höfle sent to Adolf Eichmann at RSHA Berlin was only partially intercepted. The second message to Heim was intercepted in full, on January 11, 1943. The death camps were identified only by letters.

Camps	14 Day Report to 31-12-1942	Year End 1942
L—Lublin	12,761	24,733
B—Belzec	0	434,508
S—Sobibor	515	101,370
T—Treblinka	10,335	713,555*
Totals	**23,611**	**1274,166**

In the original message the British Intelligence staff made a mistake and missed the last 5 off the Treblinka figure, it has to be 713,555 to fit the total figure. The message does not refer to the above as victims, but people sent to the camps. This decoded message is one of the most important historical finds of recent years.[163]

The figure of 434,508 for Belzec is thought to be the total for only the *Generalgouvernement* and does not include the Jews deported to Belzec from the Reich and other places, recently estimated as between 20–25,000. Thus, the likely total for the number of people murdered at the Belzec death camp is around the half a million mark. Though it is fair to say it is unlikely that the true figure will never be known.

What is interesting is that the figures for *Aktion Reinhardt* submitted by Herman Höfle in his message include the camp at Lublin (Majdanek) which was not officially part of *Aktion Reinhardt*. The camp at Lublin came under the control of the *Wirtschaftsverwaltungshauptamt (WVHA)*—Concentration Camp Inspectorate—whilst Belzec, Sobibor, and Treblinka were controlled by Odilo Globocnik. The Old Airfield camp was a storage depot for the clothing and footwear of the murdered victims in the three *Aktion Reinhardt* camps as well as from the ghettos and was due to become a sub-camp of the Lublin concentration camp. But the liquidation of the camp as part of *Aktion Erntefest* in November 1943 meant this plan never came to fruition.[164]

---

163 National Archives Kew, HW16/32.

164 Tomasz Kranz, *Extermination of Jews at the Majdanek Concentration Camp*, Panstwowe Muzeum na Majdanku, Lublin 2007, p. 64.

Epilogue

On July 4, 1944, a German anmmunition train was stationary at the Belzec railway station when it was bombed by a lone Soviet fighter plane. In the ensuing explosion the station was completely destroyed, along with a number of other buildings in the vicinity. After the fires had been put out, the Germans erected a wooden barrack near the ruins that served as the station for the next fifty years, until a new one was built in 1994. The destruction of the railway station may well be the reason why no railroad documentation of the transports to Belzec has apparently survived.

The Soviet Red Army liberated Belzec village on July 21, 1944, and a Polish War Crimes Commission, led by Judge Czeslaw Godzieszewski from the District Court in Zamosc, commenced its investigations at the former death camp site. In addition to hearing testimony from the Belzec villagers, including those who had helped construct the gas chambers, and others who witnessed transports arriving, the investigation team carried out on-site investigations at the former death camp. Nine pits were opened to confirm the existence of mass graves. The human remains found were reinterred in a specially erected concrete crypt near the northeast corner of the camp. In February 1946, officials from the District Court Zamosc returned to Belzec to interview several of the witnesses again, and the War Crimes Commission published a report on their findings on April 11, 1946.

The first monument to the victims who perished at Belzec was unveiled on December 1, 1963, but the site was neglected and rarely visited. In 1993 an agreement was reached between Poland and the United States of America concerning the construction of a new memorial at the site of the former death camp. Among the signatories were members of the Council for the Preservation of the Memory of Victims of War and Persecutions and members of the American Jewish Community.

During the years 1997 and 1999, the site of the former death camp saw a number of archeological studies under the stewardship of Professor Andrzej Kola, director of the archaeological faculty at the Nicholas Copernicus University in Torun, Poland. They located 33 mass graves, most containing crematory ashes and charcoal, as well as a number of traces of the camps buildings and unloading ramps. The team also uncovered plastic plates with the Jewish Star of David, glass and china destructs, spoons, knives, keys and padlocks, and a silver cigarette case bearing the engraved inscription "Max Munk, Wien 27."

The new memorial took the form of a symbolic cemetery designed by Polish artists Andrzej Solyga, Zdislaw Pidek, and Marcin Roszcyk. The entire area of the former camp, with its central part covered in slag and marked mass graves, constitutes a monument with a passage through it that symbolises the last stage of life. At the end of the passage there is a wall with names of over 200 Jewish communities whose members were murdered at Belzec. The memorial museum is built in the shape of a train entering the camps unloading ramp. The memorial museum was opened on June 3, 2004, by the Polish President Aleksander Kwasniewski. He was accompanied by representatives from the Polish government, the American Jewish Committee, and the United States Holocaust Museum, Washington, D.C., United States of America.

It is a fitting memorial to the hell called Belzec.

Illustrations and Sources

Photographs

Cover Photograph: SS-men outside the *Kommandantur*—(Regional Museum Tomaszow Lubelski)

Introduction: Chris Webb—Belzec Station Sign—July 2002 (Chris Webb Private Archive).

Cover Photograph With Caption: SS-men outside the *Kommandantur*—Unknown, Fritz Tauscher, Reinhold Feix, Unknown, Max Gringers, Ernst Zierke, Lorenz Hackenholt, Arthur Dachsel, and Heinrich Barbl. (Regional Museum Tomaszow Lubelski)

Fig. 1. Belzec Village (Chris Webb Private Archive)

Fig. 2. Belzec railway station—German soldiers winter 1940 (Chris Webb Private Archive)

Fig. 3. Belzec railway station—German troops by cattle car (Chris Webb Private Archive)

Fig. 4. Belzec—German soldiers 1940 (Chris Webb Private Archive)

Fig. 5. Tomaszow Lubelski (Chris Webb Private Archive)

Fig. 6. Jews from Tomaszow Lubeslski en route to Belzec labor camp (Regional Museum Tomaszow Lubelski)

Fig. 7. Jewish inmates from the labor camp pose with guard (Regional Museum Tomaszow Lubelski)

Fig. 8. Building the Otto Line (Chris Webb Private Archive)

Fig. 9. Belzec labor camp—Jew Shot at the Latrine (Regional Museum Tomaszow Lubelski)

Fig. 10. Belzec Goods Station—Winter 1940 (Chris Webb Private Archive)

Fig. 11. Belzec Gypsy camp (Ghetto Fighters House, Israel)

Fig. 12. Belzec Gypsy camp—Gypsy King Kwiek at the gates (Regional Museum Tomaszow Lubelski)

Fig. 13. Belzec Gypsy camp—Women (Regional Museum Tomaszow Lubelski)

Fig. 14. Belzec Gypsy camp—Children (Regional Museum Tomaszow Lubelski)

Fig. 15. Belzec *Kommandantur* (Regional Museum Tomaszow Lubelski)

Fig. 16. *Trawnikimänner* at the entrance to the Belzec Death Camp. From left to right: Trautwein, Samuel, Rosenholz, unknown, Kunz, unknown, unknown (Regional Museum Tomaszow Lubelski).

Fig. 17. Josef Oberhauser, Fritz Jirmann, Kurt Franz—Road entrance of the Belzec *Kommandantur* (Ghetto Fighters House, Israel)

Fig. 18. Johann Schwarzenbacher, Christian Wirth, Jurgen Lassmann (Ghetto Fighters House, Israel)

Fig. 19. Odilo Globocnik—Gauleiter of Vienna (Chris Webb Private Archive)

Fig. 20. Belzec death camp—Jewish *Kapo's* by the Sorting Sheds (Berko Nachitigall holding stick (Regional Museum Tomaszow Lubelski)

Fig. 21. Polish mechanics with Commandant Hering's car (Ghetto Fighters House, Israel)

Fig. 22. Erwin Fichtner exits the administration building—Armoury to the right (Regional Museum Tomaszow Lubelski)

Fig. 23. Belzec Death Camp—Rudolf Kamm by the sorting sheds (Regional Museum Tomaszow Lubelski)

Fig. 24. Rudolf Gockel—Reichsbahn Official for Belzec Station (Chris Webb Private Archive)

Fig. 25. Transport from Drohobycz to Belzec, August 1942 (Wiener Library)

Fig. 26. Kurt Franz and unknown SS Officer by the Sorting Sheds (Ghetto Fighters House, Israel)

Fig. 27. Rudolf Kamm without SS cap by the Sorting Sheds (Regional Museum Tomaszow Lubelski)

Fig. 28. Lorenz Hackenholt 1942 (Chris Webb Archive – courtesy of Mike Tregenza)

Fig. 29. Gottlieb Hering, Paul Groth, Unknown, Unknown, Kurt Bolender, and Ernst Zierke celebrate (Ghetto Fighters House, Israel)

Fig. 30. Heinrich Unverhau at the rear of the photo (wearing glasses) at Belzec (Ghetto Fighters House, Israel)

Fig. 31. Siegfried Graetschus (Ghetto Fighters House, Israel)

Fig. 32. Gottfried Schwarz (Regional Museum Tomaszow Lubelski)

Fig. 33. Ivan Huzjia – Ukrainian Guard – Wirth's Driver and Gassing Mechanic (Ghetto Fighters House, Israel)

Fig. 34. Johann Niemann (Ghetto Fighters House, Israel)

Fig. 35. Hans Girtzig (Ghetto Fighters House, Israel)

Fig. 36. Robert Juhrs in Italy – far right. (Ghetto Fighters House, Israel)

Fig. 37. Three *Trawnikimänner* in the Komadowski Bar Belzec; Stefan Zadziol, Pitnowy, Genrikh, and Edward Wlasiuk (Ghetto Fighters House, Israel)

Fig. 38. Two unknown Ukrainians relaxing (Ghetto Fighters House, Israel)

Fig. 39. Kessler's Mill—unknown Ukrainian officer (Ghetto Fighters House, Israel)

Fig. 40. Two *Trawnikimaner* at Belzec; Boris Kotychin and Stefan Zadziol (Regional Museum Tomaszow Lubelski)

Fig. 41. Two unknown *Trawnikimänner* with bicycles in Belzec (Ghetto Fighters House, Israel)

Fig. 42. Heini Schmidt in Italy (Chris Webb Archive – courtesy of Mike Tregenza)

Fig. 43. Three Ukrainian *Trawnikimänner* from Belzec death camp (Ghetto Fighters House, Israel)

Fig. 44. Rawa Ruska station (Chris Webb Private Archive)

Fig. 45. Belzec railway station fire drill, 1943 (Regional Museum Tomaszow Lubelski)

Fig. 46. Belzec railway station destroyed, 1944 (Regional Museum Tomaszow Lubelski)

Fig. 47. Bernard Wallerang and Heinrich Gley at Poniatowa Jewish labor camp (Ghetto Fighters House, Israel)

Fig. 48. Belzec locomotive sheds, 1944 (Regional Museum Tomaszow Lubelski)

Fig 49. Josef Oberhauser at his trial in Munich (Ghetto Fighters House, Israel)

Fig. 50. Gassing Outlet Pipe discovered at Belzec—July 2000 (Chris Webb Private Archive)

Fig. 51. Belzec Former Death Camp – Garage Foundations – July 2000 (Chris Webb Private Archive)

Fig. 52. Belzec Former Kommandantur – July 2000 (Chris Webb Private Archive)

Fig. 53. Belzec Foundations – July 2000 (Chris Webb Private Archive)

Fig. 54. Belzec Former Death Camp – General View – July 2000 (Chris Webb Private Archive)

Fig. 55. Belzec Former Death Camp – Generator Housing – July 2000 (Chris Webb Private Archive)

Fig. 56. Belzec Locomotive Sheds – July 2000 (Chris Webb Private Archive)

Fig. 57. Belzec Village – Former Bakery for the Death Camp – July 2000 (Chris Webb Private Archive)

Fig. 58. Eugeniusz Hanejko and Mike Tregenza by the former armoury in Belzec – July 2000 (Chris Webb Private Archive)

Fig 59. Former Kommandantur and SS Quarters – July 2000 (Chris Webb Private Archive)

Fig 60. Belzec Former Trawniki Bar – July 2002 (Chris Webb Private Archive)

Fig 61. Discussion with locals in the back garden of the former SS quarters in Belzec filmed by Billy Rutherford – July 2002 (Chris Webb Private Archive)

Fig. 62. Belzec Former Death Camp – General View – 2004 (Cameron Munro)

Drawings, Maps, and Sources

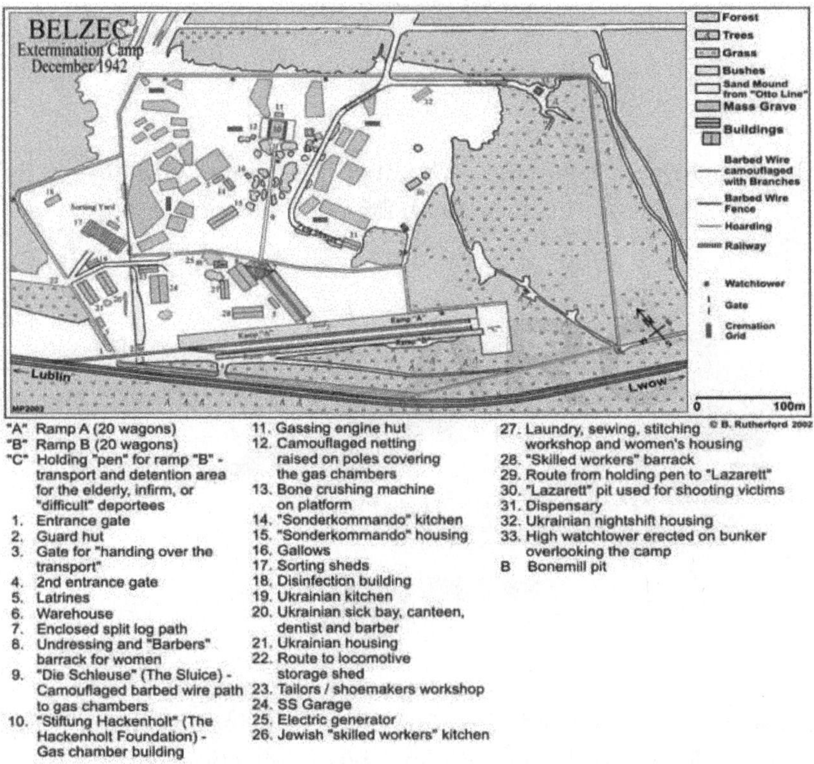

© B. Rutherford 2002

"A" Ramp A (20 wagons)
"B" Ramp B (20 wagons)
"C" Holding "pen" for ramp "B" - transport and detention area for the elderly, infirm, or "difficult" deportees
1. Entrance gate
2. Guard hut
3. Gate for "handing over the transport"
4. 2nd entrance gate
5. Latrines
6. Warehouse
7. Enclosed split log path
8. Undressing and "Barbers" barrack for women
9. "Die Schleuse" (The Sluice) - Camouflaged barbed wire path to gas chambers
10. "Stiftung Hackenholt" (The Hackenholt Foundation) - Gas chamber building
11. Gassing engine hut
12. Camouflaged netting raised on poles covering the gas chambers
13. Bone crushing machine on platform
14. "Sonderkommando" kitchen
15. "Sonderkommando" housing
16. Gallows
17. Sorting sheds
18. Disinfection building
19. Ukrainian kitchen
20. Ukrainian sick bay, canteen, dentist and barber
21. Ukrainian housing
22. Route to locomotive storage shed
23. Tailors / shoemakers workshop
24. SS Garage
25. Electric generator
26. Jewish "skilled workers" kitchen
27. Laundry, sewing, stitching workshop and women's housing
28. "Skilled workers" barrack
29. Route from holding pen to "Lazarett"
30. "Lazarett" pit used for shooting victims
31. Dispensary
32. Ukrainian nightshift housing
33. High watchtower erected on bunker overlooking the camp
B Bonemill pit

Draw. 1. Belzec Camp Dezember 1942: Drawing by William "Billy" Rutherford (Chris Webb Private Collection)

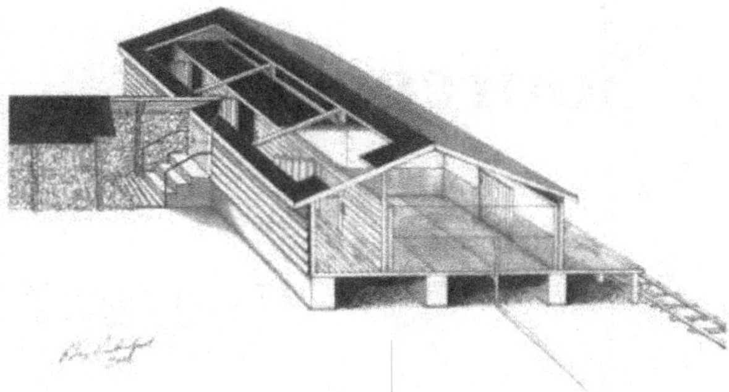

Draw. 2. Belzec First Gas Chamber Drawing: William "Billy" Rutherford (Chris Webb Private Collection)

Draw. 3. Belzec Second Gas Chamber Drawing: William "Billy" Rutherford (Chris Webb Private Collection)

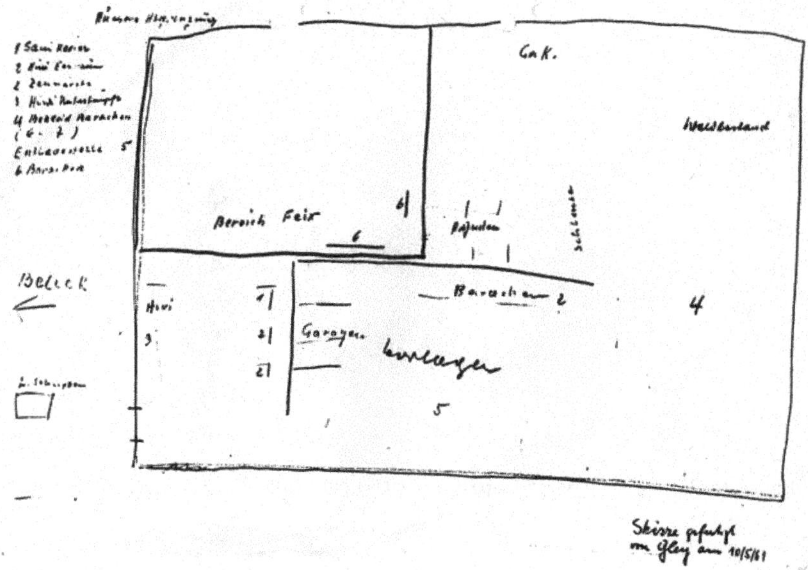

Draw. 4. Heinrich Gley Sketch of Belzec Death Camp 1961

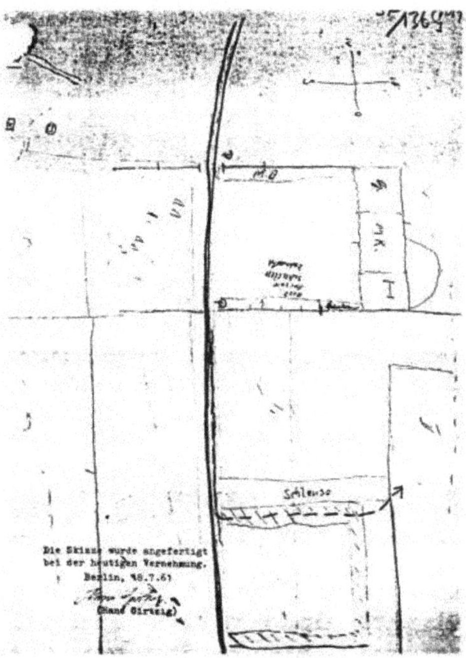

Draw. 5. Hans Girtzig Sketch of Belzec Death Camp 1961

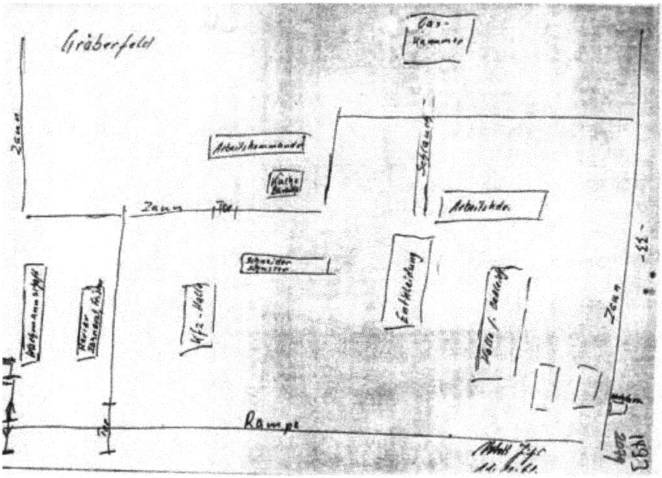

Draw. 6. Robert Juhrs Sketch of Belzec Death Camp 1961

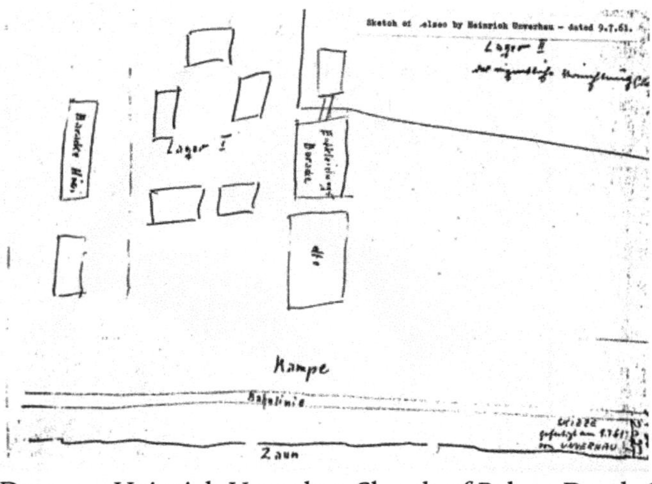

Draw. 7. Heinrich Unverhau Sketch of Belzec Death Camp 1961

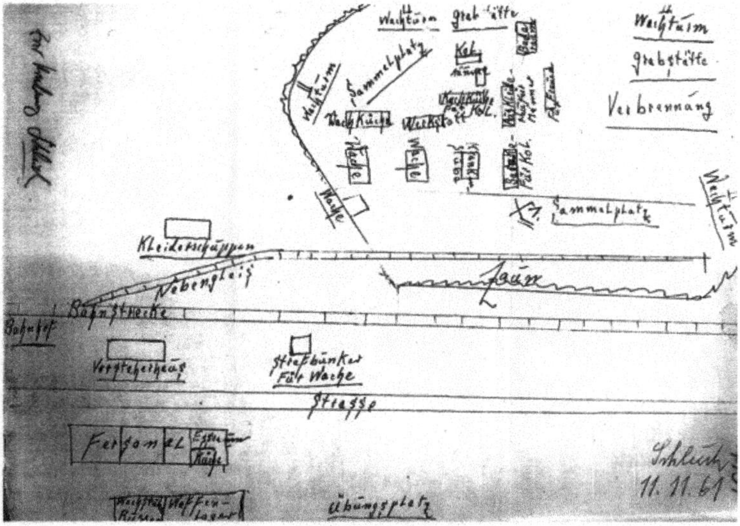

Draw. 8. Karl Schluch Sketch of Belzec Death Camp 1961 (Drawings 4–8 Holocaust Historical Society UK)

Draw. 9. Principal Deportations to Belzec Map (Used with permission from Sir Martin Gilbert)

Documents and Sources

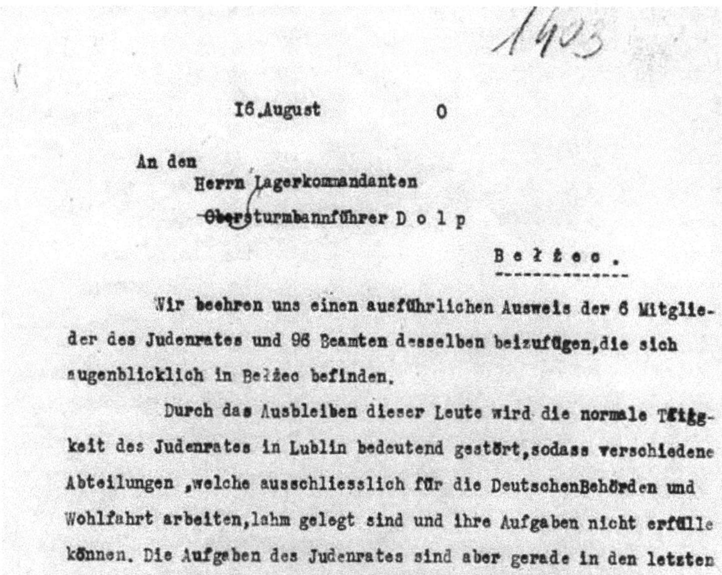

1403

16.August 0

An den
Herrn Lagerkommandanten
Obersturmbannführer D o l p

B e ł ż e c .

Wir beehren uns einen ausführlichen Ausweis der 6 Mitglieder des Judenrates und 96 Beamten desselben beizufügen,die sich augenblicklich in Bełżec befinden.

Durch das Ausbleiben dieser Leute wird die normale Tätigkeit des Judenrates in Lublin bedeutend gestört,sodass verschiedene Abteilungen ,welche ausschliesslich für die DeutschenBehörden und Wohlfahrt arbeiten,lahm gelegt sind und ihre Aufgaben nicht erfülle können. Die Aufgaben des Judenrates sind aber gerade in den letzten Tagen ganz enorm gewachsen,weil eine bedeutende Zahl Jüden aus versbhieden Ortschaften nach Lublin gebracht wurden und der Judenr t muss doch für die Einquartierung,Ernährung und Betreuung derselben sorgen. Um diese vergrösserten Aufgaben pünktlich und gewissenhaft erfüllen zu können und in erster Reihe den Anforderungen und Aufträgen der Deutschen Behörden ohne Verzögerung genügen zu können,gestatten wir uns Euer Wohlgeboren ergebenst zu bitten, die 6 Mitglieder des Judenrates und die 96 Beamten aus Bełżec nach Lublin zu entlassen,um dem Judenrat in Lublin die normale Funktionnierung zu ermöglichen.

Mit vorzüglicher Hochachtung.

Doc. 1. Lublin Judenrat Letter to Hermann Dolp (Yad Vashem)

Standort: Zamosc

Kreisstandort:

Distriktstandort: Lublin

Stand: 1. März 1942

St. = Stadtgemeinde

Lg. = Landgemeinde

	Lfd. Nr.		Gemeinde bzw. Stadtteil:	Mitgl. d. NSDAP	Mitgl. d. D. Gem.	Reichs dt.	Volks dt.	Gesamt.	Polen	Juden	Sonstige	Gesamt.	Gesamt-Einw.Z.
				Anzahl der:									
14	1	St.	Cieszanow	-	-	-	2	2	1139	4	653	1796	1798
15	2	"	Narol Miasto	1	-	-	-	-	1120	5	80	1205	1205
16	3	"	Tomaszow Lubelski	5	-	27	30	57	5569	800	531	6900	6957
17	4	"	Zamósc	88	92	465	61	528	20071	6580	155 509	27315	27841
	5	Lg.	Belzec	1	-	3	3	6	2354	18	285	2663	2663
18	6	"	Cieszanow	-	-	-	2	2	877	24	4481	5382	5384
19	7	"	Jarczow	-	-	-	-	-	3620	128	2765	6513	6513
20	8	"	Komarow	-	-	3	2	5	9714	2968	1549	14231	14236
21	9	"	Kotlice	-	-	7	-	7	5226	112	3245	8583	8590
22	10	"	Krasnobrod	-	-	4	-	4	10969	985	16	11970	11974
23	11	"	Krynice	-	-	-	-	-	8612	54	20	8686	8686
24	12	"	Labunie	-	-	27	-	27	8341	34	66	[illegible]	8468
25	13	"	Laszczow	-	-	-	-	-	5040	466	5652	11158	11158
			Übertrag a. Blatt 2:	95	92	536	100	636	82652	12178	20007	11483	115473

Doc. 2. Zamosc Area Census, March 1942 (Holocaust Historical Society UK)

Odpis z oryginału.

Lublin,den 17.III.1942.
Ref.II R./We.

V e r m e r k

Ich erhielt am 4.3.42.ein Fernschreiben der Regierung Krakau, unterzeichnet vom Herrn Abteilungspraesidenten Dr.Siebert,in welchem der Schlusssatz wie folgt lautet:
"Ich bitte,dem SS-und Polizeifuehrer in Lublin bei seinen Massnahmen beihilfisch zu sein."
Am 7.III.kam ein Anruf von der Regierung,Herrn Major Ragger,der im Zusammenhang mit der Judenaussiedlung aus Mielec in den Distrikt Lublin stand und in welchem ausdruecklich verlangt wurde, das Einvernehmen mit dem SS-und Polizeifuehrer herzustellen und zu pflegen und dass auf dieses Einvernehmen groesster Wert gelegt wird.Ich versuche nun sofort,mit Stabsfuehrer Nemez in Verbindung zu treten.Dreitaegige,kurzfristig augeinander folgende Anrufe blieben ohne Erfolg.Erst nachdem ich mich mit den Personalamt der SS in Verbindung gesetzt hatte,wurde mir der Bescheid,dass Stabsfuehrer Nemez in Urlaub ist.Am 12.3.42.wurde ich an Obersturmfuehrer Pohl verwiesen,der aber auch nicht der zustaendige Sachbearbeiter fuer Judenaussiedlungen war.Er verwies mich an Hauptsturmfuehrer Hoefle,Schreckkaserne,Telefon 1570/25/Nach Dienstschluss unter 2004 zu erreichen/.Mit Hstf.Hoefle vereinbarte ich fuer Montag den 16.3.42 eine Unterredung.und zwarum 17.30.Im Laufe der Unterredung wurde folgendes von Hstf.Hoefle erklaert:
1/Es ware zweckmaessig,die in der Distrikt Lublin kommenden Judentransporte schon auf der Abgangsstation in arbeitseinsatzfaehige und nicht arbeitseisatzfaehige Juden zu teilen.Wenn diese Auseinanderhaltung auf der Abgangsstation nicht moeglich ist, muesste man evtl.dazu uebergehen,den Transport in Lublin nach den obengenannten Gesichtapunkten zu trennen.
2/Nichteinsatzfaehige Juden kommen saemtlich nach Belzec,der aussersten Grenzstation im Kreise Zamosz.
3/Hstuf.Hoefle ist daran,ein grosses Lager zu bauen,in welchem die einsatzfaehigen Juden nach ihren Berufen karteimaessig erfasst und von dort angefordert werden koennen.
4/Piaski wird von polnischen Juden freigemacht und wird Sammelpunkt fuer aus dem Reich kommende Juden.
5/Trawnicki wird vorlaufig mit Juden belegt.
6/H.fragt,wo auf der Strecke Dęblin-Trawnicki 60000 Juden ausgeladen werden koennen.Ueber die jetzt von uns aus laufenden Judentransporte orientiert,erklaerte H.dass von den 500 in Susiec angekommenen Juden die nicht arbeitsfaehigen aussortiert und nach Belzec geschickt werden koennten.Laut Fernschreiben der Regierung vom 4.3.42 rollt ein Judentransport aus dem Protektorat mit der Bestimmungsstatim Trawnicki.Diese Juden sind nicht in Trawnicki ausgeladen,sondern nach Izbica gebracht worden.Eine Anfrage des Kreishauptmannes Zamosz,von dort 200 Juden zur Arbeit heranziehen zu koennen,wurde von H.bejaht.
Abschliessend erklaerte er,er koenne taeglich 4 - 5 Transporte zu 1000 Juden mit der Zielstation Belzec aufnehmen.Diese Juden kamen ueber die Grenze und wuerden nie mehr ins Generalgouvernement zuruckkommen.

Reuter.

Doc. 3. Reuter memorandum of a meeting with Höfle, dated 17 March, 1942 (Yad Vashem)

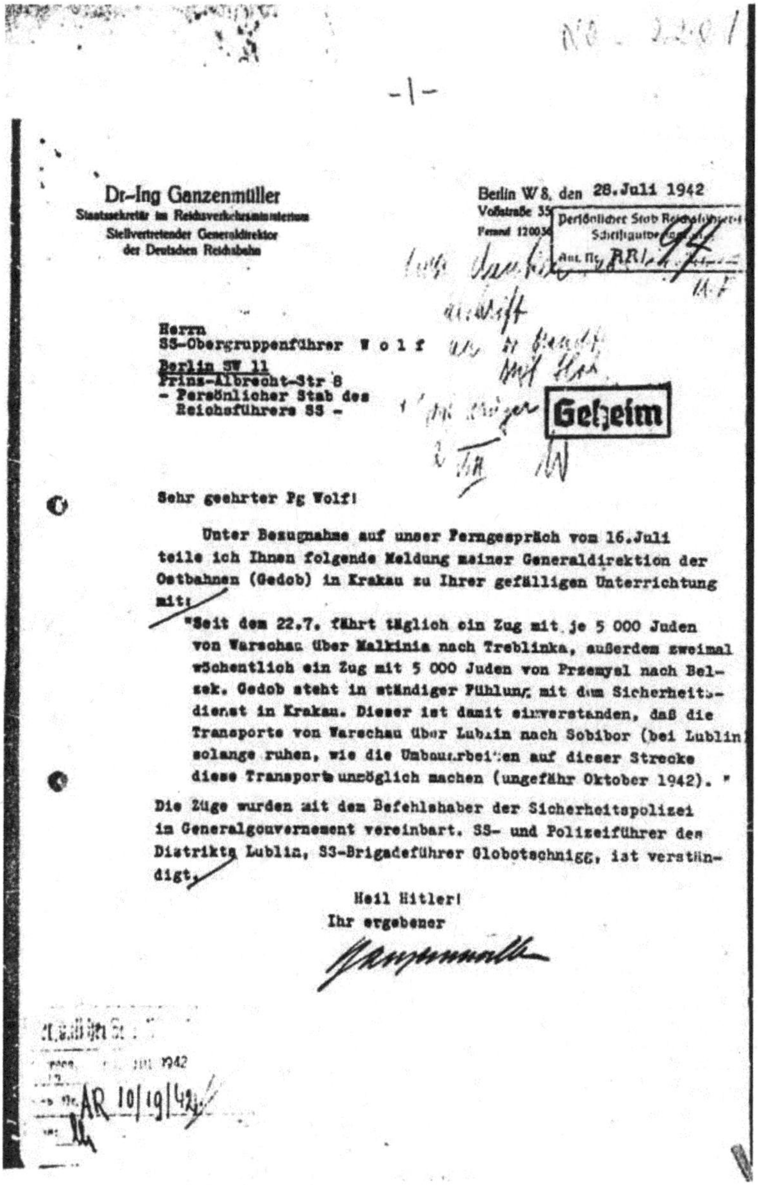

-1-

Dr.-Ing Ganzenmüller
Staatssekretär im Reichsverkehrsministerium
Stellvertretender Generaldirektor
der Deutschen Reichsbahn

Berlin W 8, den 28. Juli 1942
Voßstraße 35
Fernruf 12003

Herrn
SS-Obergruppenführer W o l f
Berlin SW 11
Prinz-Albrecht-Str 8
- Persönlicher Stab des
Reichsführers SS -

Geheim

Sehr geehrter Pg Wolf!

Unter Bezugnahme auf unser Ferngespräch vom 16. Juli teile ich Ihnen folgende Meldung meiner Generaldirektion der Ostbahnen (Gedob) in Krakau zu Ihrer gefälligen Unterrichtung mit:

"Seit dem 22.7. fährt täglich ein Zug mit je 5 000 Juden von Warschau über Malkinia nach Treblinka, außerdem zweimal wöchentlich ein Zug mit 5 000 Juden von Przemysl nach Belzek. Gedob steht in ständiger Fühlung mit dem Sicherheitsdienst in Krakau. Dieser ist damit einverstanden, daß die Transporte von Warschau über Lublin nach Sobibor (bei Lublin) solange ruhen, wie die Umbauarbeiten auf dieser Strecke diese Transporte unmöglich machen (ungefähr Oktober 1942)."

Die Züge wurden mit dem Befehlshaber der Sicherheitspolizei im Generalgouvernement vereinbart. SS- und Polizeiführer des Distrikts Lublin, SS-Brigadeführer Globotschnigg, ist verständigt.

Heil Hitler!
Ihr ergebener
Ganzenmüller

AR 10/19/42

Doc. 4. Letter from Ganzenmuller, State Secretary for Transport to Karl Wolf (Bundesarchiv Koblenz)

Sicherungsbezirk Nord
Einsatzkommando
5 Komp. Pol. B. 24

Rawa Ruska, den 31.Okt.1942.
Straße der Wehrmacht Nr.26
Tel.-Nr. 136

II./Pol. 24
Eing. [illegible] Nov. 1942

1) In der Zeit vom 25. mit 31. Oktober wurden befehlsgemäß behandelt:

a) Banditen	: -	
b) Juden	: 8	(Transportzug entsprungen)
zusammen	: 8	

In der gleichen Zeit wurden festgenommen:

a) Banditen	: 3	
b) Verbotener Waffenbesitz	: 1	
c) Geisteskranke	: 1	
d) Juden	: 20	(Umsiedlungswohnort unerlaubt verlassen u.von Transportzügen abgesprungen).
e) politisch Verdächtige	: 1	
f) Schleichhändler	: 3	
g) Arbeitsscheue	: 3	(hiervon 1 Russe).
zusammen	: 32	

In das Zwangsarbeitslager Lemberg eingewiesen: 2

Sipo.Rawa Ruska überstellt	: 1	(Russe,a.l.g).
Sipo.Sokal überstellt	: 1	
¼-Sonderkdo.Belzec zugeführt	: 5	Juden
Juden umgesiedelt	: 1	Jude.

2) Am 25.10.42 wurden in Zusammenarbeit mit dem Gend.-Zug 250 Personen und am 26.10.42 - 80 Personen festgenommen und dem Arbeitsamt Rawa Ruska zur Überprüfung wegen Arbeitseinsatz nach Deutschland überstellt.

3) Am 28.10.42 wurden in Kamionka-Strumilowa 1023 Juden umgesiedelt. Kam.-Strum. ist somit frei von Juden.

./.

Doc. 5. Polizei Battalion 24 Report from Rawa Ruska to SS Sonderkommando Belzec and others (USHMM Washington DC)

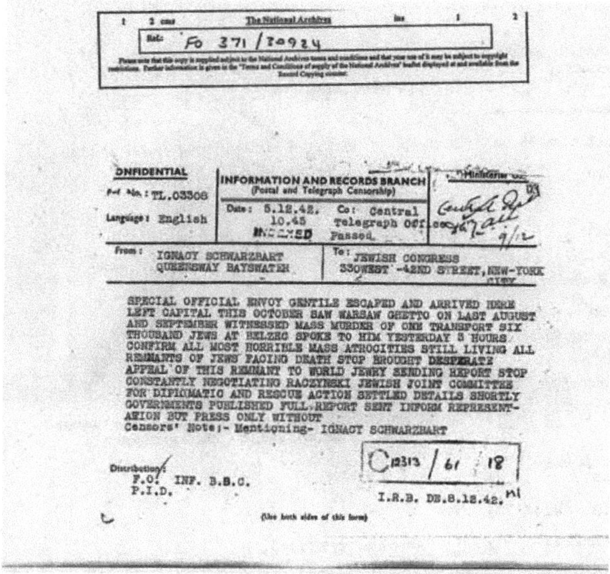

The National Archives
Ref.: FO 371/30924

ONFIDENTIAL
Ref No.: TL.03308
Language: English

INFORMATION AND RECORDS BRANCH
(Postal and Telegraph Censorship)

Date: 5.12.42. 10.45
Co: Central Telegraph Office
Passed

From: IGNACY SCHWARZBART
QUEENSWAY BAYSWATER

To: JEWISH CONGRESS
330WEST -42ND STREET, NEW-YORK CITY

SPECIAL OFFICIAL ENVOY GENTILE ESCAPED AND ARRIVED HERE
LEFT CAPITAL THIS OCTOBER SAW WARSAW GHETTO ON LAST AUGUST
AND SEPTEMBER WITNESSED MASS MURDER OF ONE TRANSPORT SIX
THOUSAND JEWS AT BELZEC SPOKE TO HIM YESTERDAY 3 HOURS
CONFIRM ALL MOST HORRIBLE MASS ATROCITIES STILL LIVING ALL
REMNANTS OF JEWS FACING DEATH STOP BROUGHT DESPERATE
APPEAL OF THIS REMNANT TO WORLD JEWRY SENDING REPORT STOP
CONSTANTLY NEGOTIATING RACZYNSKI JEWISH JOINT COMMITTEE
FOR DIPLOMATIC AND RESCUE ACTION SETTLED DETAILS SHORTLY
GOVERNMENTS PUBLISHED FULL REPORT SENT INFORM REPRESENT-
ATION BUT PRESS ONLY WITHOUT
Censors' Note:- Mentioning- IGNACY SCHWARZBART

C12313/61/18

Distribution:
F.O. INF. B.B.C.
P.I.D.

I.R.B. DB.8.12.42.

Doc. 6. Ignacy Schwarzbart Telegram regarding gassings at Belzec August 1942 (National Archives Kew)

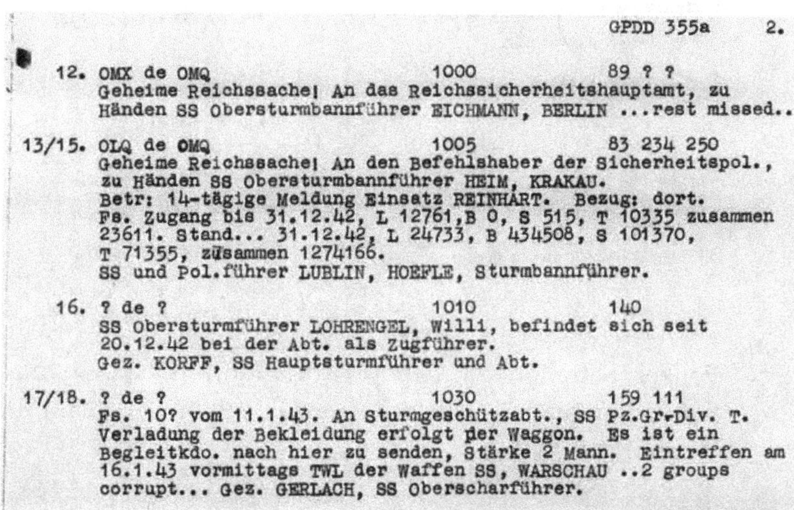

GPDD 355a 2.

12. OMX de OMQ 1000 89 ? ?
Geheime Reichssache! An das Reichssicherheitshauptamt, zu Händen SS Obersturmbannführer EICHMANN, BERLIN ...rest missed..

13/15. OLQ de OMQ 1005 83 234 250
Geheime Reichssache! An den Befehlshaber der Sicherheitspol., zu Händen SS Obersturmbannführer HEIM, KRAKAU.
Betr: 14-tägige Meldung Einsatz REINHART. Bezug: dort.
Fs. Zugang bis 31.12.42, L 12761, B 0, S 515, T 10335 zusammen 23611. Stand... 31.12.42, L 24733, B 434508, S 101370, T 71355, züsammen 1274166.
SS und Pol.führer LUBLIN, HOEFLE, Sturmbannführer.

16. ? de ? 1010 140
SS Obersturmführer LOHRENGEL, Willi, befindet sich seit 20.12.42 bei der Abt. als Zugführer.
Gez. KORFF, SS Hauptsturmführer und Abt.

17/18. ? de ? 1030 159 111
Fs. 10? vom 11.1.43. An Sturmgeschützabt., SS Pz.Gr-Div. T.
Verladung der Bekleidung erfolgt per Waggon. Es ist ein Begleitkdo. nach hier zu senden, Stärke 2 Mann. Eintreffen am 16.1.43 vormittags TWL der Waffen SS, WARSCHAU ..2 groups corrupt... Gez. GERLACH, SS Oberscharführer.

Doc. 7. Höfle—Decoded Message by British Intelligence January 1943 (National Archives Kew)

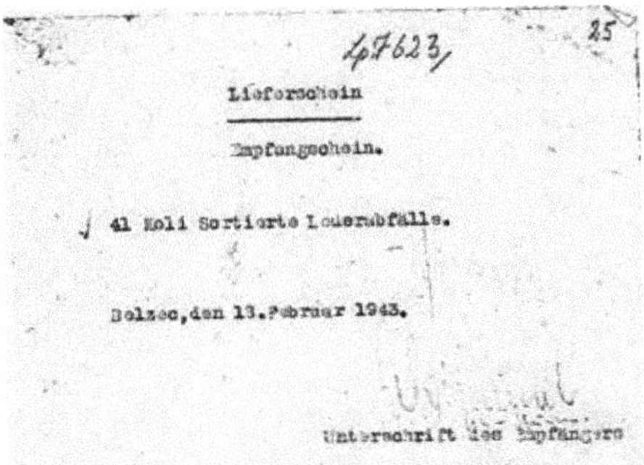

47623 25

Lieferschein

Empfangschein.

41 Koli Sortierte Lederabfälle.

Belzec, den 13. Februar 1943.

Unterschrift des Empfängers

Doc. 8. Belzec Delivery Note Sorted Leather Waste (Holocaust Historical Society UK)

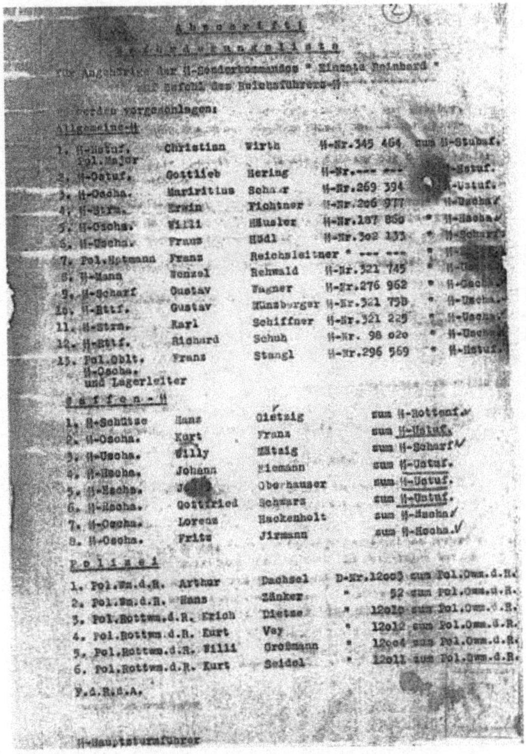

Abschrift!

Beförderungsliste

für Angehörige des SS-Sonderkommandos " Einsatz Reinhard "
auf Befehl des Reichsführers-SS

[illegible] werden vorgeschlagen:

Allgemeine-SS

1. SS-Hstuf. Pol. Major	Christian	Wirth	SS-Nr. 345 464	zum SS-Stubaf.
2. SS-Ostuf.	Gottlieb	Hering	SS-Nr. --- ---	[illegible]	SS-Hstuf.
3. SS-Oscha.	Maritius	Schw[illegible]r	SS-Nr. 269 394	[illegible]	SS-Ustuf.
4. SS-Strm.	Erwin	Fichtner	SS-Nr. 206 977	[illegible]	SS-Uscha.
5. SS-Oscha.	Willi	Häusler	SS-Nr. 187 869	"	SS-Hscha.
6. SS-Uscha.	Franz	Hödl	SS-Nr. 302 133	"	SS-Scharf.
7. Pol. Hptmann	Franz	Reichsleitner	" --- ---	"	[illegible]
8. SS-Mann	Wenzel	Rehwald	SS-Nr. 321 745	"	SS-U[illegible]
9. SS-Scharf	Gustav	Wagner	SS-Nr. 276 962	"	SS-Osch[illegible]
10. SS-Rttf.	Gustav	Münzberger	SS-Nr. 321 758	"	SS-Uscha.
11. SS-Strm.	Karl	Schiffner	SS-Nr. 321 229	"	SS-Uscha.
12. SS-Rttf.	Richard	Schuh	SS-Nr. 98 020	"	SS-Usch[illegible]
13. Pol. Oblt. SS-Oscha. und Lagerleiter	Franz	Stangl	SS-Nr. 296 569	"	SS-Hstuf.

Waffen-SS

1. SS-Schütze	Hans	Gietzig	zum SS-Rottenf.
2. SS-Oscha.	Kurt	Franz	zum SS-Ustuf.
3. SS-Uscha.	Willy	Mätzig	zum SS-Scharf
4. SS-Hscha.	Johann	Niemann	zum SS-Ustuf.
5. SS-Hscha.	J[illegible]	Oberhauser	zum SS-Ustuf.
6. SS-Hscha.	Gottfried	Schwarz	zum SS-Ustuf.
7. SS-Oscha.	Lorenz	Hackenholt	zum SS-Hscha.
8. SS-Oscha.	Fritz	Jirmann	zum SS-Hscha.

Polizei

1. Pol.Wm.d.R.	Arthur	Dachsel	D-Nr. 12003	zum Pol.Owm.d.R.
2. Pol.Wm.d.R.	Hans	Zänker	" 52	zum Pol.Owm.d.R.
3. Pol.Rottwm.d.R.	Erich	Dietze	" 12010	zum Pol.Owm.d.R.
4. Pol.Rottwm.d.R.	Kurt	Vey	" 12012	zum Pol.Owm.d.R.
5. Pol.Rottwm.d.R.	Willi	Großmann	" 12004	zum Pol.Owm.d.R.
6. Pol.Rottwm.d.R.	Kurt	Seidel	" 12011	zum Pol.Owm.d.R.

F.d.R.d.A.

SS-Hauptsturmführer

Doc. 9. Einsatz Reinhard Promotion List March 1943 (Yad Vashem)

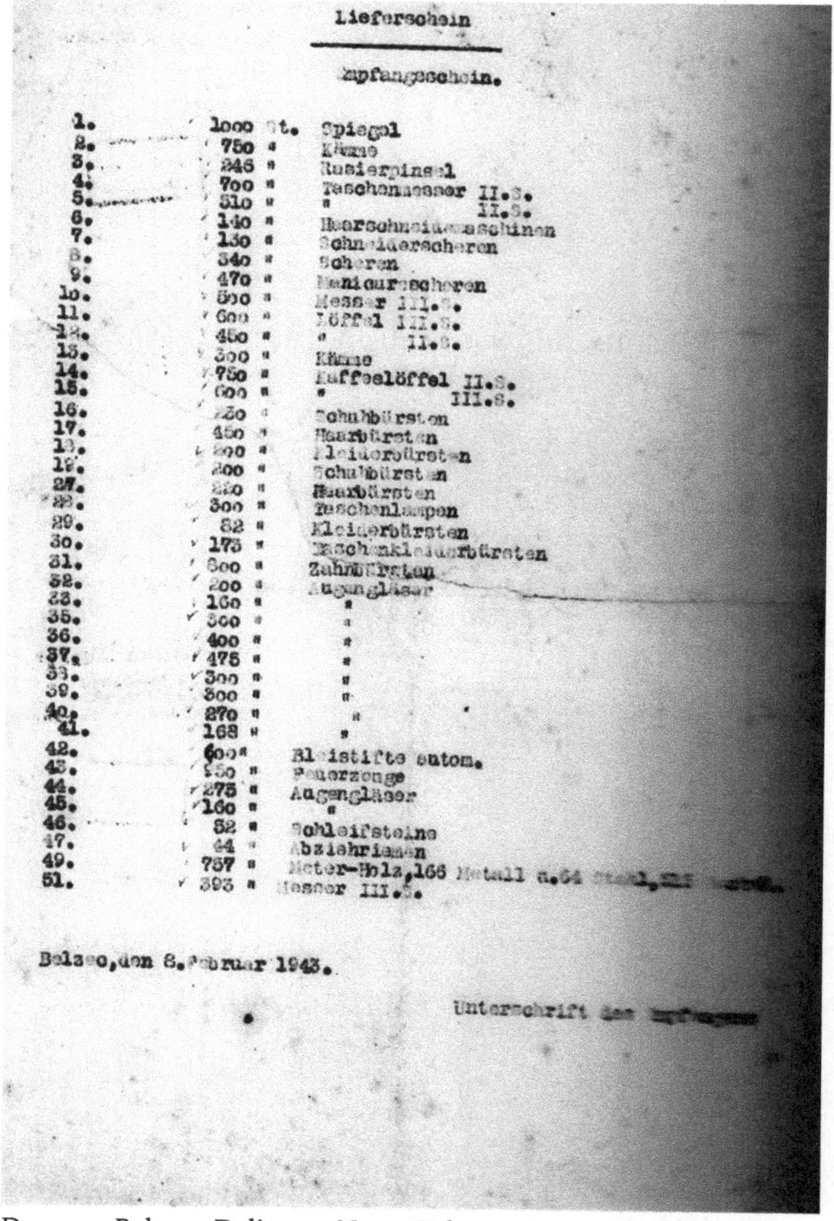

Lieferschein

Empfangsschein.

1.	1000 St.	Spiegel
2.	750 "	Kämme
3.	246 "	Rasierpinsel
4.	700 "	Taschenmesser II.S.
5.	510 "	" III.S.
6.	140 "	Haarschneidemaschinen
7.	130 "	Schneiderscheren
8.	340 "	Scheren
9.	470 "	Manicurescheren
10.	500 "	Messer III.S.
11.	600 "	Löffel III.S.
12.	450 "	" II.S.
13.	300 "	Kämme
14.	750 "	Kaffeelöffel II.S.
15.	600 "	" III.S.
16.	220 "	Schuhbürsten
17.	450 "	Haarbürsten
18.	200 "	Kleiderbürsten
19.	200 "	Schuhbürsten
27.	220 "	Haarbürsten
28.	300 "	Taschenlampen
29.	82 "	Kleiderbürsten
30.	173 "	Taschenkleiderbürsten
31.	800 "	Zahnbürsten
32.	200 "	Augengläser
33.	160 "	"
35.	300 "	"
36.	400 "	"
37.	475 "	"
38.	300 "	"
39.	300 "	"
40.	270 "	"
41.	168 "	"
42.	600 "	Bleistifte autom.
43.	150 "	Feuerzeuge
44.	275 "	Augengläser
45.	160 "	"
46.	82 "	Schleifsteine
47.	44 "	Abziehriemen
49.	757 "	Meter-Holz, 166 Metall u. 64 [illegible]
51.	393 "	Messer III.S.

Belzec, den 8. Februar 1943.

Unterschrift des Empfängers

Doc. 10. Belzec Delivery Note February 1943 (State Museum Majdanek)

Name und Vorname des SS-Angehörigen, der für sich oder seine Braut oder Ehefrau den Fragebogen einreicht:

Wirth, Christian

Dienstgrad: .... SS-Nr.

Sip. Nr.

R. u. S.-Fragebogen

(Von Frauen sinngemäß auszufüllen.)

Name (leserlich schreiben): Wirth, Christian

in SS seit .... Dienstgrad: .... SS-Einheit: ....

in SA von 30.6.1933 bis heute, in HJ von ./. bis ./.

Mitglieds-Nummer in Partei: 420 383 in SS:

geb. am 24.11.1885 zu Oberbalzheim Kreis: Laupheim.

Land: Württ. jetzt Alter: 52 Jahre Glaubensbekenntnis: evang.

Jetziger Wohnsitz: Stuttgart-S. Wohnung: Kauzenhecke 15

Beruf und Berufsstellung: Kriminal-Inspektor, Kommissariatsleiter

Wird öffentliche Unterstützung in Anspruch genommen? Nein

Liegt Berufswechsel vor? Nein

Außerberufliche Fertigkeiten und Berechtigungsscheine (z. B. Führerschein, Sportabzeichen, Sportauszeichnung):

Führerschein Klasse 3, SA-Sportabzeichen.

Staatsangehörigkeit: Deutsch

Ehrenamtliche Tätigkeit: Landeswart d. Kameradschaftsbundes Deutscher Pol. Beamten, u. Ortsgruppenwart von Stgt. des gleichen Bundes.

Dienst im alten Heer: Truppe Gren. Regt. Nr. 123 von 1905 bis 1907
" 1908 " 1910

" " XXXXX ... Res. Inf. Regt. 246 von 1914 bis 1917
" " " " 119 1917 1919

Reichswehr ... 0. von ... bis

Schutzpolizei ... Stuttgart. von 1910 bis 1913

Neue Wehrmacht 0. von ... bis

Letzter Dienstgrad: Off. Stellvertreter

Frontkämpfer: 12.10.1914 bis 6.12.1917 ; verwundet: 1 Mal, Oberarmdurchschuss

Orden und Ehrenabzeichen, einschl. Rettungsmedaille: EK. I. & II. Kl., Gold. u. Silb. Württ. M. Verd. Med. Dienstauszeichnung II. & III. Kl., Ehrenkreuz f. Frontkämpfer, Verw. Abz. i. schw

Personenstand (ledig, verwitwet, geschieden – seit wann): verh. seit 5.11.1910

Welcher Konfession ist der Antragsteller? evang. die zukünftige Braut

(Als Konfession wird auch außer dem herkömmlichen jedes andere gottgläubige Bek.

Ist neben der standesamtlichen Trauung eine kirchliche Trauung vorgesehen? Ja – nein.

Hat neben der standesamtlichen Trauung eine kirchliche Trauung stattgefunden? Ja – XXXX

Gegebenenfalls nach welcher konfessionellen Form? evang.

Ist Ehestands-Darlehen beantragt worden? XX – nein.

Bei welcher Behörde (genaue Anschrift)? ./.

Wann wurde der Antrag gestellt? ./.

Wurde das Ehestands-Darlehen bewilligt? XXXXXXX ./.

Soll das Ehestands-Darlehen beantragt werden? XXXXXX ./.

Bei welcher Behörde (genaue Anschrift)? ./.

RuSV RT SS-Druckerei ... Miesbach (Bayer. Hochland)

Doc. 11. Christian Wirth Fragebogen (Yad Vashem)

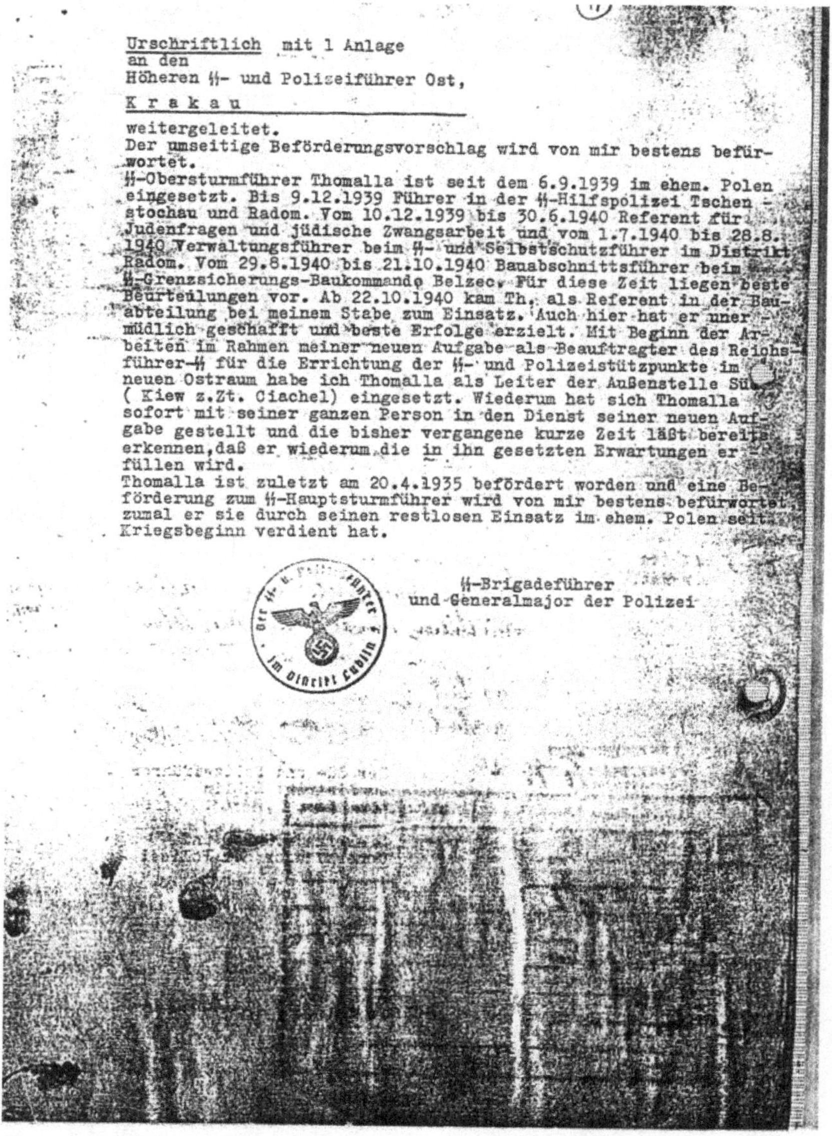

Urschriftlich mit 1 Anlage
an den
Höheren SS- und Polizeiführer Ost,

K r a k a u

weitergeleitet.
Der umseitige Beförderungsvorschlag wird von mir bestens befürwortet.
SS-Obersturmführer Thomalla ist seit dem 6.9.1939 im ehem. Polen eingesetzt. Bis 9.12.1939 Führer in der SS-Hilfspolizei Tschenstochau und Radom. Vom 10.12.1939 bis 30.6.1940 Referent für Judenfragen und jüdische Zwangsarbeit und vom 1.7.1940 bis 28.8.1940 Verwaltungsführer beim SS- und Selbstschutzführer im Distrikt Radom. Vom 29.8.1940 bis 21.10.1940 Bauabschnittsführer beim SS-Grenzsicherungs-Baukommando Belzec. Für diese Zeit liegen beste Beurteilungen vor. Ab 22.10.1940 kam Th. als Referent in der Bauabteilung bei meinem Stabe zum Einsatz. Auch hier hat er unermüdlich geschafft und beste Erfolge erzielt. Mit Beginn der Arbeiten im Rahmen meiner neuen Aufgabe als Beauftragter des Reichsführer-SS für die Errichtung der SS- und Polizeistützpunkte im neuen Ostraum habe ich Thomalla als Leiter der Außenstelle Süd (Kiew z.Zt. Ciachel) eingesetzt. Wiederum hat sich Thomalla sofort mit seiner ganzen Person in den Dienst seiner neuen Aufgabe gestellt und die bisher vergangene kurze Zeit läßt bereits erkennen, daß er wiederum die in ihn gesetzten Erwartungen erfüllen wird.
Thomalla ist zuletzt am 20.4.1935 befördert worden und eine Beförderung zum SS-Hauptsturmführer wird von mir bestens befürwortet, zumal er sie durch seinen restlosen Einsatz im ehem. Polen seit Kriegsbeginn verdient hat.

SS-Brigadeführer
und Generalmajor der Polizei

Doc. 12. Richard Thomalla –Report by Odilo Globocnik (Yad Vashem)

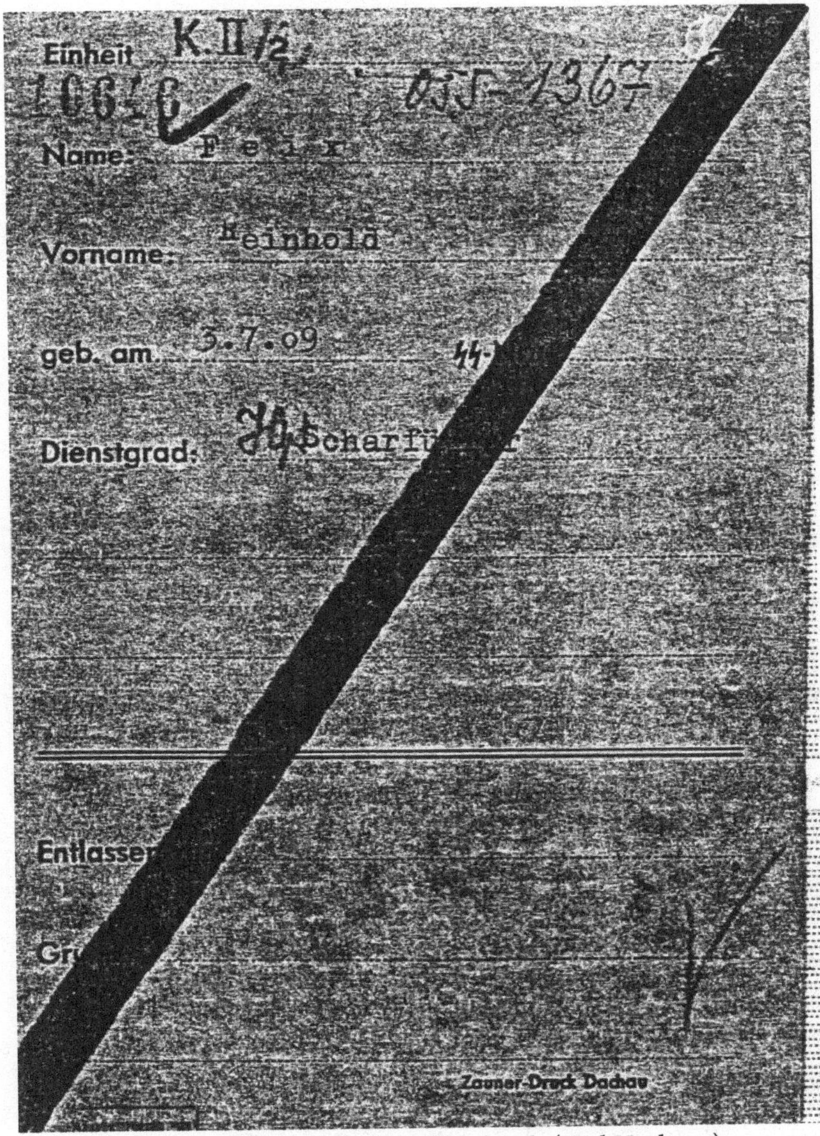
Einheit K.II/2
035-1367
Name: Feix
Vorname: Reinhold
geb. am 3.7.09
Dienstgrad: Scharfü
Entlasse
Gr
Zauner-Druck Dachau

Doc. 13. Reinhold Feix—Cover of Paybook (Yad Vashem)

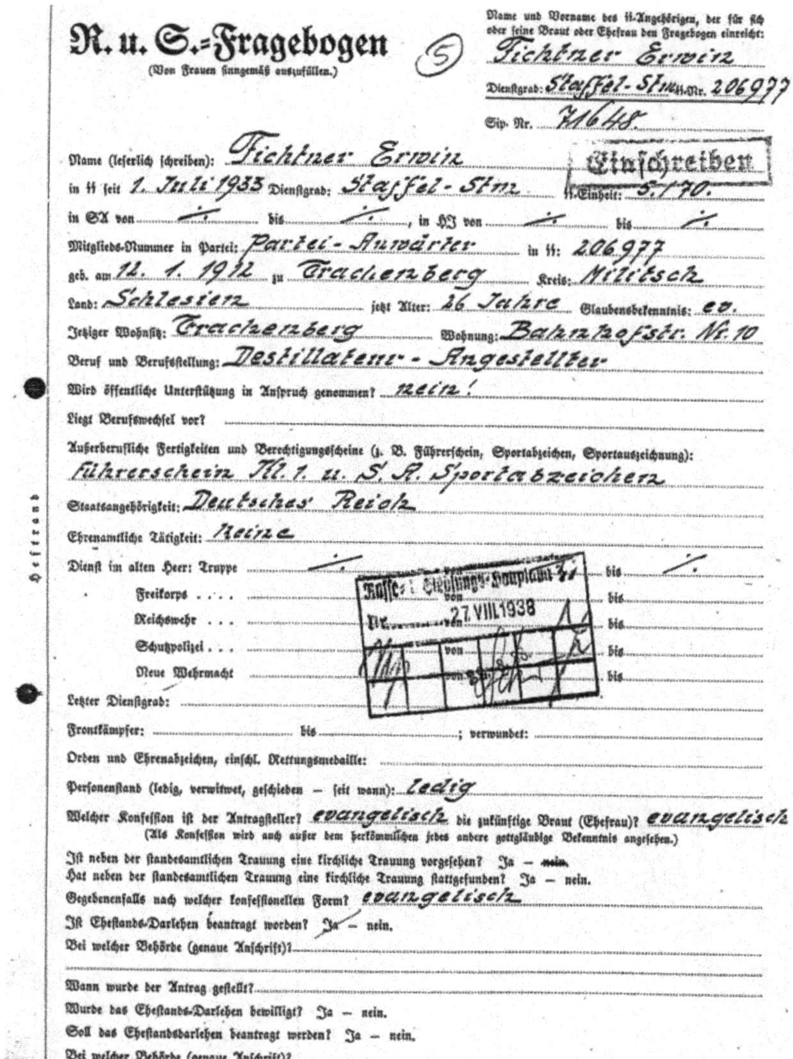

R. u. S.-Fragebogen (5)
(Von Frauen sinngemäß auszufüllen.)

Name und Vorname des SS-Angehörigen, der für sich oder seine Braut oder Ehefrau den Fragebogen einreicht: Fichtner Erwin
Dienstgrad: Staffel-Stm. SS-Nr. 206977
Sip. Nr. 71648.

Einschreiben

Name (leserlich schreiben): Fichtner Erwin
in SS seit 1. Juli 1933 Dienstgrad: Staffel-Stm. SS-Einheit: 5/70.
in SA von ./. bis ./., in HJ von ./. bis ./.
Mitglieds-Nummer in Partei: Partei-Anwärter in SS: 206977
geb. am 12. 1. 1912 zu Trachenberg Kreis: Militsch
Land: Schlesien jetzt Alter: 26 Jahre Glaubensbekenntnis: ev.
Jetziger Wohnsitz: Trachenberg Wohnung: Bahnhofstr. Nr. 10
Beruf und Berufsstellung: Destillateur-Angestellter
Wird öffentliche Unterstützung in Anspruch genommen? nein!
Liegt Berufswechsel vor?
Außerberufliche Fertigkeiten und Berechtigungsscheine (z. B. Führerschein, Sportabzeichen, Sportauszeichnung): Führerschein Kl. 1. u. S. A. Sportabzeichen
Staatsangehörigkeit: Deutsches Reich
Ehrenamtliche Tätigkeit: keine
Dienst im alten Heer: Truppe ./. bis ./.
Freikorps . . . . bis
Reichswehr . . . bis
Schutzpolizei . . . bis
Neue Wehrmacht bis

Kasse: Siedlungs-Hauptamt SS
27. VIII. 1938

Letzter Dienstgrad:
Frontkämpfer: bis ; verwundet:
Orden und Ehrenabzeichen, einschl. Rettungsmedaille:
Personenstand (ledig, verwitwet, geschieden — seit wann): ledig
Welcher Konfession ist der Antragsteller? evangelisch die zukünftige Braut (Ehefrau)? evangelisch
(Als Konfession wird auch außer dem herkömmlichen jedes andere gottgläubige Bekenntnis angesehen.)
Ist neben der standesamtlichen Trauung eine kirchliche Trauung vorgesehen? Ja — ~~nein~~.
Hat neben der standesamtlichen Trauung eine kirchliche Trauung stattgefunden? Ja — nein.
Gegebenenfalls nach welcher konfessionellen Form? evangelisch
Ist Ehestands-Darlehen beantragt worden? ~~Ja~~ — nein.
Bei welcher Behörde (genaue Anschrift)?
Wann wurde der Antrag gestellt?
Wurde das Ehestands-Darlehen bewilligt? Ja — nein.
Soll das Ehestandsdarlehen beantragt werden? Ja — nein.
Bei welcher Behörde (genaue Anschrift)?

SSV R 1 SS-Vordruckverlag W. F. Mayr, Miesbach (Bayer. Hochland)

Doc. 14. Erwin Fichtner—Fragebogen (Yad Vashem)

8763464

Fragebogen

Anlage zum Antrag auf Aufnahme in die Nationalsozialistische Deutsche Arbeiterpartei

A

Vor- und Zuname (bei Frauen auch Mädchenname): Heinrich Barbl

Beruf oder Art der Tätigkeit [1]): Hilfsmonteur

Wohnort [2]): Linz/Donau Wohnung: Landhaus Straße/Platz Nr.

Geburtsort: Sarleinsbach Geburtszeit (Tag, Monat, Jahr): 3. März 1900

Staatsangehörigkeit: Deutsch.R. Wenn staatenlos, frühere Staatsangehörigkeit: Österreich

Sind Sie erbgesund? ja

Vor- und Zuname des Vaters: Alois Schmidhofer

Geburtsort des Vaters: Lembach Geburtszeit des Vaters (Tag, Monat, Jahr): 13.5.1882

Volkszugehörigkeit des Vaters: deutsch

Vor- und Zuname der Mutter (Mädchenname!): Theresia Barbl

Geburtsort der Mutter: Sarleinsbach Geburtszeit der Mutter (Tag, Monat, Jahr): 7.2.1877

Volkszugehörigkeit der Mutter: deutsch

B

Familienstand (ledig, verheiratet, verwitwet, geschieden): verheiratet

Vor- und Zuname des Ehegatten (bei Frauen auch Mädchenname!): Maria geb. Stallberger

Geburtsort des Ehegatten: Sarleinsbach Geburtszeit des Ehegatten (Tag, Monat, Jahr): 27.9.1904

Ist der Ehegatte frei von jüdischem oder farbigem Rasseeinschlag? ja

Waren Sie früher mit einem nichtarischen Ehegatten verheiratet? nein

Wodurch ist diese Ehe beendet worden (Tod oder Scheidung)? ----

Wann? ---- Bei Scheidung, durch welches Gericht? ----

Sind Kinder aus dieser Ehe vorhanden? nein Wie viele? ---

C

Haben Sie früher einer Freimaurerloge angehört? nein Welcher? -----

Tag des Eintritts? ---- Tag des Austritts? -----

Welches Amt und welchen Grad haben Sie in der Loge bekleidet? ------

Haben Sie früher einer logenähnlichen Vereinigung (Old Fellows und Druiden-Orden) oder einem Geheimbund angehört? ---- Welcher oder welchem? -----

Fragebogen zum Aufnahmeantrag

Doc. 15. Heinrich Barbl—Fragebogen (Yad Vashem)

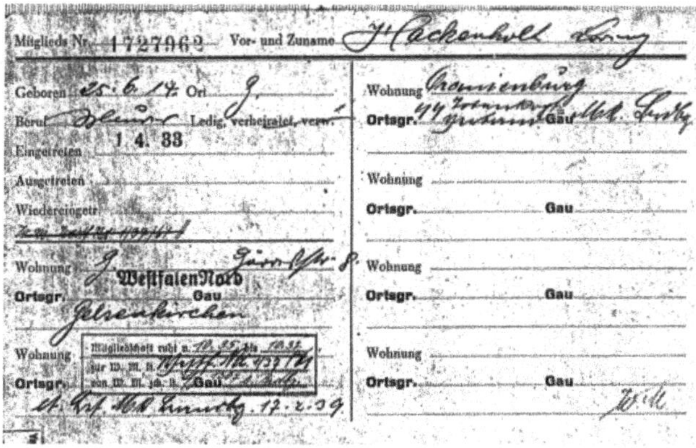

Mitglieds Nr. 1727962 Vor- und Zuname

Geboren 25. 6. 14. Ort

Beruf Ledig, verheiratet, verw.

Eingetreten 1. 4. 33

Ausgetreten

Wiedereingetr.

Wohnung Westfalen Nord

Ortsgr. Gau

Gelsenkirchen

Wohnung

Ortsgr. Gau

Wohnung

Ortsgr. Gau

Wohnung

Ortsgr. Gau

Wohnung

Ortsgr. Gau

Doc. 16. Lorenz Hackenholt (Yad Vashem)

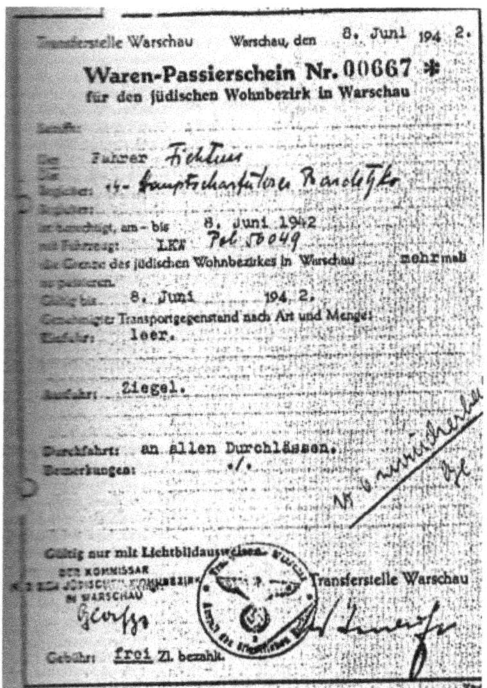

Transferstelle Warschau Warschau, den 8. Juni 1942.

Waren-Passierschein Nr. 00667 *
für den jüdischen Wohnbezirk in Warschau

Der Fahrer Fichtner

ist berechtigt, am - bis 8. Juni 1942

mit Fahrzeug: LKW Pol 50049

die Grenze des jüdischen Wohnbezirkes in Warschau mehrmals zu passieren.

Gültig bis 8. Juni 1942.

Genehmigter Transportgegenstand nach Art und Menge:

Einfuhr: leer.

Ausfuhr: Ziegel.

Durchfahrt: an allen Durchlässen.

Bemerkungen: ./.

Gültig nur mit Lichtbildausweisen.

Der Kommissar für den jüdischen Wohnbezirk in Warschau

Transferstelle Warschau

Gebühr: frei Zl. bezahlt.

Doc. 17. Transferstelle Warschau—Bricks Order June 1942 Fichtner (reproduced in *Letzte Spuren)*

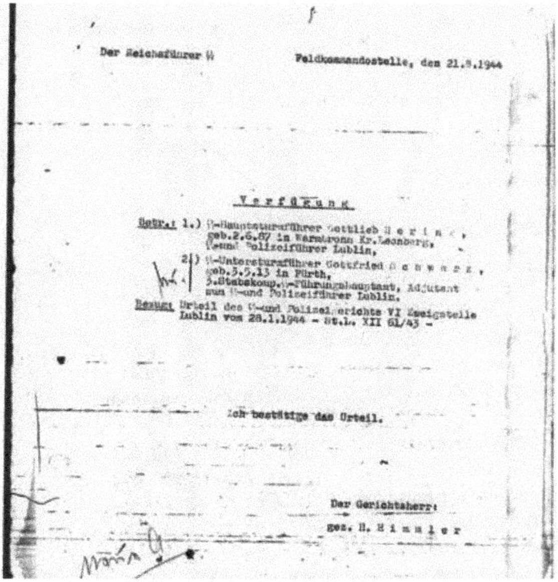

Der Reichsführer SS

Feldkommandostelle, den 21.8.1944

V e r f ü g u n g

Betr.: 1.) SS-Hauptsturmführer Gottlieb H e r i n g ,
geb.2.6.87 in Warmbronn Kr.Leonberg,
SS-und Polizeiführer Lublin,

2.) SS-Untersturmführer Gottfried S c h w a r z ,
geb.3.5.13 in Fürth,
3.Stabskomp.SS-Führungshauptamt, Adjutant
zum SS-und Polizeiführer Lublin.

Bezug: Urteil des SS-und Polizeigerichts VI Zweigstelle
Lublin vom 28.1.1944 - St.L. XII 61/43 -

Ich bestätige das Urteil.

Der Gerichtsherr:
gez. H. H i m m l e r

Doc. 18. Hering and Schwarz—Court Judgement Himmler Letter (NARA Washington)

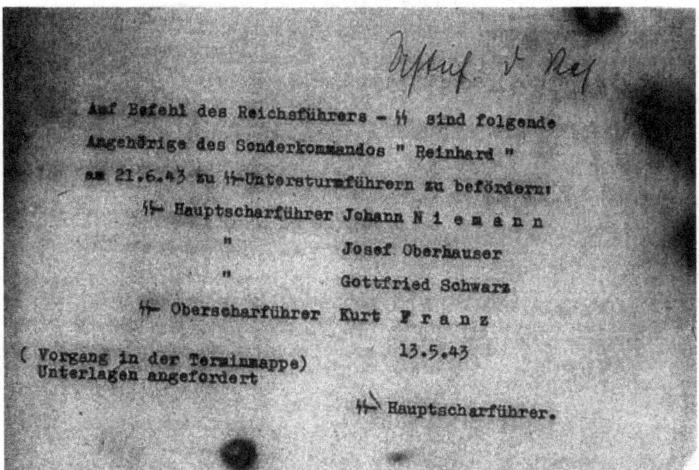

Auf Befehl des Reichsführers - SS sind folgende
Angehörige des Sonderkommandos " Reinhard "
am 21.6.43 zu SS-Untersturmführern zu befördern:

SS- Hauptscharführer Johann N i e m a n n
" Josef Oberhauser
" Gottfried Schwarz
SS- Oberscharführer Kurt F r a n z

13.5.43

(Vorgang in der Terminmappe)
Unterlagen angefordert

SS-Hauptscharführer.

Doc. 19. Johann Niemann—May 1943 (NARA Washington)

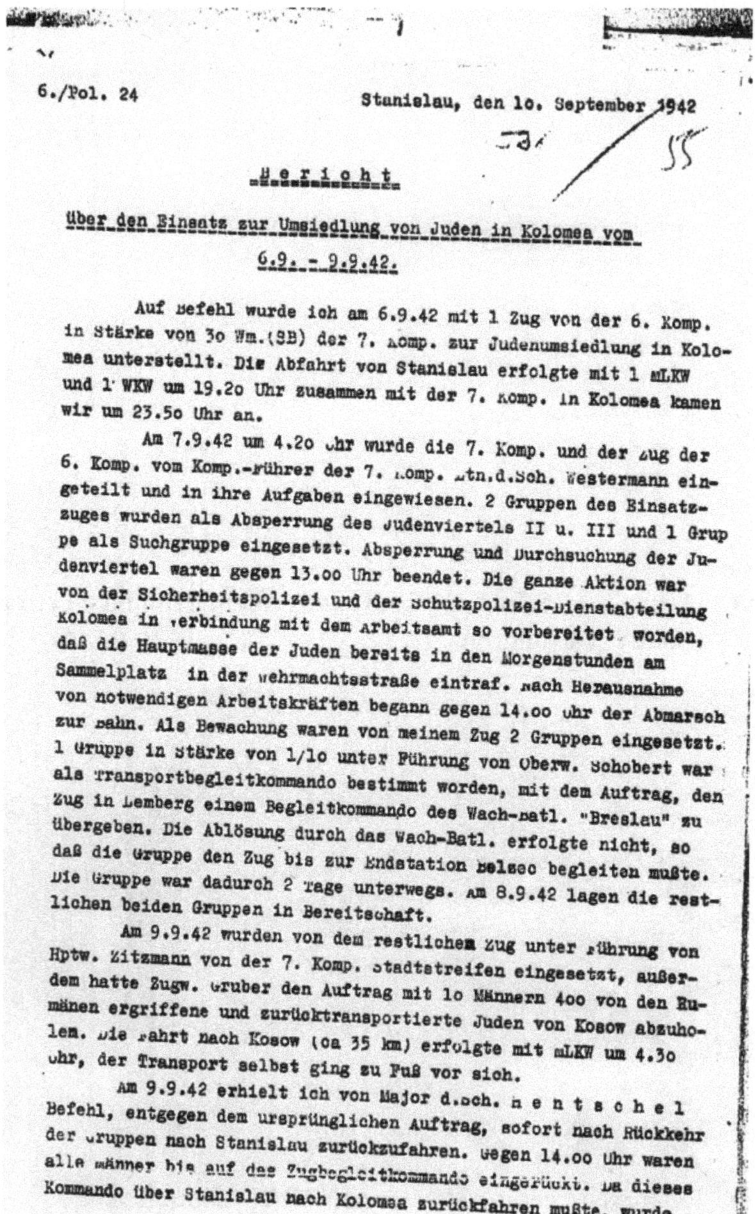

6./Pol. 24

Stanislau, den 1o. September 1942

Bericht

über den Einsatz zur Umsiedlung von Juden in Kolomea vom 6.9. - 9.9.42.

Auf Befehl wurde ich am 6.9.42 mit 1 Zug von der 6. Komp. in Stärke von 3o Wm.(SB) der 7. Komp. zur Judenumsiedlung in Kolomea unterstellt. Die Abfahrt von Stanislau erfolgte mit 1 mLKW und 1 WKW um 19.2o Uhr zusammen mit der 7. Komp. in Kolomea kamen wir um 23.5o Uhr an.

Am 7.9.42 um 4.2o Uhr wurde die 7. Komp. und der Zug der 6. Komp. vom Komp.-Führer der 7. Komp. Ltn.d.Sch. Westermann eingeteilt und in ihre Aufgaben eingewiesen. 2 Gruppen des Einsatzzuges wurden als Absperrung des Judenviertels II u. III und 1 Gruppe als Suchgruppe eingesetzt. Absperrung und Durchsuchung der Judenviertel waren gegen 13.00 Uhr beendet. Die ganze Aktion war von der Sicherheitspolizei und der Schutzpolizei-Dienstabteilung Kolomea in Verbindung mit dem Arbeitsamt so vorbereitet worden, daß die Hauptmasse der Juden bereits in den Morgenstunden am Sammelplatz in der Wehrmachtsstraße eintraf. Nach Herausnahme von notwendigen Arbeitskräften begann gegen 14.00 Uhr der Abmarsch zur Bahn. Als Bewachung waren von meinem Zug 2 Gruppen eingesetzt. 1 Gruppe in Stärke von 1/1o unter Führung von Oberw. Schobert war als Transportbegleitkommando bestimmt worden, mit dem Auftrag, den Zug in Lemberg einem Begleitkommando des Wach-Batl. "Breslau" zu übergeben. Die Ablösung durch das Wach-Batl. erfolgte nicht, so daß die Gruppe den Zug bis zur Endstation Belzec begleiten mußte. Die Gruppe war dadurch 2 Tage unterwegs. Am 8.9.42 lagen die restlichen beiden Gruppen in Bereitschaft.

Am 9.9.42 wurden von dem restlichem Zug unter Führung von Hptw. Zitzmann von der 7. Komp. Stadtstreifen eingesetzt, außerdem hatte Zugw. Gruber den Auftrag mit 1o Männern 400 von den Rumänen ergriffene und zurücktransportierte Juden von Kosow abzuholen. Die Fahrt nach Kosow (ca 35 km) erfolgte mit mLKW um 4.3o Uhr, der Transport selbst ging zu Fuß vor sich.

Am 9.9.42 erhielt ich von Major d.Sch. H e n t s c h e l Befehl, entgegen dem ursprünglichen Auftrag, sofort nach Rückkehr der Gruppen nach Stanislau zurückzufahren. Gegen 14.00 Uhr waren alle Männer bis auf das Zugbegleitkommando eingerückt. Da dieses Kommando über Stanislau nach Kolomea zurückfahren mußte, wurde

Doc. 20. Police Report on the Deportation of Jews in Kolomea to Belzec, September 6–9, 1942 (Yad Vashem)

nanym kierunku, wywołała panikę wśród nich i chęć ukrycia się na pewien, określony czas wśród ludności polskiej. Ponieważ ludność polska z reguły odmawiała , przeto Żydzi mają obecnie żal do Polaków, że w krytycznych dla nich chwilach nie przyszli z pomocą. W związku z tym daje się ~~często~~ słyszeć takie zdanie "Nu jeszcze się wojna nie skończyła, jeszcze nie wiecie, czy będziecie lepsi od nas". Za przechowanie chcieli płacić duże sumy...

W południowym terenie "1" /moje - okręgu lubelskiego/ nastąpiła przerwa w ~~z~~ wysiedleniu i wywożeniu. Wywołało to zmianę w ich usposobieniu i zabrali się do normalnych zajęć. Twierdzą z całą pewnością, że to koniec terroru wobec nich. Datę ustania wywożenia przewidzieli dokładnie. Mówią, że ujęła się za nimi Ameryka, grożąc Niemcom, że podobnie będą postępować z Niemcami w Ameryce.

... W związku z zabiciem w Wąwolnicy kieownika filii ~~urz~~ Urzędu Pracy Władysława Kota, Niemcy w drodze represji rozstrzelali 72 Żydów i 2 Polaków. Prócz tego 20 Polaków aresztowano. Kot był ~~grubsey~~ gorliwy przy rekrutowaniu robotników do Niemiec.
/rzecz działa się w kwietniu 1942 - moje/.

S. 147 Raport z obozu w Bełżcu

"... Obóz wykończono całkowicie na kilka dni przed 17.III.42... Obserwacje ludności /obóz jest w zasięgu wzrokowym i słuchowym mieszkańców budynków kolejowych/ doprowadziły wszystkich do jednego wniosku, że Żydzi w obozie są masowo zabijani. Swiadczą o tym fakty następujące:"...

Wymienia się 11 punktów na dowód wniosku, głównie, że nie ma

(30)

- 53 -

dowozu żywności, do obozu przywozi się wapno, wywozi się wagony z ubraniem, w ciepłe dni daje się odczuć silny smród /to były argumenty na 6 punktów/.

"...7/ Widziano na terenie obozu Żydów w bieliźnie.

8/ na terenie obozu znajdują się trzy baraki, które nawet w dziesiątej części Żydów nie pomieszczą.

9/ W rejonie obozu w cieplejsze dni daje się odczuć silny smród.

10/ Selbstschutze płacą za wódkę, którą piją w dużych ilościach, każdą żądaną sumę, często zegarkami i kosztownościami.

11/ Przybyli do Bełżec Żydzi, którzy szukali świadka, któryby stwierdził, że Żydzi są uśmiercani. Chcieli zapłacić 120 000 zł. Amatora nie znaleźli...

.... Kierownictwo obozu spoczywa w rękach 12 SS-manów; /Kom, Manplmann, Wirth/, którzy mają do pomocy 40 Selbstschutz.

S. 172 Sprawozdanie bez daty z Tomaszowa Lubelskiego.

"... W okolicy Tomaszowa Lubelskiego operują trzy bandy, jedna sowiecka, doskonale zorganizowana i świetnie uzbrojona. Ta banda potrafiła zabrać z rzeźni cały ubój tygodniowy, innym razem - mąkę z młyna znajdującego się w samym mieście w pobliżu posterunku policji polskiej. Pozostałe bandy, jedna złożona z Polaków, ludzi z najróżniejszych środowisk, wytrąconych z normalnego życia, druga mieszana: Polacy i Żydzi, w tej przewodzą raczej typy kryminalne...

Doc. 21. Delegatura Report to the Polish Government in exile on Belzec April 1942 (Yad Vashem)

Appendix 1

Alphabetical List of Ukrainian Guards—Belzec

Name	Additional Information
ALEKSEJEV, Peter	
BARTELS, Iwan	*Volksdeutscher*
BAUMANN, Maks	
BENDER, Ivan	*Volksdeutscher*
BERG	*Volksdeutscher*
BIALAKOW, Wasyl	
BUDZIAK	
BULJI, Waslyl	
DALKE, Heinrich	*Volksdeutscher*. Also served at Sobibor death camp
DYNER	
FLEISCH	*Volksdeutscher*
GRUZIN, Wasyl	
HAWRYLUCH	
HAZDICKI	
HUBER, Michal	*Volksdeutscher*
HULEYT, Vasyl	
HUTYT, Wasyl	
HUZIJA, Iwan	
JADZIOL, Stefan	
JAKOVEVITS, Diner	
JESCHKE, Adolf	*Volksdeutscher*
KOBAWCZENKO	
KOLISYN, Borys	
KOLONKO, Adolf	*Volksdeutscher*
KOSTENKOW, Kyril	
KOTYCHYN, Borys	
KOZENDE, Mikolaj	
KOZLOWSKI, Iwan	
KUCZERCHA, Iwan	
KULYCHIN, Wasyl	
KUNZ, Samuel	*Volksdeutscher*. Arrested but died before he could stand trial in 2010. See Chapter 17
LAZARENKO	
LITUS, Petro	

LUSSE	
LYNGKIN	
MALAGON, Nikolai	Also served at Treblinka death camp
MAMCZUR	
MATWIJENKO, Nikolai	
MOTYGULAN, Sagudula	
NIKOFOROW, Iwan	
OLEJNIK, Taras	
OLJIEWSKI	
ORLOVSKIJ, Vasily	
OSTER, Peter	*Volksdeutscher*
PAMIN, Franz	*Volksdeutscher*
PAVLI, Nikolai	
PECZENYT, Grygory	
PIECZONY, Gregorz	
PIETKA, Alexej	
PITKONYT	
PITNOWY, Genrikh	
POCHOLENKO, Michal	
PODIENKO, Wasyl	
PODIONAK, Wasyl	
POHL	*Volksdeutscher*
POKOLENKO, Michal	
PROCHENKO, Wasyl	
PROCHIN, Dymytri	
PRUS, Alexander	*Volksdeutscher*
PRYMAK	
ROGOSA, Boris	Also served at Treblinka death camp, as head of the Ukranian guards
ROHLE, Heinrich	*Volksdeutscher*
ROSENHOLZ	*Volksdeutscher*
ROSENKO, Arnold	
SABAT, Viktor	
SAMUEL	
SCHARF	
SCHMIDT, Heinrich	*Volksdeutscher* from the Baltic States. Remembered by Rudolf Reder 'as the worst of the thugs. Went to Italy after the conclusion of *Aktion Reinhardt*. He committed suicide in Italy.
SCHMITZ	*Volksdeutscher*
SCHULTZ, Alexander	*Volksdeutscher*
SIEVERT, Reinhard	*Volksdeutscher*
SIMIONOW, Alexander	
STEINER	*Volksdeutscher*
STEPANOW, Peter	

STETCZENKO	
STURM	*Volksdeutscher*
SYSTOLA, Jakub	
SZACHOLIJ, Wasyl	
SZPAK, Dimitri	
SZPAK, Profiry	
SZWAB, Alexander	
TICHONOWSKI, Iwan	
TRAUTTWEIN, Karol	*Volksdeutscher*
TRUBENKO, Wasyl	
TWERDOCHLIB, Alexander	
VEITH	*Volksdeutscher*
WANOCHA	
WEDRYHAN, Fiodor	
WEDRYHAN, Petro	
WERDENIK, Ivan	
WLASIUK, Edward	
WOLOSZYN, Iwan	
WONK, Michal	
WOWK, Viktor	
WYSOTA, Jakub	
ZAGREBAJEW	
ZAJCZEW, Iwan	
ZAPLAWNYJ, Iwan	
ZIMBERT	*Volksdeutscher*
ZUJEW	
ZUK, Ignatz	

Appendix 2

Glossary of Nazi Terms

Abteilung: A branch, section or sub-section of a main department or office (*Hauptamt, Amstgruppe* or *Amt,* q.v.) Also a military or paramilitary unit of up to battalion strength, i.e. approximately 700 men.

Aktion Reinhardt: The code name used in honor of Reinhard Heydrich for the mass murder of Polish Jewry program

Allgemeine-SS: General body of the SS consisting of full-time, part-time, and inactive or honorary members, as distinct from the *Waffen-SS* (see entry for *Waffen-SS*).

Amt: A directorate or an office of a ministry.

Amtsgruppe: A branch of a *Hauptamt.*

Anschluß: Annexation of Austria to the German Reich in March 1938

Arbeitslager: Labor / Work Camp.

Außenstelle / Außendienststelle: Out-station of an office, agency or ministry.

Befehlshaber der Sicherheitspolizei und des SD: Commander in Chief of the SIPO and SD.

Deutsche Ausrüstungswerke (DAW): German Armaments Factories

Gau: One of 42 main territorial divisions of the Nazi Party.

Gauleiter: The highest ranking party official in a *Gau,* responsible for all political and economic activity, mobilization of labor, and civil defence.

Geheime Staatspolizei (Gestapo): Secret State Police which became Amt IV of the RSHA in September 1939. Headed by *SS-Obergruppenführer* Heinrich Müller.

Generalgouvernement: German-occupied Poland administered by Hans Frank from his headquarters in Krakow.

Hauptamt: A main or central office.

Höhere SS- und Polizeiführer: Higher SS and Police Leader. Himmler's personal representative in each military region. Also established in the occupied territories. Nominally the commander of all SS and police units in his area, as well as acting liaison officer with the military and senior regional authorities.

Judenrat: Jewish Councils established by the Nazis for Jewish self-administraton, in all its various facets, food, housing, labor allocation, welfare, police, economic, and social, etc.

Kapo: A prisoner-functionary in the Nazi camps who was assigned by the SS camp staff to supervise labor brigades, maintain discipline, or fulfil administrative tasks.

Kanzlei der Führers: Hitler's Chancellery.

Kommando: A brigade, squad, or detail.

Kommissariat: A Regional HQ of the police; also a political administration in the occupied eastern territories (e.g. *Reichskommissariat Ukraine*).

Kreishauptmann: The principal district official in the *Generalgouvernement* and occupied territories.

Kriminalpolizei (Kripo): Criminal Police, the plainclothes detective squads which together with the *Gestapo* formed the *Sicherheitspolizei*. In 1939 the *Kripo* became *Amt V* of the *Reichssicherheitshauptamt (RSHA)*. Headed by *Reichskriminaldirektor* Arthur Nebe.

Lagerältester: Camp elder, a senior prisoner in a Nazi camp.

Leitstelle: A Regional HQ of the *Gestapo* or *Kripo* established at the HQ of a Military District or capital of a county.

Oberkapo: Senior *Kapo* in a Nazi camp.

Oberzugführer: Senior platoon leader; in charge of the platoon leaders.

Ordnungspolizei (Orpo): Order Police. The regular uniformed police, comprising the *Schutzpolizei (Schupo)*, *Gendarmarie* (rural constabulary), and *Feuerschutzpolizei* (fire-fighting police), together with certain technical and auxiliary services.

Organisation Todt: A paramilitary government organization used mainly for the construction of strategic highways and military installations.

Reichsgau: One of eleven regions formed from territories annexed to the Reich.

Reichskanzlei: Chancellery of the Reich directed by Hans Lammers.

Referat: A sub-section within a *Gruppe*.

Referent: The official in charge of a *Referat*.

Reichsführer-SS: Reich Leader of the SS. Heinrich Himmler's SS title from June 1936.

Reichskriminalpolizeiamt (RKPA): Berlin HQ of the *Kriminalpolizei (Kripo)* which in September 1939 became *Amt V* of the *Reichssicherheitshauptamt (RSHA)*.

Reichssicherheitshauptamt (RSHA): Reich Security Main Office, formed in September 1939 and combined the *Sicherheitspolizei* and the *Sicherheitsdienst (SD)*. It was both an *SS-Hauptamt* and a branch of the Reich Ministry of the Interior.

Schutzpolizei (Schupo): Protection Police. The regular uniformed municipal constabulary forming the bulk of the *Ordnungspolizei*.

Sicherheitsdienst (SD): Security Service. The intelligence branch of the SS headed by Reinhard Heydrich.

Sicherheitspolizei (Sipo): Security Police, comprising the *Kripo* and *Gestapo*, headed by Reinhard Heydrich.

Sonderkommando: A special unit of the SS employed for police and political tasks in occupied territories. Also used to denote the special brigades of prisoners in Auschwitz who dealt with the corpses.

SS-Leibstandarte "Adolf Hitler": Hitler's bodyguard regiment. The oldest of the SS militaized formations, established in 1933. Commanded by Joseph "Sepp" Dietrich.

SS- und Polizeiführer: SS and Police Leader. In command of a district in the eastern occupied territories, subordinate to a *Höhere SS- und Polizeiführer*.

Standarte: SS or SA formation equivalent to a regiment, i.e. approximately 3,000 men.

Sturmabteilung (SA): Storm Detachment, also called the "Brown Shirts" after their uniform. The original Nazi paramilitary organization founded in 1921.

Sturmbann: An SA or SS unit, equivalent to a battalion, i.e. 750–1,000 men.

Volksdeutsche: Ethnic Germans.

SS-Totenkopfverbände: SS Death's Head units that guarded the concentration camps. In 1939 they formed the nucleus of the *SS-Totenkopf* division, one of the first field formations of the *Waffen-SS*.

SS-Verfügungstruppen: The prewar militarized formations of the SS, renamed the *Waffen-SS* in 1939.

Volksdeutsche: Ethnic Germans.

Vorarbeiter: Foreman of a team of workers.

Waffen-SS : Fully militarized SS formations. Initially composed of the *SS-Verfügungstruppen* and the *SS-Totenkopf* units. During the Second World War it comprised of 40 divisions, both German and non-German units.

Wehrkreis: Military region, usually indicated on maps by a Roman numeral.

Wehrmacht: The German Armed Forces, i.e. the army, air force, and navy.

Wirtschafts- und Verwaltungshauptamt (WVHA): Administration and Economic Main Office of the SS, formed from the *SS-Hauptamt Haushalt-und Bauten* in 1940. Headed by Oswald Pohl, the WVHA supervised the SS economic enterprises and administered the concentration camps.

Zugführer: Military term for platoon leader.

Appendix 3

Table of Equivalent Ranks

SS-Reichsführer	Reichs Leader
SS-Oberstgruppenführer	General
SS-Obergruppenführer	Lieutenant General
SS-Gruppenführer	Major General
SS-Brigadeführer	Brigadier General
SS-Oberführer	Senior Colonel
SS-Standartenführer	Colonel
SS-Obersturmbannführer	Lieutenant Colonel
SS-Sturmbannführer	Major
SS-Hauptsturmführer	Captain
SS-Obersturmführer	First Lieutenant
SS-Untersturmführer	Second Lieutenant
SS-Sturmscharführer	Sergeant Major
SS-Hauptscharführer	Master-Sergeant
SS-Oberscharführer	Sergeant First Class
SS-Scharführer	Staff Sergeant
SS-Unterscharführer	Sergeant
SS-Rottenführer	Corporal
SS-Sturmmann	Acting Corporal
SS-Oberschutze	Private First Class
SS-Schutze	Private

Selected Bibliography

ARAD, Yitzhak: *Belzec, Sobibor, Treblinka—The Aktion Reinhard Death Camps* (Indiana University Press, Bloomington and Indianapolis 1987).

BERGER, Sara: *Experten der Vernichtung: das T4 Reinhardt-Netzwerk in den Lagern Belzec, Sobibor und Treblinka*, Hamburger Institut fur Sozialforschung, Hamburg, 2013.

BLATT, Thomas (Toivi): *Sobibor The Forgotten Revolt* (H.E.P Issaquah 1988).

BLATT, Thomas (Toivi): *From the Ashes of Sobibor* (Northwestern University Press, Evanston, Illinois 1997).

BÖHM, Dr. Boris: *Nationalsozialistische Euthanasiaverbrechen in Sachsen:* Kuratorium Gedenkstätte Sonnenstein, Dresden / Pirna 1996.

BÖHM, Dr. Boris: *Sonnenstein Heft 3*: Kuratorium Gedenkstätte Sonnenstein-Pirna 2001.

COWDERY, Ray & VODENKA, Peter: *Reinhard Heydrich*: *Assassination (*USM Inc, Lakeville 1994).

CZECH, Danuta: *Auschwitz Chronicle* (Henry Holt, New York 1989).

CZERNIAKOW, Adam: *The Warsaw Diary of Adam Czerniakow.* Editors Raul Hilberg, Stanislaw Staron, and Josef Kermisz (Ivan R. Dee, Chicago 1999).

GILBERT, Martin: *Final Journey* (George Allen & Unwin Ltd., London 1979).

GILBERT, Martin: *The Holocaust—The Jewish Tragedy* (William Collins, London 1987).

GRABITZ, Helge and SCHEFFLER, Wolfgang: *Letzte Spuren* (Hentrich Edition, Berlin 1993).

HILBERG, Raul: *Die Vernichtung der europäischen Juden, Band 2* (Fischer Taschenbuch Verlag, Frankfurt am Main 1990).

HILBERG, Raul: *The Destruction Of The European Jews* (Holmes & Meier, New York & London 1985).

HOFFMANN, Dr. Ute Hoffmann and SCHULZE, Dietmar: *Gedenksatte Bernburg*, Dessau, 1997.

JORGENSEN, Torben: *Stiftelsen-Bolerne fra Aktion Reinhardt* (Gyldenals, Bogklubber, Gylling 2003).

KLEE, Ernst: *Das Kulturlexikon zum Dritten Reich* (Fischer S. Verlag GmbH 2007).

KLEE, Ernst: *Was sie Taten—Was sie Wurden* (Fischer Taschenbuch Verlag 1986).

KLEE, Ernst, DRESSEN, Willi, RIESS, Volker: *The Good Old Days* (Hamish Hamilton, London 1991).

KRANZ, Tomasz: *Extermination of Jews at the Majdanek Concentration Camp* (Panstwowe Muzeum na Majdanka, Lublin 2007).

KUWALEK, Robert: *From Lublin to Belzec* (Ad Rem, Lublin 2006).

KUWALEK, Robert: Oboz Zaglady W Belzcu, (Panstwowe Muzeum Majdanku 2010).

LANZMANN, Claude: *Shoah* (Pantheon Books, New York 1985).

LONGERICH, Peter: *The Unwritten Order—Hitler's Role in the Final Solution* (Tempus, Stroud 2001).

MACLEAN, French L. *The Camp Men* (Schiffer Military History, Atglen PA 1999).

MARSALEK, Jozef: *Majdanek* (Interpress, Warsaw 1986).

NOVITCH, Miriam: *Sobibor Martydom and Revolt* (Holocaust Library, New York 1980).

O'NEIL, Robin: *Belzec Stepping Stone to Genocide* (Jewish Gen, New York 2008).

O'NEIL, Dr. Robin: *Oskar Schindler Stepping Stone to Life*, susaneking.com 2010.

PIRO, Anna: *The Krakow Ghetto 1941—43*, The Historical Museum of the City of Krakow, Krakow 2005.

POPRZECZNY, Joseph: *Hitler's Man in the East Odilo Globocnik*, McFarland and Company, Jefferson and London 2004.

REDER, Rudolf: *Belzec*, Brzenka Panstwowe Muzeum, Oswiecim 1999.

REITLINGER, Gerald: *The Final Solution* (Vallentine, Mitchell, London 1953).

SCHELVIS, Jules: *Sobibor A History of a Nazi Death Camp* (Berg, Oxford, New York 2007).

SCHOENBERNER, Gerhard: *The Yellow Star* (Corgi Books, London 1978).

SERENY, Gitta: *Into That Darkness—From Mercy Killing To Mass Murder* (Pimlico, London 1974).

TREGENZA, Michael: *Belzec Death Camp*, The Wiener Library Bulletin 1977, volume XXX 41 / 42; pp. 8–25.

TREGENZA, Michael: *Christian Wirth and the First Phase of Einsatz Reinhard*, Zeszyty Majdanka Vol XIV, Panstwowe Muzeum na Majdanka Lublin 1992.

TREGENZA, Michael: *Christian Wirth: Inspekteur des SS-Sonderkommandos Aktion Reinhard*, Zeszyty Majdanka Vol Xv, Panstwowe Muzeum na Majdanka Lublin 1993.

WELICZKER, WELLS, Leon: *The Janowska Road* (USHMM, Washington DC, USA 1999).

Published Papers and Unpublished Works / Correspondence

Published:

GILBERT, Sir Martin: Maps of *Aktion Reinhardt*

GUTH, Karin: Interview in Hamburg. Available online from http://www.deathcamps.org

TOPPING, Alexandra: *The Guardian* online, 22 November, 2010: "Suspected Nazi death camp guard Samuel Kunz dies before trial." http://www.Guardian.co.uk

TREGENZA, Michael: Belzec—*The Unknown Death Camp of the Holocaust*, Fritz Bauer Institut Jahrbuch 2000. (Revised and updated 2006)

Unpublished:

TREGENZA, Michael: Private Report, Allötting Germany 1972

TREGENZA, Michael: Christian Wirth The Exemplary Officer

WEBB, Chris: The ARC Trips to Poland 2002 and 2004 (Holocaust Historical Society)

Correspondence:

BRIGHT, Frank: Private correspondence with the author 2014

HANEJKO, Eugeniusz: Private correspondence with the author 2008

HANEJKO, Tomasz: Private correspondence with the author 2013–2014

IMICH, Jan: Private correspondence with the author April 2003

RUTHERFORD, William: Private correspondence with the author 2003–2005

STADLER, Harry: Interview and correspondence with the author 2003

TREGENZA, Michael: Private correspondence with author

Archival Sources

Belzec Memorial Museum, Poland
Bundesarchiv Koblenz, Außenstelle Ludwigsburg (formerly the Zentrale Stelle der Landesjustizverwaltungen, Ludwigsburg.
Bundesarchiv Koblenz, Außenstelle Berlin-Lichterfelde (formerly the Berlin Document Centre).
Chris Webb Private Archive, UK
Ghetto Fighters House, Israel
Holocaust Historical Society, UK
Majdanek Museum, Lublin, Poland
Michael Tregenza Archive, Lublin, Poland
National Archives Kew, London , UK
National Archives, Washington DC , USA
Regional Museum Tomaszow Lubelski, Poland
Staatsarchiv Munchen, Germany
United States Holocaust Memorial Museum , Washington DC, USA
Wiener Library , London , UK
Yad Vashem, Jerusalem, Israel

Websites

Action Reinhard Camps (ARC)
Das Bundesarchiv Gedenkbuch. de—Memorial Book
Guardian online
Holocaust Education & Archive Reasearch Team (H.E.A.R.T)
Holocaust Historical Society (HHS)
Jewish Gen
Nizkor—Adolf Eichmann Complete Trial Transcripts
Yad Vashem Central Database of Shoah Victims Names

Acknowledgements

ADLER, John; ARORA, Surinder; BIEDKA, Lukasz; BIERSCHNEIDER, Robert (Staatsarchiv Munchen); **BOHM, Dr. Boris** (Sonnenstein / Pirna Memorial); **BOWLES, Paula; BRIGHT, Frank** (Holocaust Survivor); **CONSTANDY, Michael** (Westmoreland Research Alexandria VA); **EKSTEIN - HELFGOTT**, Anita; **FELDMAN, Professor Matthew** (Teesside University, UK); **FERRERO, Shaul** (Yad Vashem); **GILBERT, Sir Martin** (Author and Historian); **GROSMAN, Judy** (Ghetto Fighters House, Israel); **HANEJKO, Eugeniusz** (Director Regional Museum Tomaszow Lubelski; **HANEJKO, Tomasz** (Head of Belzec Memorial Museum; **HOJAN, Artur** (T4 Association); **IMICH, Jan; JAROS, Marek** (Wiener Library London); **KATZ, Lilli-Mai; KUWALEK, Robert** (Former Belzec Museum Director); **LISCIOTTO, Carmelo** (H.E.A.R.T) ; **LUGNER, Hans; MUNRO, Cameron** (T4 Association); **O'NEIL, Dr Robin** (Author and Historian); **OREN, Zvi** (Ghetto Fighters House, Israel), **PRESTON, Trevor, RUTHERFORD, William (Billy); SPYRAKIS, Clare; SPYRAKIS, Heather; SPYRAKIS, Nicky; STADLER, Harry** (Kinder Transport); **TREGENZA, Michael** (Author and Historian); **TYAS, Stephen; WEBB, Shirley; WITTE, Peter. WOOD, Melanie**

Index of Names

C

D

E

F

G

H

I

J

K

L

M

N

O

P

R

S

T

U

V

W

Z

ibidem-Verlag / *ibidem* Press
Melchiorstr. 15
70439 Stuttgart
Germany

ibidem@ibidem.eu
ibidem.eu